8

COLUMBIA UNIVERSITY STUDIES IN ENGLISH
AND COMPARATIVE LITERATURE

THE ORIENT
IN
AMERICAN TRANSCENDENTALISM

THE ORIENT IN AMERICAN TRANSCENDENTALISM

A STUDY OF
EMERSON, THOREAU, AND ALCOTT

BY

ARTHUR CHRISTY

1963
OCTAGON BOOKS, INC.
NEW YORK

OCTAGON BOOKS, INC.
175 FIFTH AVENUE, NEW YORK 10, NEW YORK

LIBRARY OF CONGRESS CATALOG CARD NUMBER: 63-20888

Printed in U.S.A. by
NOBLE OFFSET PRINTERS, INC.
NEW YORK 3, N. Y.

TO

MY FATHER

AND

MY MOTHER

PREFACE

This book is a study of the beginnings of American interest in Oriental thought. Traffic with the Orient began when Yankee clipper-ships entered the China trade, but for decades the traffic was almost alone in economic values. It was not until about Emerson's time that the Oriental was more than a heathen and his religious literature more than foolishness. The tide turned with the growth of the Transcendental Movement in the large sense, for which Emerson, a man fundamentally individualistic and unfettered by the creed of any school, was nevertheless the chief literary spokesman. Puritanism lost its hold and men became tolerant of the hoary, occult, Asiatic faiths, for Transcendentalism was not merely negative in effect, breaking Puritan intolerance; in its own tenets was inherent sympathy with Oriental thought, and spiritual values were added to the silks and spices which Americans imported.

An awareness of the fact that the Emersonians were a very potent factor in bringing the Oriental into American life has been increasing. "It would be a matter of deep interest to know exactly how far the American spirit had been impregnated, directly or indirectly, by the infiltration of Hindu thought during the XIXth century," writes Romain Rolland in his recent *Prophets of the New India,* "for there can be no doubt that it has contributed to the strange moral and religious mentality of the modern

United States. . . . I do not know whether any historian will be found to occupy himself seriously with the question. It is nevertheless a psychological problem of the first order, intimately connected with the history of our civilization." This book may be considered as an attempt to write the first chapter of the general study Romain Rolland suggests, a study which he himself realized must commence with Ralph Waldo Emerson, Henry David Thoreau, and Amos Bronson Alcott, three men at one time intimate friends and neighbors in Concord.

But it should be clearly understood that the limiting of this study to the Concord men is arbitrary. There were other members of the Transcendental communion, Theodore Parker, Convers Francis, James Freeman Clarke, and Samuel Johnson, to mention a few, who were interested in the Orient. They also should logically be included in any study which bears the title of this book. However, the Orientalism of the Concordians was a unique entity representative of Transcendentalism as a whole, and ample justification can be found for studying it alone. The Concord approach was not that of the theologian, metaphysician or specialist in comparative religions. It was the approach of the poet and mystic. Our interest, therefore, will largely be in the literary and mystical results of the Oriental influences in the Transcendentalism which flowered in Concord.

Readers familiar with the correspondence of Emerson and Carlyle may remember that in 1844 Emerson responded to his friend's chiding of his other-worldliness with these surprising words: "You sometimes charge me with I know not what sky-blue, sky-void idealism. As far as it is a partiality, I fear I may be more deeply infected than you think me. I have very joyful dreams which I cannot bring to paper, much less to any approach to practice, and I blame myself not at all for my reveries, but that they have not yet got possession of my house and barn. . . . I only worship Eternal Buddh in the retirements and intermissions of Brahma." These words are typical of much that Emerson and his Concord friends wrote. Now it is a difficult task to account for the dreams and ecstasies of mystics. They are men who crush the centuries as the sections of a telescope, and staunchly declare that they must get beyond time and space and rely more on intuition than reason. Yet no estimate of American Transcendentalism will be complete until the Oriental aspects of the mystical elements in the movement are examined. This is obvious if any serious credence can be given to Emerson's confession to Carlyle.

The vogue of the Oriental in New England Transcendentalism was the result of distinct causes. The first was Emerson's inability to find at home a complete refutation of the eighteenth-century rationalism against which his idealistic temperament revolted. The Sensationalist psychology of Locke and Hume dominated the thought of the period in which he grew to intellectual maturity. It was a philosophy very uncongenial to him; and there was no help in the church. Christianity in general had come to the sorry pass where, according to Richard Garnett, "it could be written out at examinations." All the old grounds of religious certitude had been cut away. Unitarian liberalism itself had become a bare-faced orthodoxy as narrow as the old. Transcendentalism and the theology of which

the Harvard faculty of divinity was the chief representative crossed swords when George Ripley and Professor
Andrews Norton championed the respective causes after
Emerson's "Divinity School Address" had brought the issues to the front. Norton centered the controversy in the
miracles of the Bible. Ripley countered, in *"The Latest
Form of Infidelity" Examined*, by stating that it was not
a question as to whether the miracles were valid and the
Bible authentic, but whether or not they were the only
evidences of Christianity. Eighteenth-century rationalism,
combined with a natural desire to defend dogma, had
forced the pastors of hungry flocks into the "position of
an antiquarian, spending all his time proving the validity
of miracles and the Bible, instead of *being* a Christian."
In a time of rationalism, men who cared for the spirit
but rejected the proof were naturally driven to revolt.
When they came into contact with the catholicity of the
Indian scriptures and the emphasis these books placed on
the inner spiritual resources, they naturally read them
avidly.

Another reason for the cordial reception accorded the
Orientals was the adoption, consciously or unconsciously,
of the eclectic method of Victor Cousin by the Transcendental thinkers. Eclecticism may be described as the
method of a truce-maker with a sound head and feeling
heart, sympathetic with the points of view of passionate
adversaries and desirous of bringing about reconciliation
and peace. Cousin lived on the Continent at the time when
Germany was terminating the era of idealism whose repre-
sentatives had been Kant, Fichte, Hegel and Schelling;
and France was taking up the movement after the exclu-

sive sensationalism of the Encyclopedists, Condillac and
Helvetius. Cousin tried to be the arbitrator between intuition and reason. Since it was impossible for him to abide
completely by either one of the systems, he argued that
the logical thing was to reject all the exclusive views that
could not be admitted, and to reconcile what was left to
a comprehensive point of view capable of including and
thus explaining and complementing all acceptable facts.
The eclectic method was admirably adapted to the needs
of a group of American intellectuals. However, the extent
varied to which the Transcendentalists adopted the philosophy of the French eclectics who had been introduced by
several translators during the first decades of the century.
The most extreme idealists murmured; the more practical
minds found it useful. But in varying degrees it became
the method of the men who were encouraging a renais-
sance.

It might even be said that eclecticism is the method
of cosmopolitanism. It is naturally best suited to men who
wish to range the whole gamut and history of human
thought, accepting the congenial and rejecting that un-
suited to their ends. The composite Orientalism of Concord was itself a result of an eclectic synthesis. Emerson
and his friends read the Hindus for their idealistic philosophy, a philosophy naturally congenial to the Transcendental mind. But they were also practical Yankees fac-
ing the demands of a work-a-day world; so they read
Confucius, a sage as shrewd as any Yankee, and found in
him effective precepts whereby to regulate their affairs
with men. The Mohammedan Sufis provided poetry for
their urbane and artistic needs. These three Oriental cul-

tures were eclectically blended, despite their inherent contradictions, into a composite which in miniature is an
excellent representation of that larger Transcendentalism
composed of borrowings from Greek, English, French,
German and native thought.

Personal temperament must also be considered. As
Transcendentalists, Emerson, Thoreau, and Alcott shared
many common enthusiasms and characteristics, but their
natural aptitudes and training led to different ends. These
are clearly seen as one studies the men in perspective.
Emerson's Orientalism is explained by his eclectic theology. All his important theories of art and poetry, and
his rules for the conduct of life, are implicit in the doctrine of the Over-Soul, a term so broad that it embraced
his cosmos. Thoreau was not a doctrine-maker. He sought,
rather, to immerse himself completely in nature, never considering any purpose in his life more important. In doing
so, he compared himself to the Hindus. Alcott's Orientalism eventually expanded into an enthusiasm for the
world's scriptures and for active work in disseminating
information about them. In these three interests—eclectic
theology, immersion in nature, and the universal scriptures, lie the differences and results in the Orientalism of
the three friends.

Since books were the medium of the Oriental influence,
and they naturally receive emphasis in this study, all the
bibliographical and chronological facts that it has been
possible to gather together regarding the Oriental readings
of Emerson, Thoreau, and Alcott will be found in an appendix. To the facts produced by the drag-net of the usual
methods of scholarly research are added those provided by

the opportunity, graciously granted, to examine the personal libraries of Emerson and Alcott which still remain in Concord. The records of the Harvard College Library and the Boston Athenæum also disclosed evidence of the extensive use the Concord men made of the Oriental volumes in these institutions. In this appendix, furthermore, will be found many of the comments which were written by the Concordians upon the Oriental books, the quotations which they deemed sufficiently memorable to be transcribed into their diaries, and such explanatory notations as will enable the reader to evaluate the importance of each volume.

In this connection rises the problem of citing Oriental texts and rendering the Anglicized Oriental proper name with its varied spelling. Wherever the determination of the specific text that was used is of importance, as in the discussion of Emerson's poem "Brahma," or the sources of Thoreau's interest in the Yoga, the exact editions of the works they read are cited. When, however, the discussion is an explanation of a specific Oriental doctrine, use has been made of the most readable translations and the expositions of modern scholars, particularly those of Professors Dasgupta and Radhakrishnan, Hindus widely read in the philosophies of both the East and West. In some instances the translations read by the Concord men, which are listed in the appendix, were the work of early scholars primarily interested in philology, and the pages are littered with cumbersome, parenthetical notes that are of small appeal to readers of an Emersonian temper. This is the reason for the frequent quotations from Professor R. E. Hume's superb translation *The Thirteen Principal*

Upanishads. Furthermore, the Concord men often used several forms for the same word, and the reader should be aware that it was their habit often to refer to a book such as the *Bhagavadgita* as *The Bhagvat*, the *Bhagavad Geeta*, or the *Bhagavat Gita*. These old and varied spellings occur only in quotations, however; the modern renderings are consistently given elsewhere. Other possibilities of confusion for the reader are the respective old and new spellings of *Menu* and *Manu* and the designation of the Hindu deity as the *Brahman* or *Brahma*.

The introductory chapter is an attempt to present very briefly a few of the subjects which are in the nature of background. The story of Concord Orientalism is inextricable from the rise of the English and French Oriental Societies and the work of the early translators. The introduction also attempts to provide the reader with the main facts regarding the Hindu, Chinese and Persian literatures with which Emerson and his friends were acquainted. They read far more widely in the Oriental books than is suspected, and it is difficult to understand Transcendental enthusiasm for the Orientals without understanding the Orientals themselves. I have, therefore, provided as much of this background material as space allowed.

It seems necessary to state that this book is neither propaganda for any modern theosophical movement nor in the spirit of those sanguine reformers who decry the so-called materialism of the West and find in the East the sole haven of the waning spirituality of the world. I have tried to limit myself strictly to the proper function of a literary historian—simply to record and analyze the work of three men who were preëminently poets and informal essayists, basing my discussion upon their published writings and such critical works about them as offered material pertinent to my purpose. I have also been granted the rare privilege of access to unpublished manuscripts. I cannot adequately express my gratitude to Mrs. F. Alcott Pratt of Concord, Massachusetts, for permitting me to enter her home and for days browse through Alcott's library and the fifty volumes of his unpublished diary. Practically the entire chapter on Alcott is thus based on unprinted material. Dr. H. W. L. Dana assisted me in every possible way, when I asked for the privilege of making a compilation of the Oriental books in Henry Wadsworth Longfellow's library, after I had learned through Alcott's diary that he had been supplied from this source. Professor Edward Waldo Forbes, acting in behalf of the Emerson family, graciously granted me permission to make use of such marginalia as I found in the Oriental books in Emerson's library, and to print for the first time two of his translations from Hafiz. I must add that Mrs. Flora Livingston, custodian of the Widener Memorial Collection in the Harvard College Library, made it possible for me to edit Thoreau's unpublished translation from the *Harivansa,* entitled *The Transmigration of the Seven Brahmans,* which has already appeared in book form; and to use excerpts from a rich collection of miscellaneous Thoreau manuscripts. This material forms a valuable supplement to existing knowledge of Thoreau's interest in Oriental asceticism.

Finally, I should state that since this book was undertaken upon my own initiative, and worked out largely according to my own ideas, I am solely responsible for its conclusions, and those members of the faculties of Columbia University whom I have the honor to acknowledge as masters must in no way be blamed for my indiscretions. To Professors Ralph Leslie Rusk and Jefferson Butler Fletcher, who have been my most exacting critics and benevolent advisers, I owe suggestions that have been of inestimable value. Professors Robert Ernest Hume and A. V. Williams Jackson were the inspiration of my interest in Oriental thought, an interest which was my birthright and the partial result of boyhood years of experience in Oriental countries, but latent until they awakened it. I am grateful also for the timely counsel and friendly encouragement given to me by Professors Ashley Horace Thorndike, Samuel Lee Wolff, and Herbert Wallace Schneider. Professors Robert E. Spiller of Swarthmore College, Clarence L. F. Gohdes of Duke University, and Arthur W. Hummel of the Chinese Division at the Library of Congress have graciously read this book in manuscript and offered helpful suggestions. The Houghton Mifflin Company has granted me permission to quote from books for which it holds the copyright. Nor must I fail to acknowledge the uniform courtesies extended to me, a stranger, at the Boston Athenæum and the Harvard College Library. I also owe particular thanks to the reference assistants of the Columbia University and New York Public Libraries for help in securing access to rare volumes of Oriental translations. But my deepest indebtedness is to my father and mother, and to my wife. The memory of their sympathetic aid will be a benediction on all my years.

ARTHUR CHRISTY

COLUMBIA UNIVERSITY
    10 May, 1932

CONTENTS

CONTENTS

PART ONE

INTRODUCTION

All philosophy, of East and West, has the same centripetence.
—Emerson, *Works,* IV, 48.

PART ONE

INTRODUCTION

INTRODUCTION

I

No careful reader of the pages of Emerson, Thoreau, and Alcott needs to be informed, either by Romain Rolland or by any one else, that these writers were deeply influenced by a wide acquaintance with Oriental books. They confessed their indebtedness in unmistakable terms at almost every turn. But it remains for an expositor to tell *why* Concord men read the Orientals and to *what end;* and most important of all, the *sources* from which they took Oriental ideas and ornamentation for some of the classic pages of American literature. This is the task before us.

The key to Emerson's workshop was the essay "Quotation and Originality."[1] He borrowed from innumerable men and books, and his borrowings found their way into his prose and verse. It was in no "stealthy or shame-faced way" that he worked, "but proudly, royally, as a king borrows from one of his attendants the coin that bears his own image and superscription."[2] Emerson confessedly believed in quotation. On one occasion he quoted, "It is no more according to Plato than according to me."[3] He carried his doctrine almost to the point of heresy. A great man quotes bravely, he wrote, and will not draw on his invention when his memory serves him with a word as good. This is analogous to his excusing a great mind from consistency. He saw no dishonor in mental indebtedness.

It had the same virtue as pecuniary indebtedness: the capitalist was as eager to lend as the consumer to borrow. Such a transaction in the realm of thought indicated no more intellectual turpitude than the simple fact of the borrower's debt indicated bankruptcy. In the vast number of cases the transaction was honorable to both. Should another's words describe the fact, use them as freely as the language and the alphabet. Thus ran the argument of the essay "Quotation and Originality."

But would not a practical use of this theory spell suicide and the death of originality? Emerson would have answered no. In proportion to one's reality of life and perception would be the difficulty of finding the replica of one's own thought in another's words. Furthermore, it was the approved method of history. Search the world and it would be found that borrowing was a universal method well approved through many ages. He explained his thought in greater detail in the *Journals:*

The apparently immense amount of debt to the old. . . At first view, 'tis all quotation,—all we have. But presently we make distinction: first, by wise quotation. . . . One quotes so well that the person quoted is a gainer. The quoter's selection honors, and celebrates the author. . . . For good quotation, then, there must be originality in the quoter,—bent, bias, delight in the truth, and only valuing the author in the measure of his agreement with the truth, which we see, and which he had the luck to see first. . . .[4]

In perfect agreement with Emerson was Bronson Alcott. "If the ancients left us ideas," he wrote in *Table-Talk*, "to our credit be it spoken that we moderns are building houses on them."[5] And in *Tablets* he wrote in the same tenor: "Very desirable it were since the gates of the East are now opening wide and giving the free commerce of mind with mind, to collect and compare the Bibles of the races for general circulation and careful reading."[6] Out of what Alcott called the Theban night came the light of his day to blend with thought. The method of blending was to quote and compare.

But one passage in this connection need be quoted from Thoreau. His method was Emerson's and Alcott's. There is an elusive intent in his words, however, when he writes: "Like some other preachers, I have added my texts—derived from the Chinese and Hindoo scriptures —long after my discourse was written."[7]

Moot questions arise from the adoption of this method of quotation by these men. If Thoreau could derive texts for his thought from the Chinese and Hindu scriptures, and if Emerson used the words of Orientals because he saw in them a deeper sense than the speakers put into them, what was the relation of their thoughts to the foreign texts? Holmes stated the obvious when he wrote that Emerson, "reading as he did . . . must have unconsciously appropriated a great number of thoughts from others."[8] But a recent critic, who could see no relation between Thoreau's Yankee nature and Oriental nature, differs essentially with Holmes as to the effects of reading the books of the East. "Thoreau took figures and sentences," he writes, "not ideas, from his Oriental reading."[9] The line between figures and ideas is in most instances very shadowy. Our task will be to examine both.

Obviously there must have been some relationship between ideas and texts, however subtle; and the only valid approach to this relationship is to understand the attitude of the Concord men toward the Oriental scriptures. It was thus that Thoreau wrote of the *Rigveda* and the work of scholarly commentators:

Reading the hymns of the Rig Veda, translated by Wilson, which consist in a great measure of simple epithets addressed to the firmament, or the dawn, or the winds, which mean more or less as the reader is more or less alert and imaginative, and seeing how widely the various translators have differed, *they regarding not the poetry, but the history and philology,* dealing with very concise Sanscrit, which must always be amplified to be understood, I am sometimes inclined to doubt if the translator has not made something out of nothing,—whether a real idea or sentiment has been thus transmitted to us from so primitive a period. I doubt if learned Germans might not thus edit pebbles from the seashore into hymns of the Rig Veda, and translators translate then accordingly, extracting the meaning which the sea has imparted to them in very primitive times. While the commentators and translators are disputing about the meaning of this word or that, I hear only the resounding of the ancient sea and put into it all the meaning I am possessed of, the deepest murmurs I can recall, *for I do not the least care where I get my ideas, or what suggests them.*[10]

Emerson's attitude was very similar to Thoreau's. Apropos of the Hindus he wrote: "I want not the metaphysics, but only the literature of them."[11] The cue should be taken and never forgotten. The Concord men were interested only in the tones and over-tones of the literatures of India, China, and Persia.

A passage in Emerson's essay "Books" presents further specific mention of some of the Orientals and their writings which were considered important:

There is no room left,—and yet I might as well not have begun as to leave out a class of books which are the best: I mean the Bibles of the world, or the sacred books of each nation, which express for each the supreme result of their experience. After the Hebrew and Greek Scriptures, which constitute the sacred books of Christendom, these are, the Desatir of the Persians, and the Zoroastrian Oracles; the Vedas and Laws of Menu; the Upanishads, the Vishnu Purana, the Bhagvat Geeta, of the Hindoos; the books of the Buddhists; the Chinese Classic, of four books, containing the wisdom of Confucius and Mencius. Also such other books as have acquired a semicanonical authority in the world, as expressing the highest sentiment and hope of nations. Such are the Hermes Trismegistus, pretending to be Egyptian remains; the Sentences of Epictetus; of Marcus Antoninus; the Vishnu Sarma of the Hindoos; the Gulistan of Saadi; the Imitation of Christ, of Thomas à Kempis; and the Thoughts of Pascal.[12]

This was high praise indeed! But in other contexts Emerson freely vouchsafed even more intimate comment. In "Books" he did not mention the *Bhagavat Purana,* but in conversation with Moncure Conway he said, "Ah! there is a book to be read on one's knees!"[13] Even of Oriental romances was his praise extravagant: "Thus Milman's translation of *Nala and Damayanti* is nearer to my business and bosom than is the news in to-day's *Boston Journal.* And I am admonished and comforted, as I read. It all very nearly concerns me. We are elevated by beauty. I walk in marble galleries and talk with kings the while."[14]

Thoreau, too, speaks of his literary preferences at Walden in words pregnant with meaning:

My residence was more favorable, not only to thought, but to serious reading, than a university; and though I was beyond the range of the ordinary circulating library, I had more than ever come within the influence of those books which circulate round the world, whose sentences were first written on bark, and are now merely copied from time to time onto linen paper.[15]

How carefully did the Concordians read books? As a boy barely in his majority, Emerson confessed that his "cardinal vice of intellectual dissipation" was "sinful strolling from book to book, from care to idleness."[16] He added that with this malady he belonged to the incurables. Over two decades later, in 1843, he was still uncured. Some one must have taunted him with the remark, "Your reading is irrelevant." Emerson's answer was defiant. "Yes, for you, but not for me. It makes no difference what I read. If it is irrelevant, I read it deeper. I read it until it is pertinent to me and mine. . . . A good scholar will find Aristophanes and Hafiz and Rabelais full of American history."[17] Elsewhere he explained his meaning in other terms. "Only so much of Arabian history can I read as I am Arabian within."[18] Such a sentence may legitimately be applied to the *Bhagavadgita* and the reading of the Chinese and Persians as well.

With minute, pains-taking reading Emerson had no patience. "Books are like rainbows," he wrote, "to be thankfully received in their first impression, and not examined and surveyed by theodolite and chain, as if they were part of the railroad."[19] It may be pertinent to note also Cabot's words on Emerson's tastes in other literatures:

French literature he did not love, though he was a reader of Sainte-Beuve and of George Sand. On a journey he liked to have Martial or a treatise of Cicero in his handbag, partly because he did not read them at home. At home he read no

Latin or Greek, though he retained his knowledge of Greek sufficiently to be able, in his later years, to compare the old translation of Plutarch's Morals (a favorite book of his) with the original. Mystic writings—Swedenborg, Behmen, and the like—came always well recommended to him, though they did not engage him very deeply. The New Platonists (in Thomas Taylor's translation) and the Oriental (particularly the Hindoo) religious books, the Bhagavat Gita, the Puranas, and Upanishads, were among his favorites. He often quotes the so-called Chaldæan Oracles, and the like, without troubling himself with any question of their authenticity. . . . In general, after he began to write and publish, his reading was 'for the lustres',—for a touch of suggestion that might help to crystallize the thoughts that were floating within him.[20]

Emerson's reading seemingly served to confirm or at most modify lines of thought already discovered rather than suggest new departures.

Thoreau frankly confessed what his tastes were when he wrote, "I never read a novel, they have so little real life and thought in them. The reading which I love best is the scriptures of the several nations, though it happens that I am better acquainted with those of the Hindoos, the Chinese, and the Persians, than of the Hebrews, which I have come to last. Give me one of these bibles, and you have silenced me for a while."[21] This was an unusual confession from a man of Thoreau's reticence. Such words have great significance for anyone who believes in Thoreau's sincerity and would see him in an Oriental light.

Sanborn's statement of Thoreau's ability is as interesting as Cabot's on Emerson:

When I first knew him, at seven-and-thirty, he read Latin

and French as readily as English; Greek without difficulty; German, Italian and Spanish more or less; and had some knowledge of several dialects of the American Indians. Without a knowledge of Persian, Sanscrit, or Chinese, he had much acquaintance, through translations, either French or Latin, of writers in those languages, and could have competed with J. R. Lowell at the same age. He was at forty-four a much better scholar, in the classic sense, than Emerson, Channing, or Hawthorne.[22]

It remains only to speak of Alcott. Junius Alcott, a brother, gave the most valuable information regarding Bronson's training and activity. "His reading," writes Junius, "during this residence in and near Philadelphia, was indeed immense; the libraries, public and private, were open to him."[23] The list of authors whose "unnumberable works on education, morals and religion" were read prominently includes that of Degérando, an ideal preparation for the man whose road was to lead to Concord, whose good star had fixed for him the destiny of being neighbor to Emerson and Thoreau. In the scholarly sense Alcott was handicapped in being deprived of college discipline. In every way he was a self-educated man, yet in no sense could he be considered untutored in the literatures of the world. There exists an account of Alcott's expressions at a Bible Convention held in 1842:

That he certainly considered the religious writings of the Brahmins and of Mahometans were inspired in like manner as the Christian Scriptures; though no books contain so full and faithful an exposition of eternal truth as do the Old and New Testaments. He hoped a collection of the Sacred Books of all races would be made, that we might then have the fullest revelation of God's word, as uttered by the inspired writers of all past time. He spoke of the inspiration of Christ and of the Scriptures; and said he had come to consider the authenticity of all scripture,—not merely that of the Old and New Testament,—to consider the nature of scripture, its absolute grounds and objects.[24]

When the three neighbors approached the sacred scriptures of other races in this temper, it was not probable that they would find points about which to quarrel. Nor is it surprising to find many Oriental reflections in their own work.

One of the earliest results of the neighborly sharing of books in Concord was the editing of the "Ethnical Scriptures" for the *Dial*. The first selections appeared in July, 1842, when Emerson chose sentences from Charles Wilkins' translation of the *Hitopadesa* for publication. More interesting, in some ways, than the selections themselves was Emerson's introduction to the series:

We commence in the present number the printing of a series of selections from the oldest ethical and religious writings of men, exclusive of the Hebrew and Greek Scriptures. Each nation has its bible more or less pure; none has yet been willing or able in a wise and devout spirit to collate its own with those of other nations, and sinking the civil-historical and ritual portions to bring together the grand expressions of the moral sentiment in different ages and races, the rules for the guidance of life, the bursts of piety and of abandonment to the Invisible and Eternal;—a work inevitable sooner or later, and which we hope is to be done by religion and not by literature.[25]

After reading such words one naturally wonders what portions of Hindu sacred literature Emerson will select to "collate" with his own. The initial sentence of the entire series was the following: "Whatever cometh to pass, either good or evil, is the consequence of a man's own actions, and descendeth from the power of the Supreme Ruler."[26] This seems to be an echo of Emerson's law of Compensation. Two more passages may be quoted from the list to indicate the nature of his selections. The following was brief but obviously to his taste: "The mind of a good man does not alter when he is in distress; the waters of the ocean are not to be heated by a torch of straw."[27] And finally the following series of catechetical queries and answers:

What is religion? Compassion for all things which have life. What is happiness? To animals in this world, health. What is kindness? A principle in the good. What is philosophy? An entire separation from the world.[28]

The January, 1843, number of the *Dial* contained selections by Thoreau from the *Laws of Menu*. In contrast with Emerson's choices, note Thoreau's passages: "The resignation of all pleasures is far better than the attainment of them."[29] "The organs, being strongly attached to sensual delights, cannot so effectually be restrained by avoiding incentives to pleasure, as by a constant pursuit of divine knowledge."[30] "Whatever is hard to be traversed, whatever is hard to be acquired, whatever is hard to be visited, whatever is hard to be performed, all this may be accomplished by true devotion; for the difficulty of devotion is the greatest of all."[31] Assuredly Thoreau's hand and temper are as clearly seen in these selections as Emerson's is in his.

Alcott took no hand personally in the selection of the "Ethical Scriptures"; instead he contributed his own

"Orphic Sayings," which, one cannot but remark in passing, were at times less intelligible than the Hindus, Chinese
and Persians. His friends, however, made up for his in-
activity. After the July, 1842, number of the magazine in
which Emerson introduced the new feature to the American public, scarcely a number appeared that did not contain sentences from the Orientals. Following Emerson's
and Thoreau's selections for the July, 1842, and January,
1843, numbers respectively (which have already been
noted) there appeared Confucian passages of Thoreau's
choosing in April, 1843; and in July of the same year,
extracts from the *Desatir*, accredited by G. W. Cooke to
Emerson.[32] Thoreau again chose Confucius for the October number of the same year, continuing the rôle as the
compiler of the sayings in the next number, that of January, 1844, when he entitled his selections "The Preaching
of Buddha." These were culled from the work of Burnouf,
an eminent French translator. The Egyptian Hermes
Trismegistus also received a conspicuous place in this
number. Emerson concluded the series with selections
from the so-called Chaldæn oracles.[33] The differences in
the contributions made to the *Dial* by the Concord friends
were essentially the same as the differences to be found in
their personal uses of Oriental thought. These will be
examined after we survey briefly the various Oriental
literatures with which they were acquainted.

II

The history of Indian literature is the history of the
mental activity of a race for at least three thousand
years.[34] It embraces everything which the word *literature*

connotes—epic, lyric, dramatic and didactic poetry that is religious as well as secular, and narrative and scientific prose. The religious aspect stands in the foreground, for the Indian mind is essentially of this temper. A people who permitted theological treatises to be woven into their greatest epics, the *Mahabharata* and the *Ramayana,* were impelled by their very nature to produce a literature that would stand for centuries a great monument to their groping after God. Western scholarship has only of late turned its attention to the vast storehouse of fable and dramatic work which still remain locked in the Sanskrit. For decades it ignored the secular, and not without reason concerned itself with the religious works, because these predominated. This was the reason why the American Transcendentalists read almost exclusively in the *Puranas* and *Upanishads*. There was no alternative. Fortunately they desired no other. The translations European scholars produced for them could hardly have been more congenial or better chosen.

Practically all histories of Indian literature commerce with the *Rigveda*. It rightly takes precedence here also, for it belongs to the dim twilight which preceded the dawn of Indian literature, and was well known in Concord. It is the earliest poetry of the Aryan race, a collection of hymns to the forces of nature. What renders these hymns so valuable is that they are a mythology in the making. The reader sees the gods created before his eyes. The hymns are not merely apostrophes to literary personages and to philosophical concepts, such as the sun-god, the moon-god, the fire-god, the gods of the air, earth, and sea.

Instead, they are chiefly addressed to the shining sun itself, the moon in its nocturnal sky, the fire in the sun, in
the lightning and on the hearth, the clouds and rain, roar-
ing storms and rivers, and the fruit-granting earth. Gradually the transformation of natural phenomena into mythological figures appears. The sun was named Surya; the
moon, Soma; fire, Agni. The Maruts were the storms;
Dyaus was the sky; and Vayu the wind. It is of these phenomena and their deification that the *Rigveda* sings.

A singular cosmic sense and acquaintance with the forces
of the universe abetted the natural speculative tendencies
of the Indian mind. Its idealism was latent. Although the
mythological importance of the *Rigveda* is far greater
than the philosophical, there are hymns in the collection
which form an unmistakable bridge to the philosophical
speculations of the *Upanishads*. The following verses will
indicate the nature of early Indian philosophy which accompanied the birth of both myths and gods:

Then was not non-existent nor existent; there was no realm
of air, no sky beyond it.
What covered in and where? and what gave shelter? was water
there, unfathomed depth of water?

Death was not then, nor was there aught immortal: no sign
was there, the day's and night's divider.
That one thing, breathless, breathed by its own nature: apart
from it was nothing whatsoever.

Darkness was there: at first, concealed in darkness, this All
was indiscriminated chaos.
All that existed then was void and formless: by the great
power of warmth was born that unit.

Thereafter rose Desire in the beginning, Desire, the primeval
    seed and germ of spirit.
Sages who searched with their heart's thought discovered the
    existent's kinship in the non-existent.

Transversely was their severing line extended; what was above
    it then, and what below it?
There were begetters, there were mighty forces, free action here
    and energy up yonder.

Who verily knows and who can here declare it, whence it
    was born and whence comes this creation?
The Gods are later than this world's production. Who knows
    then whence it first came into being?

He, the first origin of this creation, whether he formed it all or
    did not form it,
Whose eye controls this world in highest heaven, he verily
    knows it or perhaps he knows it not.[35]

Here in early bloom is the power of subtle questioning
that so characterizes the Indian mind. It was inevitable
that such speculation, once begun, would continue. The
Indian could not rest content with his unknown God. A
wonder regarding His nature drove him on. Primitive
magic and superstition submerged it, but every once in a
while it crept out. The three other Vedas—the *Atharva,
Sama,* and *Yajur* were filled with incantations against evil
spirits, magic spells, and the ritual and directions for sacrifices, with songs to accompany them. Mystery-mongering
crippled philosophy. As the decades passed, the universe
for the Hindus became populated with dark demoniacal
powers and ghostly beings which brought disease and misfortune. The gods who had embodied the benevolent forces
of nature had receded to the background. Trained wizards

attempted to protect men from hostile spirits with the charms and flattering speeches of the later *Vedas*.

Brahmanizing became such a profitable business that the Brahman priesthood gave itself more enthusiastically to the study of sacrifice-ceremonies than to the gods. It developed an elaborate science of sacrifice which was expounded in the texts known as the *Brahmanas*.

An example given by Winternitz of the conduct of four priests in accompanying a sacrifice will indicate better than anything else how ritual and priest came between man and the God he strove to reach.[36] A *Hotar,* or caller, was required to recite the verses of hymns in order to praise the gods and invite them to the sacrifice. The *Udgatar,* or singer, accompanied the preparation and presentation of the sacrifices, especially of the Soma libations, with songs. The *Adhvaryu,* or executor, performed all the sacrificial acts, muttering prose prayers and sacrifice formulae. And finally came the *Brahman,* or high priest, whose office it was to protect the sacrifice from harm. Every sacred act, in the priestly view, was exposed to danger. If it was not performed exactly in accordance with the ritualistic prescription, or if a spell or prayer formula was not spoken correctly, or if a singer rendered a tune incorrectly, the sacred act was apt to bring destruction upon the originator of the sacrifice. It was therefore the duty of the Brahman to sit south of the sacrifice, for the south was the haunt of the god of death and other demons hostile to men. His duty was to follow the whole procedure, and when he noticed the least mistake in any detail, or an irregularity on the part of the three other priests, to pronounce sacred words which would make good the harm. In order to fill the office of the Brahman, the priest was necessarily "full of the veda," knowing perfectly all that was required of the other priests, who themselves were highly trained in their respective rôles.

But a knowledge of the four *Vedas* was not all that was required of the priest. Every sacrificial act was treated with extreme circumstantiality. Great importance was attached to such matters as whether a movement was to be made to the right or to the left, whether a pot was to be placed on this or that spot, whether a blade of grass was to be laid with its point to the north or north-east, and how the sacrificial cake was to be divided. The *Brahmanas* were the "explanation or utterance of a learned priest, of a doctor of the science of sacrifice, upon any point of the ritual."[37] Besides these explanations, there were a few redeeming legends, or *Puranas*, and speculative reasons for the ceremonies and their connection with the prayer formulae. It is easy to see why Radhakrishnan once declared that the religious history of India proved that the dative case held no comfort for the human heart.

The *Brahmanas*, as we may surmise, mark a dolorous period in Indian literature. It is only fair, however, to remind the Occidental that *Leviticus* preceded *Isaiah* and *Jeremiah*. The *Brahmanas* are noteworthy because they formed the background for the *Upanishads*. Emerson and his friends read much of this Brahmanical literature. That they were not repelled by it is a monument to their tenacity of purpose and faith in the inherent power of men to speak truth in sincerity. Max Müller, enthusiastic Orientalist though he was, did not write with compliments of these ecclesiastical texts in *Chips from a German Workshop:*

However interesting the Brahmanas may be to students of

Indian literature, they are of small interest to the general reader. The greater portion of them is simply twaddle, and what is worse, theological twaddle. No person who is not acquainted beforehand with the place which the Brahmanas fill in the history of the Indian mind, could read more than ten pages without being disgusted.[38]

As has already been intimated, philosophy in ancient India was not developed among the priests. Indeed, Hindu philosophy in no way abetted the cause of the priests, who were emphasizing the sacrifices and their efficacy againts the gods. No Brahman was apt to doubt the existence of the divine pantheon, or raise the question whether there were any sense in sacrificing. The early speculations of the *Rigveda* received scant encouragement.

It was through others than members of the Brahman priestly caste, even through the Kshatriyas and through sceptics and unbelievers, obnoxious fellows to the priesthood, for they neither sacrificed nor gave gifts, that India continued to probe for Reality. The epics, particularly the *Mahabharata* and the *Ramayana,* contain numerous descriptions of ascetics who had retired to the forests to find peace. Many of these recalcitrant forest seers had undoubtedly been trained by the Brahmans. But they could not brook a mercenary life whose spiritual expression was an elaborate liturgy alone. In the forests they turned to the thoughts which became crystallized in the *Upanishads,* a word literally meaning "to sit down near a teacher," and suggesting a pupil sitting near a teacher for confidential communication.

Much of the Brahmanical tradition was naturally retained in these books. Charms and mysteries of all sorts

were mixed with the purest idealism. Nor did they necessarily contain the thoughts of single teachers. Various
schools of thought were mixed in single volumes. But fundamental doctrines stand out, lending an appearance of
philosophical uniformity. Such are the doctrines of Maya
and Karma. The chief preachment is well stated in these
words: "The universe is the Brahman, but the Brahman
is the Atman." The portentous philosophical and religious
implications of this basic principle will become more apparent when it is restated as—The world is God and God
is the soul.

It was this principle, permeating as it does a great part
of Indian literature from the *Upanishads* down, that appealed to the mystic minds of Emerson and Thoreau. To
show its affinities with the Transcendental doctrine of the
Over-Soul, no better words can be found than those by
Deussen, who wrote in *The Philosophy of the Upanishads:*

The *Brahman,* the power which presents itself to us ma-
terialised in all existing things, which creates, sustains, preserves,
receives back into itself again all worlds, this eternal infinite
divine power is identical with the Atman, with that which, after
stripping off everything external, we discover in ourselves as our
real most essential being, our individual self, the soul.[39]

Indeed, just as all Emerson's work seems but a variation
of the fundamental doctrine of the Over-Soul, so the philosophic literature of India repeats similar variations on
the doctrine of the Supreme Cosmic Brahma.

Prometheus *stealing* the fire from the gods and bringing
it to man is an illustration of the average Occidental Cal-
vinist's attitude toward the Divine, an attitude of estrange-

ment. Emerson's Over-Soul, which absorbed man in an all-enfolding Divinity, expressed the Oriental view. It is probably fair to say that in so far as men escaped the Promethean—or Calvinistic—sense of hostility in God, and felt that the Divine was open to them at all times, in that sense they were becoming sympathetic with the Oriental. Though the more advanced theology of Emerson's time had largely freed itself from Calvinism, and had already emancipated itself from the concept of an arbitrary deity, in the doctrine of the Over-Soul the theological pendulum had swung as far toward the Oriental pole as it was possible in New England.

Of course no informed writer will be blind to two grave objections legitimately raised against a loose comparison of the American Transcendentalist and the Vedantist. The first objection is that which the West has charged against Hindu thought since its first disclosure—an inherent pessimism. The second is implicit in the first: the seeming impossibility of Yankees, bred from the soil, shrewd, individualistic, embracing any thought which insisted on negating all that contributed to the civilization in which they lived. This objection is removed by the recognition of one fact. Emerson and his friends were not engaged in a wholesale taking-over of Hindu thought. And the first, that of pessimism, is, for the Hindu, logical rather than literary.

It was a learned Orientalist who definitely declared that the doctrines of the *Upanishads* were basically not pessimistic, supporting his assertion with such quotations as, "He who knows the joy of the Brahman, for him there is no fear"; "Where is delusion, where sorrow, for him who knows the Unity?" and "Consisting of joy is the Atman. And like a song of triumph, of optimism, sound the words of an Upanishad: Joy is the Brahman. For truly, out of joy arise all these beings, by joy they live after they have arisen, and when they pass away they are again absorbed into joy."[40]

The contention that Hindu philosophy is essentially pessimistic arises from the fact that it is only a small step from a belief in the non-reality of the world to contempt for the world. The usual concept of a "future" life is not predicated in philosophic Hinduism, since there is really only one life. Possibly it is true that the greater the fervor with which the joys of the Brahman are praised, the more worthless does earthly existence appear; and in India the practical consequence was wholesale neglect of the material necessities of civilization and life. The pessimism of the Hindu masses, which was the result of the inexorable doctrine of transmigration and the hopelessness of escape, is not to the point here.[41] There is an expressive illustration of the varying effects of Hindu thought in the romantic pantheism of such writers as Deussen and Winternitz, and the contrasting pessimism of Schopenhauer. All three of these men read the Hindu books, yet how differently they viewed the world! The explanation for this difference, of course, lies in what they *selected*.

The latent pessimism of the *Upanishads* never came to the surface in America. Reading selectively for the choice passages that would corroborate their own instinctive beliefs, Emerson, Thoreau and Alcott but built their own dreams on the hoary Indian texts.

III

No one Oriental volume that ever came to Concord was more influential than the *Bhagavadgita*. This is evident from the manner and frequency in which the Concordians spoke of it. Sanborn states that for years Emerson was one of the very few Americans who owned a copy, and that his was even more widely used than that in the Harvard College Library.[42] To this little classic of Hindu literature Emerson gave the highest praise:

I owed—my friend and I owed—a magnificent day to the *Bhagavat Geeta.*—It was the first of books; it was as if an empire spoke to us, nothing small or unworthy, but large, serene, consistent, the voice of an old intelligence which in another age and climate had pondered and thus disposed of the same questions which exercise us.[43]

He was not unwilling to study the book critically, but he insisted on one reservation: "Let us not now go back and apply a minute criticism to it, but cherish the venerable oracle."[44]

Thoreau, too, when writing of the book at Walden used metaphors that suggest profound possibilities of interpretation:

Thus it appears that the sweltering inhabitants of Charleston and New Orleans, of Madras and Bombay and Calcutta, drink at my well. *In the morning I bathe my intellect in the stupendous and cosmogonal philosophy of the Bhagvat-Geeta*, since whose composition years of the gods have elapsed, and in comparison with which our modern world and its literature seem puny and trivial; and I doubt if that philosophy is not to be referred to a previous state of existence, so remote is its sublimity from our conceptions. I lay down the book and go to my well for water, and lo! there I meet the servant of the Bramin, priest of Brahma and Vishnu and Indra, who still sits in his temple on the Ganges reading the Vedas, or dwells at the foot of a tree with his crust and water jug. I meet his servant come to draw water for his master, and our buckets as it were grate together in the same well. The pure Walden water is mingled with the sacred water of the Ganges.[45]

A book that could inspire such fervor in undemonstrative Yankees must have been exceptional. What has been its appeal for centuries to mystics of both hemispheres is hard to say. Even Hindus of the present time who have been educated in the West are said to praise the *Vedas* and often leave them unread. But the *Gita,* as it is familiarly called, is intimately known to them and loved; its Krishna has been claimed as seeming a worthy rival of the Christ of the *Gospels.*[46] Perhaps these words from a recent translator come close to an explanation:

The Bhagavad-gita makes its prime appeal to reflective mind, depressed and perplexed by the spectacle of life. Such a mind, after bitter experience of the meanness of power, the imperfections of institutions, the sadness of knowledge, inevitably raises the questions: Why do one's duty, in such a world as the present? How is it possible, in such a world, to see any profit or joy in duty alone? Partial answers may be found in Homer, Ecclesiastes, Lucretius, the New Testament, and elsewhere; the full answer, satisfying both intellect and spirit, is given in the Song of the Blessed One.[47]

These words are not entirely partial, as any one who has read the *Bhagavadgita* knows. And yet it is a book of serious contradictions and inconsistencies, for it is a merging of the Yoga and Sankhya philosophies;[48] and it advocates ways of life that are inherently incompatible.

The book is about as long as the *Gospel of St. John*. It is an interlude in the great *Mahabharata* epic, narrating the actual dialogue between Krishna, or God incarnate in a charioteer, and Arjuna, the strongest fighter of an army, just prior to a battle between the Kurus and Pandavas. The substance of the dialogue would justify calling the *Bhagavadgita* a verse *Upanishad*.

Arjuna hesitated to order the fighting to continue, as the reader knows from the beginning of the first chapter. It was a fratricidal war. The hostile forces were his kinsmen. Why should he be the instrument of their death? Law and order perish with the destruction of the family stock. Women turn to sin and the castes are mixed. To slay one's kinsman for the sweet fruits of kingship and thus invite the consequent evils is a heavy sin. With this mood of doubt the book opens. Arjuna turns to Krishna for counsel. Krishna bids him lay aside his scruples, for souls are without beginning and end, and of no importance in the connection of body and soul. There is no real slaying in war, for in death the soul but puts off its outward body for another, as a man changes his clothes. Grief over death is not for the wise. Pleasure and pain pertain not to the soul, but to transitory matter. Let Arjuna do the duty of his caste, engage in battle, fight and conquer. Let him be resolute, let him do his duty, and the joys of the earth will be his. This, said Krishna, was in accordance with the doctrines of the Sankhya.

Now let Arjuna approach his problems with the doctrines of the Yoga. Works must be done, but without the thought of reward. Even in activity a man may be of a quiet mind. "The man who casts off all desires and walks without desire with no thought of a *Mine* and an *I* comes into peace."[49] This is not new teaching. Krishna, himself, as incarnated deity, works and is workless. Wise is the man who does the same. The lower road of sacrifice, of mortification of the flesh, of controlling the breath is acceptable; but the highest road is that of knowledge. It was at this stage of the discourse that Krishna delivered one of the most powerful passages in the whole poem:

Children only, and not the learned, speak of the speculative and practical doctrines as two. They are but one, for both obtain the self-same end, and the place which is gained by the followers of the one, is gained by the followers of the other. That man seeth who seeth that the speculative doctrines and the practical are one.[50]

Significantly enough, Emerson copied this very passage into his *Journals*,[51] for it neatly expressed his own philosophy. By virtue of the law of identity, he probably said to himself, the approach to the Over-Soul and the development of the individual perfection are the same. He could admire great doers as well as great thinkers, for both accomplished their ends by the self-same laws of the world.

But to continue with the thought of the poem. In merging the Sankhya and Yoga, Krishna did not reject the method of flight from the world as a means of salvation, but he offered what purported to be a new and better way which all men could follow. This was the behest that men should work, and perform the practical duties of the world, but in the spirit of the Yoga, without hope of reward, and without attachment to the fruit of the work. "He who does my work, who is given over to me, who is devoted to me, void of attachment, without hatred to any born being, comes to me."[52] The duty of each man was his caste. Arjuna, of the warrior or Kshatriya caste, was to realize that "there is nothing more blest than a lawful strife."[53] To each man was a special duty, and this duty was to be performed. Thus it was possible for one to be redeemed from the world while in the midst of the world's activities. He could accumulate merit by his good deeds and the law of Karma, or Compensation, would be fulfilled. If he did his work without being trammelled by it, he could also be a true Yogi. This was a better way of salvation, this blending of the two formerly separate ways, than the complete renunciation of all activity. "Casting off of works and the rule of works both lead to bliss, but of these the rule of works is higher than the casting off of works."[54] Such a sentence is sufficient proof that the Yoga unworldliness of the *Upanishads* had been tempered in the *Bhagavadgita* to suit the practical needs of life—and Concord.

But the point where the *Bhagavadgita* departed most abruptly from the Vedantic tradition was in the new concept of *bhakti* or loving devotion. The God of the Vedanta, an impersonal and contentless infinity, had become a personal, loving God, a God who graciously bade men to come and share His grace, to find refuge in Him. "Exceedingly dear am I to the man of knowledge and he to Me."[55] And he was a God who participated actively in the affairs of the world. "Though birthless and unchanging of essence, and though Lord of born beings, yet in My sway over the nature that is Mine own I come into birth by My own magic. For whensoever the law fails and law-lessness uprises, then do I bring Myself to bodied birth. To guard the righteous, to destroy evil doers, to establish the law, I come into birth age after age."[56]

This aspect of the God of the *Bhagavadgita* is clearly theistic, as it would be in any system in which there is a personal God. The invitation accorded to Arjuna even had possibilities of Christian interpretation. "As thou hast come into this unstable and joyless world, worship Me; have thy Mind on Me; thy devotion to Me, thy sacrifice to Me, do homage to Me. To Me shalt thou come."[57] At the same time He is the taste in the water, the light of the moon, the mystic syllable *Om* of the Vedas, the under-standing of them that understand, and the splendor of all that is splendid. These were but a few of the "essences of beings" which Krishna claimed to be in the tenth chap-ter. Thus the book contains an irreconcilable medley of personal theism and impersonal pantheism. It presents a personal God, knowing and loving His followers; at the same time it presents the Brahma of the *Upanishads*, a pantheistic All. No reader approaching the book objec-tively can deduce a consistent philosophy from it.

The great influence of the *Gita* lies in its eclecticism. By recognizing the irreducible diversities in human nature, and accommodating itself to idealists and materialists, men of contemplation and men of action alike, the book ap-pealed to many minds. Every road, it said, led to the same goal; and it approved all of them, in no patronizing and indifferent manner, but with the sanction and reason-ableness of age-old philosophies. Thus few books could have been more congenial to the Concordians who had adopted the eclectic method. It took up the very issues which they raised among themselves—the "same questions which exercise us," as Emerson said[58]—and it answered them in much the same manner as they were answered in Concord. It emphasized the place of *bhakti,* or loving devotion to God—no uncongenial emphasis, this, for mystics—and it endorsed all life and labor, whether scholarly, contemplative, or manual. The *Bhagavadgita* even approved of the hobbies of Emerson, Thoreau and Alcott—from trances to vegetarianism. No book could have done more. There is little reason to wonder at its popularity.

IV

The contribution of China to American Transcendentalism was largely in practical ethics. The Vedanta emphasized man's relationship to God, not man's relationship to man. Philosophy and poetry of the kind provided by India and Persia were not to be found in the books of Confucius and Mencius. That Emerson and his friends read these Chinese books extensively and found their own lives reflected in them is proof of the truism that no man can be a total mystic all the time or ever get beyond a certain measure of dualism. The body, for one thing, is not to be denied by the practically minded man. And in practice it is impossible to act, wish, strive for, think at all, without implicitly postulating duality. Philosophizing seems most unnatural to the Chinese people today, but the history of the nation, until the turn of the twentieth century, expressed a magnificent attempt to govern all society by a philosophic principle in the moral and ethical sense. Chi-

nese wisdom expressed itself in the outward symbolical relation of each individual to the Emperor and the Tao, not
in thoughts about the Tao; for the early spirit of Lao Tsu
had died in the letter. In government, Plato's ideal of the
philosopher-king came perhaps as close to being realized
in China as human society will ever permit. All that is
symbolized by the rice-bowl triumphed, however, and
withered the ideal, leaving a practical code for very practical men.

Now, although idealism was most congenial to the
American Transcendentalists' intellectual life, the century
in which they lived presented social problems which men
with a Puritan penchant for reform could not ignore. The
cruelties of slavery and the increasing harshness of life
under the smoky encroachments of industrialism were
only two regnant causes for a descent from the ideal world
to consider man's relations to his fellows. In practical ex-
tremities neither the Hindus nor the Persians could speak
with the wisdom of Confucius, who refused to speculate
about the unknown, assuming the traditional Tao, an ineffable unity behind the universe.[59] Rather than metaphysical doctrines he preached the necessity of every person's
simply doing his proper duty in the immediate affairs of
life. If what he taught is a religion, it is a religion emphasizing a social morality obligatory on all persons, and
teaching the potency of the fundamental goodness of human nature in the moral supervision of the world. Confucius also taught the doctrine of the invincible human
will, of inescapable social duties, of reciprocal social responsibilities, of the value of the family and the efficacy
of the good example of the superior man.[60] What Massa-

chusetts citizen of the nineteenth century would not have endorsed such teaching, when he could interpret it in his own way?

The Confucian scriptures are unusual in that no theological doctrine of inspiration or supernatural authority has ever been evolved to give them greater influence.[61] Confucius has never been deified by his followers as have Buddha and Mohammed. His utterances antedated the arrival of Buddhist missionaries in China,[62] and received no tinge from India. The chief religious postulate that can be deduced from the thought of this unspeculative teacher of practical men is that of the inherent goodness of human nature as implanted by a force whose nature it was not necessary to define.[63] "The great God has conferred on inferior people a moral sense, compliance with which would show their nature invariably right," he said.[64] Mencius, the St. Paul of the system, continued preaching his master's doctrine: "The tendency of man's nature is to good. . . . There are none but have this tendency to good."[65] This recognition of the moral nature of men as set against the Calvinistic insistence on total depravity was probably one of the first things in Confucianism that drew Emerson's attention. It is possible to see in his insistence on man's essential morality as he expressed it in the "Divinity School Address," the reflection of the early reading of the Confucian books, although the belief is inherent in the concept of Immanence. In writing of Reality in the essay "Experience," he indicated how he interpreted the thought of Mencius.

Fortune, Minerva, Muse, Holy Ghost,—these are quaint names, too narrow to cover this unbounded substance. The baffled intellect must still kneel before the cause, which refuses to be named,—ineffable cause, which every fine genius has essayed to represent by some emphatic symbol, as, Thales by water, Anaximenes by air, Anaxagoras by (Nous) thought, Zoroaster by fire, Jesus and the moderns by love; and the metaphor of each has become a national religion. The Chinese Mencius has not been the least successful in his generalization. "I fully understand language," he said, "and nourish well my vast-flowing vigor."—"I beg to ask what you call vast-flowing vigor?" said his companion. "The explanation," replied Mencius, "is difficult. The vigor is supremely great, and in the highest degree unbending. Nourish it correctly and do it no injury, and it will fill up the vacancy between heaven and earth. This vigor accords with and assists justice and reason, and leaves no hunger. . . ." We give to this generalization the name of Being, and thereby confess that we have arrived as far as we can go. Suffice it for the joy of the universe that we have not arrived at a wall, but at interminable oceans. Our life seems not present so much as prospective; not for the affairs on which it is wasted, but as a hint of this vast-flowing vigor.[66]

Emerson's quotation was from Collie's translation. The rendering by Legge, perhaps more scholarly and faithful to the original, suggests that there is not the divinity in the Confucian passage which Emerson read into it. But inherent differences bothered him little. How else explain such strange team-mates as the Holy Ghost and Mencius' cosmic vigor? The following is Legge's translation:

Mencius told him, "I understand words. I am skilful in nourishing my vast, flowing passion-nature." Ch'ow pursued, "I venture to ask what you mean by your vast, flowing passion-nature!" The reply was, "It is difficult to describe it. This is the passion-nature;—It is exceedingly great, and exceedingly strong.

Being nourished by rectitude, and sustaining no injury, it fills up all between heaven and earth. This is the passion-nature;— It is the mate and assistant of righteousness and reason. Without it, man is in a state of starvation."[67]

A Chinese scholar has given an apt, general summary of Confucian thought which will most clearly show its relationship to American Transcendentalism:

According to Confucianism, Heaven signifies the source of the laws which govern the world. More precisely, Heaven is the symbol of the unity which permeates the universe. Law is only a human concept. In nature, without the human mind, law has no existence. A law of nature is only a short description of a train of phenomena briefly and graphically summarized. The deity in the Confucian sense is Nature. Heaven endows humanity with reason and intelligence. Therefore, the operations of the mind are, in fact, an indirect manifestation of the will of Heaven. Destiny, natural sequence of events, is then a matter which cannot be avoided but must be watched, for heaven works without bias.[68]

The author of these words was careful to qualify his statements and explain that Confucius' "ethical system is based on the assumption of the natural character of cosmic evolution and only in a vague way has reference to theism."[69] This is an important qualification, for the theistic quality of Transcendental thought varied with each individual, but it was probably never absent. Men bred in the Puritan tradition could hardly escape its influence.

Since Emerson's term *Over-Soul* was seemingly broad and loose enough to embrace both the Hindu's Brahma and Confucius' cosmic unity, all students of his Orientalism should be aware of the differences between them. The

Vedantic Brahma has been sufficiently described already. Of the Confucian concept, it is first important to note that there was in it nothing resembling the Hindu concept of Maya. Confucius' Heaven was integrally related to nature and society. The Tao was the Source, but the Emperor served as its liaison on earth. He was the apex of the divinely ordered social pyramid. He represented the governing principle, and also the Chinese nation, the Middle Kingdom, the hub of the Universe, socially more than metaphysically. Thus cosmic solidarity expressed itself in social solidarity, having evolved itself into an elaborate social hierarchy. As such, its preservation was dependent on a faithful observation of all the rules which would preserve a united state. Propriety and filial piety became corner stones in the Confucian's ideal of conduct, and an elaborate social ethic grew up. It was this ethic which became crystallized in the books of the Confucian canon and attracted Emerson and his friends.[70]

V

The third and probably the least influential system of Oriental thought which must be considered is that of the Mohammedan mystics, commonly called Sufism. The Persian poets whose works were read in Concord were inextricably connected with this system—so much so, in fact, that to understand the one, it is necessary to understand the other.

In his *Literary History of Persia* Professor Edward Browne gives four theories regarding the origin of Sufism.[71] He states that it might have incorporated the esoteric doctrines of the Prophet of Islam; that it might have arisen as a reaction of the Aryan mind against a Semitic religion; that it might have been the result of the Neo-Platonic influence on Mohammedanism; and, finally, that it might have simply been of independent origin, a spontaneous growth of mysticism.[72] The essential thing is that Sufism was a form of mysticism, and as such possessed a common denominator with all other forms of mysticism, such as belief in the illusory nature of the tangible world and man's forlorn sense-fettered state of separation from the ineffable Source of all things.[73]

The particular feature of Sufism which should be immediately noted is that it evolved an elaborate poetic symbolism which was extensively used by such poets as Hafiz, Saadi, Enweri, and Kermani, whom Emerson read and seemed to admire. Sufis, being Mohammedans, very naturally adopted the concepts of their faith in describing the bliss of Paradise. Few readers need be reminded that the Mohammedan conceived of heaven in terms of sensuous delights and beautiful houris. The Prophet had promised these to his faithful followers. Mohammedan poetry consequently came to be generally written in figures and imagery which the Western reader knows principally through the *Song of Solomon*.

It is unfortunate that the eroticism of a crude form of Mohammedanism has tinged this symbolism to such a degree that many Occidentals have been unwilling to see back of the symbol the spiritual longing of devout souls. The erotic symbols were but a small part of the entire legend, but a few flies seem to have spoiled the ointment for many.

The following examples, culled to represent something

of the variety used, will show that all the symbols were not erotic, and that those who see mystical divinity in them may have grounds for doing so.[74] The *nightingale* represented the mortal pilgrim as he travelled the allegorical Path. *Autumn* stood for the end of life; a *barque* for a soul in a body bound by earthy ties; the *breeze of paradise* for God's blessing, the *breeze of death* for the Angel of Death, death being the true dawn or awakening to the true Life; and the *camel driver* for fate or destiny. There were numerous other symbols of a like nature. *Night* represented the world or this life, a dark night through which all must pass before the light can be reached. The voice of the *reed* and the melody of the *harp* were taken as the instructions of the Spiritual Guide. A *tress*—and here we approach the *Song of Solomon*—stood for the attractiveness of God's grace, for the heart bound by the tress knew the Life Absolute. Tresses were symbolic of all that conceals the Divine, just as a tress of hair may contain perfume. The *veil* was anything which hindered the union with the Beloved and stifled devout thought and desire. Even more specific, and to the Westerner more far-fetched, were other symbols. The *eyebrow* of the Beloved was often compared to the domed or arched recesses of a mosque where prayers were offered with the face toward Mecca; *musk* was the perfume of the Beloved, or better yet, it stood for the fragrant message which the True Beloved sends by death to those who love him. *Down* on the female cheek signified the attraction of Divine Love, or stood as a symbol of the verdancy of spiritual growth. The *lips* of the Beloved were the opening to the inscrutable mysteries of God's essence. Even the *mole,* in the East considered a beauty spot on a woman's face, represented aspects of the attractiveness of God for the devout. Two bacchanalian symbols were often used: the *tavern* was the call to contemplation, and *wine* the intoxication of the Spirit.

Some scholars have concluded that the Sufis invented their figurative style in order to mask mysteries which they wished to keep secret. They lived in times when plain statements of what they believed might have endangered their lives, and were driven to preserve their esoteric doctrine in this way. Other scholars point out that knowledge of the Infinite revealed to a mystic in his moments of ecstasy needs the artificial disguise of emblems from the world of sense. Imperfect though these emblems be, they suggest a deeper meaning than appears on the surface.[75] Finally, of course, come the great multitude who see in the *Beloved* nothing but the Mohammedan's houri. To this charge of sensuality in Sufi poetry, Professor Nicholson, probably the foremost interpreter, writes:

No intelligent and unprejudiced student of their writings could have made it, and we ought to have been informed on what sort of evidence it is based. There are black sheep in every flock, and amongst the Sufis we find many hypocrites, debauchees, and drunkards who bring discredit on the pure brethren. But it is just as unfair to judge Sufism in general by the excesses of these impostors as it would be to condemn all Christian mysticism on the ground that certain sects and individuals are immoral.[76]

But more specific are the words of another modern critic: "There are some who maintain there is no hidden, mystical, spiritual meaning at all in the works of Hafiz, and denounce them as erotic love songs. I cannot understand any

thoughtful Persian scholar, who has really studied Hafiz
... entertaining such a view."[77] This may be accepted as
the general opinion of Persian scholarship.

VI

The Asiatic Society of Bengal was the first organized
effort on the part of the English speaking world systema-
tically to devote itself to what Sir William Jones, its first
president, called in his inaugural address the "History,
civil and natural, the Antiquities, Arts, Sciences, and
Literatures of Asia."[78] The idea of forming the Society was
conceived by Sir William Jones, who had come out to Calcutta in October, 1783, as a judge of the supreme court
in Bengal.[79] A distinguished scholar and linguist, already
familiar with some of the classics of India and enthusiastically devoted to Oriental research,[80] he felt the need of a
thorough understanding of Hindu polity on the part of
British administrators, and accordingly dedicated himself
to the great task of translating the *Laws of Menu* in order
that the legal system of the natives of India might be
understood. This work was monumental and still stands
an eloquent memorial to the father of English Oriental
studies. His own scholarly interests had shown Jones the
great need of coöperation among the leaders in India, in
order that personal stimulus, a common interest, and publicity might advance the work. He consequently called a
meeting in Calcutta on January 15, 1784, of all those who
were interested in the project.[81] Thirty men attended,
among them Francis Gladwin, the translator of the *Gulistan* for which Emerson wrote the introduction of the
American edition.

The presidency was first offered to Warren Hastings, who declined on the ground that the superior talents of his colleagues would shine with such lustre that his would be dimmed.[82] He urged the election of Sir William Jones, who became the first president and served until his death on April 27, 1794.[83]

The work of the Society, its meetings, its membership, and its activities in translating manuscripts belong to the story of English Orientalism instead of American. The complete account of the work of the Society will be found in the *Centenary Review*, which covers its activities from 1784 to 1883. The primary interest of this study in the Society lies in the translations which came to Concord because of its activities. In this connection it should be noted that though Sir William Jones was himself actively engaged in translating, the Society seems to have met for the benefit of its members alone and entertained no idea of taking up the task of printing Oriental texts or translating them.[84] The first proposal to do so came from Baptist missionaries at Serampore, who offered to undertake the publication of a series of Sanskrit works with translations. The Society agreed to coöperate with the missionaries, and in 1806 the Hindu epic *Ramayana* was chosen for the purpose.[85] Emerson and his friends read portions of this great epic with delight. After this start the complexion of the Society's work changed, and through the years which followed the English reading world was offered a rich series of books. Sir William Jones contributed no less than twenty-nine papers to the first four volumes of the Society's *Transactions;* and besides his famed Manu he translated into English the *Sakuntala* of Kalidasa, which was known in Concord, and the *Gitagovinda* of Jaya-deva.[86]

A reference to the Oriental titles in the reading of the Concordians will also show the importance of the name of Henry Thomas Colebrooke,[87] a president of the Society for nine years, from April, 1806, to February, 1815, and founder of the Royal Asiatic Society of Great Britain and Ireland. He wrote on Hindu mathematics, was a profound Sanskrit scholar and zealous astronomer, and, in the words of the *Centenary Review*, produced "nothing that did not at once command the highest attention from the public, and notwithstanding the great advance that has been made in oriental researches of late years, his papers are still looked upon as models of their kind."[88]

It is Sir Charles Wilkins who must always be connected with the *Bhagavadgita* and Concord Orientalism.[89] He was the first Englishman to acquire a thorough mastery of Sanskrit, and in 1779 published a grammar of the language.[90] The translation of the *Bhagavadgita*, for which he is best known, was published in 1785 under the direction of Warren Hastings.[91] It was the first time this philosophical classic had been translated into a European language.[92] The climate of Bengal was not kind to so persevering a scholar, however, and Wilkins was forced to retire from the Indian Service at the close of the century. But his activities continued in England, and he published a translation of the *Hitopadesa*, from which Emerson culled passages for the "Ethnical Scriptures" which appeared in the *Dial* of July, 1842.[93] Several extracts of the *Mahabharata* also came in translation from Wilkins' pen, and it is not impossible that it was these which were read in Concord.

Of the original members of the Asiatic Society of Bengal, only two more need mention. They are Horace Hayman Wilson[94] and Brian Houghton Hodgson. Wilson came to India in 1808 as a member of the Medical Service of the East India Company. He first attracted public notice with the exquisite translation of the *Meghaduta,* which was published in 1813.[95] This book also found its way to Concord. It was followed by the *Theatre of the Hindus,*[96] not only in publication but in arriving in Concord. As a visitor of the Sanskrit College of Calcutta, Wilson superintended the publication of a large number of Sanskrit books, and with the assistance of a native staff, had the bulk of the eighteen *Puranas* translated into English. From these he selected the *Vishnu* for publication. This volume also in a short time crossed the water to Concord. Wilson became the first incumbent when the chair of Boden Professor of Sanskrit was created at Oxford in 1832.[97] Almost to the day of his death his labors continued. Within a week of his decease he completed the fourth volume of his translation of the *Rigveda* and a critical review of Max Müller's work. No name stands higher in the history of Oriental research, or as the medium through which Vedanta philosophy entered and permeated American Transcendentalism.

Brian Houghton Hodgson[98] is most significant because it was as a result of his work that Thoreau selected the passages for the *Dial* of January, 1844, which were entitled "The Preaching of Buddha." Coming to India in 1819, Hodgson spent the greater part of his time in the Himalayas, holding for several years the office of Resident at the Court of Khatmandu, Nepal.[99] In an utterly unworked field, he devoted himself assiduously to scientific and literary research. His contribution to the men of Concord was an introduction to Buddhism, and to the world at large a series of one hundred and twelve papers printed in the *Transactions* of the Society, together with the discovery of valuable manuscripts.[100]

After having served for nine years as a president of the Asiatic Society of Bengal, Henry Thomas Colebrooke founded the Royal Asiatic Society of Great Britain and Ireland for the benefit of retired nabobs and all who were interested in Oriental matters at home. The Bengal society functioned in the East alone. The need of a similar society was felt in England, and in 1823, Colebrooke, who had organized the project, was appointed a director. The *Centenary Volume*[101] of this society covers its history and work. Its significance here lies in the fact that it sponsored the Oriental Translation Fund in 1828[102] and thus continued the work of introducing the literature of the Orient to the Occidental world. Practically all of the translators and editors whose names appear in the formidable list of Oriental books read in Concord were members of one, and sometimes both, of these societies. They were the first leaders in English investigation of Oriental literature.

One cannot but wonder at the singular dearth, among the Concord men, of interest in German research into Oriental literature. A Batavian society had been founded as early as 1779,[103] and German investigation continued with characteristic thoroughness. But Von Hammer-Purgstall is the only German name of consequence to be found among those who sent Oriental translations to Concord. It was he who introduced Emerson to Persian poetry.

Despite the fact that the contribution of the English

Orientalists was predominant, and that of the Germans practically nil, there are yet other prominent Orientalists to be mentioned. These are the French. Three names stand out in this group: Jean Pierre Abel Rémusat, Anquetil Duperron, and Eugène Burnouf. They, too, were pioneers in Oriental research. The years of their lives will show how they overlapped those of the Concordians. Rémusat lived from 1788 to 1832; Duperron from 1731 to 1805; and Burnouf from 1801 to 1852.

The career of Duperron was the most unusual.[104] Born a Parisian, he spent several years at the university, where he became acquainted with Hebrew. This language introduced him to Persian and Arabic, studies which he pursued for a time in Holland. Duperron's education had prepared him for either the Church or the Consulates, and between these he hesitated for a period. His Oriental studies had in turn introduced him to the Avesta and the Zoroastrian scriptures. A scholar by temperament far more than a churchman or a diplomat, he was anxious to undertake the investigation of that vast body of literature. So, eschewing the comfortable life in the Church and all possible political preferment that might have come to him through the Consular service, he enlisted as a plain soldier in 1754 to serve in the army of the French trading company in India, with the hope that thus he would be able to go where he might find manuscripts and information. Friends who heard of his action came to his aid, securing for him an annuity of five hundred francs from the king and the privilege of free travel in India. No stroke of fortune could have suited Duperron better. He went to India and worked assiduously in Zoroastrian research among the Parsees, until in 1757 war broke out between the British and the French and he was forced to flee, in order to avoid capture and deportation. In disguise he allied himself to pilgrim bands and wandered over India.

Duperron found the manuscripts he sought. His importance here, however, lies not in these but in a book entitled the *Oupnek'hat*, which Schopenhauer declared to be "the production of the highest human wisdom."[105] This book was an imperfect Perso-Latin translation of Vedic and Upanishadic material, but it was one of the most important links in the early contacts of Western intellectuals with Hindu thought. Moriz Winternitz, a great German historian of Indian literature, writes that it was through this book that the philosophers Schelling and Schopenhauer became interested in the East.[106] The *Oupnek'hat* was not the *Upanishads* as these are now known and explained, but neither was it a poor introduction to Hindu mysticism. When Schopenhauer received the book with such extravagant praise, it is not surprising that its reception in Concord was cordial.

Eugène Burnouf, it was, who won enduring fame among Orientalists by deciphering the Zend-Avesta manuscripts which Duperron brought back to France. As early as 1826 he had published his *Essai sur le Pali*, and in 1840-47 brought out the Sanskrit text and French translation of the *Bhagavata Purana* in three folio volumes. His last works were the *Introduction à l'histoire du Buddhisme indien* and *Le Lotus de la bonne loi*. These works came out in 1844 and 1852 respectively.[107] The last, in particular, was a favorite with Thoreau. Burnouf's greatest influence, however, was as a teacher. He laid the foundation of Vedic study in Europe by gathering around him a group of students who later became prominent. Among these was Max Müller.[108]

Rémusat was one of the indefatigable pioneers who was self-taught. He took up Chinese and, unaided, published in 1811 his *Essai sur le langue et le littérature chinoises*. When, in 1814, the College de France created the chair of Chinese, Rémusat was called. He was also one of the principal founders of the Société Asiatique in 1822 and long its secretary.[109] His principal works are *L'Invariable milieu*, published in 1817, and the *Iu-kiao-li,* which appeared in 1826. Rémusat's activities were entirely in the field of Chinese, one that exerted less influence in Concord than the Hindu, but his name was often on the tongues of the Concordians.

In conclusion, it is only necessary to repeat that American Transcendentalists owed most to the English Orientalists. The reason was probably their preference for English books if translations were available in this language. Their willingness to read the French enriched them. Had they likewise read the German Orientalists, the entire output of Western research into the literatures of the East might have found its way to New England by the various channels which connected the publishing houses of Europe with Emerson's study in a little provincial American town.

VII

In the connection of sources, there is perhaps no better way of indicating how enthusiastically Oriental books were received in Concord during the heyday of Transcendentalism than to restate the story of the arrival of the Cholmondeley collection in 1855. It was an event of great significance, for it brought Thoreau forty-four Oriental volumes in one consignment.

Thomas Cholmondeley, a friend of Arthur Hugh Clough at Oxford, had come to Concord in September, 1854, with letters which introduced him to Emerson. It does not appear that he had ever heard of Thoreau until he met him at dinner in Emerson's home. When the latter learned that Cholmondeley wished to remain in town he advised him to apply to Thoreau's mother, who took lodgers. The young Englishman did so. He was received into the family and the intimate acquaintance with Thoreau began. Upon Cholmondeley's return to England, a few weeks later, an important correspondence between the friends ensued.[110] It was the time of the Crimean War, and Cholmondeley enlisted. Just before sailing with his regiment he sent the following letter to Thoreau:

October 3, 1855.

My dear Thoreau,—

I have been busily collecting a nest of Indian books for you, which, accompanied by this note, Mr. Chapman will send you, and you will find them at Boston, carriage paid (mind that, and don't let them cheat you), at Crosby and Nichols'. I hope, dear Thoreau, you will accept this trifle from one who has received so much from you, and one who is anxious to become your friend and to induce you to visit England. I am just about to start for the Crimea, being now a complete soldier; but I fear the game is nearly played out, and all my friends tell me I am just too late for the fair. When I return to England (if I do return), I mean to buy a little cottage somewhere on the south coast, where I can dwell in *Emersonian leisure,* and where I have a plot to persuade you over.

. . . .

Adieu, dear Thoreau, and immense affluence to you.

Ever yours,

THOS. CHOLMONDELEY.[111]

Franklin Benjamin Sanborn writes that the books arrived in Concord on November 30, 1855, when he saw them in the attic chamber where Thoreau kept his small library in cases made by his own hands, not failing to mention that upon the receiving of the first announcement of their coming Thoreau had "fashioned for these treasures a new case, out of driftwood that he had brought home in his voyages along the Musketaquid, thus giving Oriental wisdom an Occidental shrine."[112]

On December 9, writing to his friend Blake, Thoreau described the books in brief:

I have arranged my books in a case which I made in the meanwhile, partly of river boards. I have not dipped far into the new ones yet. One is splendidly bound and illuminated. They are in English, French, Latin, Greek and Sanskrit. I have not made out the significance of this godsend yet.[113]

And again, writing on December 25, to Daniel Ricketson of New Bedford, he said that he had "a royal gift in the shape of twenty-one distinct works (one in nine volumes— forty-four volumes in all) almost exclusively relating to ancient Hindoo literature and scarcely one of them to be bought in America. I am familiar with many of them and know how to prize them. I send you this information as I might of the birth of a child."[114] These books Thoreau cherished until the day of his death. After his decease they passed into the hands of his friends.

It is quite possible to argue that since by 1855 Transcendentalism was on the wane, the Cholmondeley collection could not have greatly affected the fundamental doctrines of the movement. But such an argument ignores certain facts. Alcott and Thoreau caught the Oriental contagion from Emerson, who had commenced his browsing about 1834. All three men had read the Orientals before they published a single book. Manu, Confucius, and Zoroaster, assuredly representative of the Hindus, Chinese, and Persians, had passed through Emerson's hands before the publication of *Nature,* or the delivery of his famous lectures, "The American Scholar" and "The Divinity School Address." In these the Oriental echoes are not faint.

Long before Cholmondeley came to Concord, the interest in Eastern thought had flamed. The forty-four volumes sent by this English friend deserve particular mention not because of the time of their arrival, but because they *did* arrive. Cholmondeley later confessed to Thoreau the reason for his choices. "I had indeed studied your character closely," he wrote, "and knew what you would like."[115] Emerson, Thoreau, and Alcott had been gladly welcoming each new translation of the Oriental classics as it came to the libraries of the cities. Cholmondeley's gift merely did away with the tedious journey to Cambridge and Boston for these books. The exciting unpurchasable discoveries of youth had become fireside friends.

VIII

As yet there does not exist a single comprehensive study of the Oriental influence on Occidental thought. In the

American field, save for fugitive articles and pamphlets which will be found listed in the notes, the only book devoted to the subject is Frederic Ives Carpenter's recent *Emerson and Asia,* a valuable, pioneering work. In the European field will be found Marie de Meester's very slight monograph entitled *Oriental Influences in the English Literature of the Nineteenth Century,* J. Hoops's *Orientalische Stoffe in der englischen Literatur,* Martino's *L'Orient dans la littérature française au XVIIe et au XVIIIe siècle,* Paul Hoffman's *Der Indische und der Deutsche Geist,* and Adolf Reichwein's *China and Europe, Intellectual and Artistic Contacts in the Eighteenth Century.* Professor Schwartz of Stanford in 1927 published *The Imaginative Interpretation of the Far East in Modern French Literature, 1800-1925.* The learned periodicals of comparative literature and the publications of the Oriental Societies also contain significant, brief articles, an example of which is Rémusat's "Extrait d'un mémoire sur Lao Tseu," appearing in the *Journal Asiatique* of 1823. This article dealt with the parallels of Taoism, Plato, and Pythagoras. But these titles in themselves will indicate the paucity of intensive research. The scholars of the West have been far more home-keeping than its poets.

There is little doubt that, since the Transcendental and Romantic Movements were practically contemporaneous, the question of their parallel interests in the Orient will be raised. It is a moot point whether or not there is a relation between the Oriental interests of Emerson and Thoreau and those of Coleridge and Southey, Tom Moore, Byron, and Shelley, to mention only a few outstanding English writers who were long fascinated by the East. So far as I am able to judge, there seems in this respect to be no important connection between the English and American writers. For the American Transcendentalists, the Orient was the home of the oldest philosophic truths; for the English Romanticists, it was a source of poetic glamor. The connection between the two is slight.

Ours, then, is fundamentally a problem of studying the meeting of American and Oriental idealism alone, a meeting brought about by no European middlemen save the translators. To state our problem thus is to suggest the influence of Plato and Plotinus. Harrison, in his *Teachers of Emerson,* and Carpenter, in *Emerson and Asia,* have examined this influence with such completeness that little can be added. No one, however, has pointed out the parallels between the Hindus and the writers carefully read by the American Transcendalists. To do so briefly is to suggest broadly another reason why Concord welcomed Oriental thought.

It is not too sweeping a generalization to say that when men start with the same premises they are likely to arrive at very similar conclusions. The results of comparative research bear out the generalization, as we shall see. There is no doubt that it was a dogma with Emerson. It will be remembered that he divided all men into two groups —idealists and materialists. He sided with the former unequivocally, believing that they all started with what he called the spirit, and that they all said substantially the same thing. On this basis there can be little doubt that he found the various bodies of idealistic thought with which he came in contact stepping stones to others. Platonism and Neo-Platonism were for him an introduction and corroboration of the Hindus.

His essay on Plato is the best evidence of the fact. Indeed the essay is almost as much on the fundamentals of Hindu thought as it is on the Greek philosopher. Emerson was definite in his conviction that the basis of Plato's thought was Oriental. Witness the following: "Meantime, Plato, in Egypt and in Eastern pilgrimages, imbibed the idea of one Deity, in which all things are absorbed. . . . The excellence of Europe and Asia are in his brain."[116] Witness other sentences from this essay on a representative Greek: "All philosophy, of East and West, has the same centripetence."[117] "The country of Unity . . . the seat of a philosophy delighting in abstractions . . . is Asia."[118] "The raptures of prayer and ecstasy of devotion lose all being in one Being. This tendency finds its highest expression in the religious writings of the East, and chiefly in the Indian Scriptures, in the Vedas, the Bhagavat Geeta and the Vishnu Purana."[119] There seems but one explanation for the presence of these sentences and numerous quotations from the Hindu scriptures in the essay. He drew no other distinction between Platonism and Indian thought than that which he drew in a Harvard lecture on Neo-Platonism and its dependence on the East. In that lecture he is reported to have said, "When Orientalism in Alexandria found the Platonists, a new school was produced. The sternness of the Greek school, feeling its way forward from argument to argument, met and combined with the beauty of Orientalism."[120] In view of Emerson's evident merging of Hindu and Greek thought, it would seem a legitimate task to examine the results of investigations by competent scholars in the subject, to see how sure a guide were his intuitions.

The historical possibility that Greek philosophy was influenced by India through the medium of Persia is generally granted. The intercourse between the Ionic inhabitants of Asia Minor and the dwellers of the countries to the East was so varied during the decades preceding and following the Persian wars, that abundant occasions must have presented themselves for the exchange of ideas between Greeks and Indians.[121] Investigators who are pressed for proof of the indebtedness of Greek philosophy to Oriental thought generally fall back on the argument that the "bitter prejudice" following the great War led the Greeks to suppress the indebtedness.[122] Scholars have differed widely with each other on the issue. The debate has yielded a great deal of fruit, and the number who have been convinced of an Oriental influence in Greek philosophy seems larger than those who would deny it. Actual intercourse is hard to prove. Eventually one falls back on analogies based on racial affinities, common temperament, and a primitive association. The period in which the Greek and Oriental parallel each other most closely and reproduce Upanishadic doctrines is between 800 B.C. and the time of the Buddha.[123] With Buddhistic pessimism the period of the Vedanta ended and agnosticism supplanted the faith in Brahma, which is broadly synonymous with the Greek Nous.

Simultaneous with the first returns of Oriental research came the pointing out of parallels. Sir William Jones himself, the father of English Oriental study, found as sweeping parallels between all the schools of thought as anyone would care to mention. Witness such words as:

Of the philosophical schools it will be sufficient here to remark, that the first Nyaya seems analogous to the Peripatetic, the second, sometimes called Vaiseshica, to the Ionick; the two Mimansas, of which the second is often distinguished by the name of Vedanta, to the Platonick, the first Sankhya, to the Italick; and the second, or Patanjala, to the Stoick, philosophy; so that Gautama corresponds to Aristotle; Canada, with Thales; Jaimini with Socrates; Vyasa with Plato; Capila with Pythagoras; and Patanjali, with Zeno. But an accurate comparison between the Grecian and Indian schools would require a considerable volume.[124]

After Jones came Colebrooke, with even a greater emphasis on the idea that the doctrines of Pythagoras might be rooted in India. He wrote: "Adverting to what has come to us of the history of Pythagoras, I shall not hesitate to acknowledge an inclination to consider the Grecian to have been . . . indebted to Indian instructors."[125]

It was Professor Richard Garbe of Tübingen who most optimistically found parallels between the Vedanta and representative Greeks. His chief point was the correspondence of the Vedantic One with the concepts of the Eleatics. "Xenophanes," he writes, "teaches that God and the Universe are one, eternal, and unchangeable; and Parmenides holds that reality is due alone to this universal being, neither created nor to be destroyed, and omnipresent; further, that everything which exists in multiplicity and is subject to mutability is not real; that thinking and being are identical."[126] Garbe continues with parallels in Anaximander, Heraclitus, Empedocles, Anaxagoras, and Democritus. His demonstrations are too general to be entirely convincing, but they are of much interest.[127]

In this connection there is no writer who is of greater assistance than Professor F. W. Bussell, whose book,

Religious Thought and Heresy in the Middle Ages, offers
a wealth of material not suggested by its title. His exposition of the difficulties confronting the scholars of both
schools and the parallels he himself draws between Plato
and the Hindus are the clearest that have yet been published. With regard to the all-important problem of evil,
Bussell points out the fact that the dualism man finds in
himself he attributes to all Nature and to God himself. In
the Zoroastrian *Avesta,* for instance, evil or the "untruth,"
admittedly one side of God's character, is paralleled by
Maya; and Brahma in the Vedanta with Being or Non-
being in the philosophy of Parmenides.[128] And in Plato's
Statesman (273) is discovered the corresponding Upanishadic belief that God is not the author of evil, but that
the Evil Principle, or Maya, exists in Him from time im-
memorial, in a manner analogous to the "dark spot in God"
which Boehme found.[129]

Plato's doctrine in the *Phaedo* (67 and elsewhere) that
death is the only portal to perfect knowledge (for after
death, the soul is no longer trammelled by the flesh) is
compared to the Hindu thought of the dreamless slumber
into which the soul enters when freed from its organs and
faculties and united with the supreme knowledge.[130] The
famous eulogy of the soul as the *prime mover* in *Phaedrus*
recalls the Upanishadic descriptions of the soul as "the
self, agent and actuator of all the world, of things that
move and move not."[131] The chariot simile Bussell also
refers to the East; and the concept of the colorless, in-
tangible Essence (*Phaedrus* 247) he finds paralleled in
the "supreme purusa, which, beyond the undeveloped principle pervades all things and is without character or form

. . . its shape is not seen in anything visible and no man hath seen this self with his eyes, though it is seen as heart, mind, intuition can reveal it."[132] Again, the *Philebus* doctrine of the highest life is paralleled with the Upanishadic notion that the wise who recognize the Self bid farewell to pleasure and pain, and becoming passionless, attain the life eternal. For, Plato has it (*Philebus* 65), truth and the pure mind are one, and he who has fathomed himself, recognizing within the highest, at once and without further effort attains all wisdom.[133]

The Hindu depreciation of public life, which Bussell calls their *incivisme,* is set against the doctrine of the *Republic* that the Guardian's true life in the State—though it be perfected to suit the purpose—lies in the private world of knowledge and the self.[134] In further support, the cave allegory of the *Republic* is offered, and the philosopher's portrait in *Theaetetus.* The *Mundaka Upanishad* scornfully speaks of those who "infatuate, deem revealed rites and works for the public good the best and highest thing in life, failing to find that other thing which is better and higher still."[135]

The detached, impartial temper with which Bussell writes renders his suggestions of great worth, for he presses no point to prove a thesis. He finds the analogies he offers suggestive but in no way conclusive of actual and conscious borrowing. Although he admits that he has not strictly proved anything, his reader feels with him, that "it is at least likely that some obscure vehicles and *media* carried eastern speculation westwards; that the exotic orphism and Pythagoras' eclectic and foreign system were somehow indebted to oriental sources."[136]

In Germany, it was Professor Lassen, who in his *Indische Alterthumskunde* flatly denied every Indian influence upon Greek philosophy of pre-Christian times.[137] However, he accepts it for Christian Gnosticism and Neo-Platonism. His opinion is that the Indian elements in the Gnostic system were derived from the Buddhism, which in a secondary and modified form had exerted an influence upon the intellectual life of Alexandria. The relations between Alexandria and India are sufficiently proved to make the contention seem valid.[138] The influence, according to Lassen, is most clearly perceptible in the Gnostic doctrines of the many spiritual worlds and numerous heavens, which in turn were derived from the fantastical cosmogony of later Buddhism.

In the thought of Plotinus, chief of the Neo-Platonists, Lassen finds a Hindu parallel in the insistence that the soul itself is free from sorrow and passion, untouched by all affection or pain, for the suffering of the world belongs to matter.[139] Another connection is established between Vedantic thought and Plotinus in the latter's insistence that one may be happy when sleeping, for the soul does not sleep, and the Hindu insistence that the dreamless sleep is homogenous with redemption.[140] A greater parallel probably is Lassen's comparison of Plotinus' and the Vedantic theories of emanation and the development of the world.[141]

Richard Garbe, building on the work of Lassen, finds the closest parallels between Plotinus and the East in the ascetic nature of Plotinus' morality. This asceticism might be explained, Garbe thinks, by an inclination toward Stoicism. But when he compares it with the Yoga system he has little doubt of its indebtedness. Here are the reasons:

Plotinus pronounces all *worldly* things to be vain and void of value, and he therefore calls upon us to throw off the influence of the phenomenal world. If we keep off all external impressions and by way of concentration of thinking overcome the multiplicity of ideas, resulting from these impressions, the highest knowledge will fill our mind, in the form of a sudden ecstatic perception of God. There is not the slightest difference between this theory and the doctrines of the Yoga philosophy.[142]

In Porphyry, the most distinguished disciple of Plotinus, the Indian influence can be proved directly, for he made use of the treatise of Bardesanes, from which he copied an important passage concerning the Brahmans. Bardesanes in turn had acquired his information about India from the Indian ambassadors at the court of the Emperor Antoninus Pius.[143]

Numerous as have been the scholars who have debated the question as it affects the ancients, there has been only one outstanding modern writer who has paid attention to the modern parallels. This is Professor W. S. Urquhart, whose *Vedanta and Modern Thought* appeared in 1928.[144] A brief exposition of the Oriental parallels which Urquhart has discovered in the philosophy of Spinoza and Fichte will be ample warrant for an attempt to discover parallels in Emersonianism. Urquhart endeavors in no way to prove that Spinoza or Fichte ever read or adopted Orient doctrine to their own uses. His effort is purely to demonstrate similarities, not inter-dependence.

Professor Urquhart finds in Spinoza the speculative tendencies of both Plato and Aristotle, and of both Sankara and Ramanuja, the greatest interpreters of the Vedanta. Spinoza shows his affinity with Sankara in that he regarded God as a characterless infinite; with Ramanuja, in "conceiving of God as the abode of all the auspicious qualities, as that which 'has absolutely infinite attributes of which each expresses infinite essence in its own kind.' "[145] And like the Hindus, Spinoza is negative in his attitude toward the world and God. The root idea of the Vedanta is the identification of the soul with God, the Atman with Brahma. With Spinoza, likewise, it is by obedience to the higher knowledge that men are to turn from the things of this world, withdraw into the depths of the soul, and in the self within attain unity with the Universal Self or God.[146]

Where the passage from the undifferenced unity of Substance to its varied attributes actually is, how the transition from the non-qualitative to the qualitative Brahma actually takes place, neither Spinoza nor the Hindus have adequately explained, and their interpreters have faced baffling difficulties and interminable disputes.

Professor Urquhart's words will state the issue and Spinoza's Oriental affinity clearly:

Do the attributes constitute the essence of Spinoza's substance or are they only fictions of the human intellect? If the former, what becomes of the doctrine of the undifferenced unity of the Brahman; if the latter, whence came the minds capable of constructing the fictions? If all ordinary experience belongs to the region of names and forms—to borrow a Vedantic phrase —will not the imaging intellect also be a mere reflection, and partake of the general illusoriness, and whence can come the energy necessary for framing the illusion and becoming dissatisfied with it, as well as that general capacity for persistence which is so fundamental an element in Spinoza's philosophy. If it is suggested in reply that these difficulties are themselves illusory, and will disappear with the disappearance of illusion, we are simply compelled to press the question farther back and ask whence came the illusory point of view at all, for even an illusion must have a cause.[147]

In attempting to deal with the question of illusion, Spinoza faces difficulties similar to those which confronted Sankara in relation to the doctrine of Maya. If the Absolute is defined as undifferentiated and changeless, then it is impossible to get any creative energy out of it.[148] But here is man with his experiences which demand explanation of their relation to the ultimate reality. "This demand can be speciously satisfied only by a conception which, like the Vedantic Maya, hovers between being and non-being; or, like the infinite modes of Spinoza, bridges only very ineffectively the gulf between static unity and dynamic multiplicity."[149] Both explanations, says Urquhart, are "illogical attempts to prevent the finite world from becoming . . . a mere impertinence in the system."[150]

Fichte, in turn, seems to have thought on practically identical terms with Spinoza on this score. Urquhart quotes Professor Rudolf Otto in an address delivered in 1925 as finding the likeness between Sankara and Fichte as "being so striking that one might almost speak of the rebirth of Indian philosophical speculation in a German personality."[151] Professor Otto declared there was no direct relationship, but the gaze of both thinkers was in the same direction. Both thought of the pure Being as an absolute unity without variety. Relationship with it was to be attained by a higher kind of knowledge, or intuition, which must be carefully differentiated from the ordinary operations of the understanding. In a universe in which the Ultimate is unchangeable and without creative energy, the passage from it to the ordinary world is the power resembling Maya, which Fichte describes in near-Vedantic language. To both professors Otto and Urquhart this is the most striking parallel of all. These are the words they quote from Fichte: "There is only the One, unchangeable and eternal, and there is nothing beyond Him. All changeable and alterable is therefore most certainly nothing. And its appearance is most certainly empty illusion. That I know."[152]

In the speculative sense there is as much nihilism in these words from Fichte, and in Spinoza's thought for that matter, as in the Vedanta. And it will be seen that the Emersonianism, to which Thoreau and Alcott largely subscribed, is in many of its cardinal tenets as close to the Orientals as are those of the Greeks and the Germans which Professor Urquhart has discovered. It is true that in life there is a broad chasm between Eastern and Western thinkers. Just why men whose gaze is in the same direction should in the end differ so radically about the value of the human personality is a question which has never been answered. They will both agree that an absolute God is the only Reality, but in their living, one will seek release and the Nirvana or a state of *no* life, and the other will seek to be a representative man, never forgetting himself, always inviting his soul in the Whitmanian sense.

We proceed to the Concord Transcendentalists and an analysis of their beliefs.[153]

PART TWO

EMERSON AND THE OVER-SOUL

In the sleep of the great heats there was nothing for me but to read the Vedas, the bible of the tropics, which I find I come back upon every three or four years. It is sublime as heat and night and a breathless ocean. It contains every religious sentiment, all the grand ethics which visit in turn each noble and poetic mind, and nothing is easier than to separate what must have been the primeval inspiration from the endless ceremonial nonsense which caricatures and contradicts it through every chapter. It is of no use to put away the book: if I trust myself in the woods or in a boat upon the pond, nature makes a Bramin of me presently: eternal necessity, eternal compensation, unfathomable power, unbroken silence,—this is her creed.
—Emerson to Samuel Gray Ward, July 18, 1840, *Letters from Ralph Waldo Emerson to a Friend,* edited by C. E. Norton.

The true doctrine of omnipresence is that God reappears with all his parts in every moss and cobweb.
—Emerson, *Works,* II, 101.

PART TWO

EMERSON AND THE OVER-SOUL

EMERSON AND THE OVER-SOUL

I

On October 16, 1823, Ralph Waldo Emerson, then a boy
not yet of age, addressed a significant letter to his favorite
aunt—Mary Moody Emerson. In the questions of this
letter is the germ of his Orientalism, in fact, of all his
maturest thought. Had he not been driven by an inner
necessity to grope for their answer, the sacred books of
the Hindus, Chinese, and Persians would never have been
more than provinces in his general information and culture. It was because these books answered his probing
questions in a way which Western writers never approached that they became to him a dear delight. Although
the Orientals are not specifically mentioned in the letter,
there is no better approach to their influence.

"I have a catalogue of curious questions," the boy wrote
his aunt, "that have been long accumulating, to ask you.
. . . I ramble among doubts, to which my reason offers no
solution."[1] Books were dull and old and unsatisfactory. He
wished an answer from a living witness and faithful lover
of the mysteries of Providence. Such an answer, could he
but procure it, would seem of more worth than all the books
of all the centuries. "Now what is the good end answered,"
ran the first question, "in making these mysteries to puzzle
all analysis?" Was not the ordinary effect of an unex-
plicable enigma opposition, ridicule, and bigoted scepti-

cism? After all, was he to be driven to the conclusion that the universe, great and glorious in its operation, aimed "at the sleight of a mountebank who produces a wonder among the ignorant by concealing the causes of unexpected effects?"[2] He realized that his questions were youthful, starting "in the infancy of inquiry," but he was mature enough to know that they were also "the longest stumbling-blocks in philosophy's way."[3]

These were only general queries. There was a host of specific problems that baffled him. What weapons had Aunt Mary prepared in active meditations for her metaphysical armory against the problem of evil? What became of a slave, born in chains, beaten and toiling incessantly, ignorant of virtue and never practicing it, who died cursing God and man? Was his lot eternal darkness because he had lived in the shadow of death on earth? And what of the millions of worldly and impure, born upon earth generation after generation, never coming up to the best rules of human virtue? They could not possibly find favor in the spiritual world toward which they were travelling. "How is it, then, that a Benevolent Spirit persists in introducing onto the stage of existence millions of new beings in incessant series to pursue the same wrong road and consummate the same tremendous fate?" As to the old knot of human liberty, "our Alexanders must still *cut* its Gordian twines." Next came the "Scotch Goliath, David Hume . . . this uncircumcised"; but where was the stripling who could stand before him, confound him, and with adroit wit prove the existence of the universe and its Founder? The years had produced a long, dull procession of reasoners; they "challenged the awful shade to duel, and struck the air."

Daily the youthful inquirer was referred to his own feelings as a triumphant refutation of the "glazed lies of this deceiver," but never would he feel safe until he had a "victorious answer set down in impregnable propositions."[4]

Now Emerson had known something of the Orientals before he wrote this letter, but it was not until after its writing that he turned his face Eastward. Perhaps it is truer to say that he turned both inward and Eastward. David Hume, "this uncircumcised," ruled the Occidental world with his Sensation philosophy. Where but within himself and in the East was a young mystic to find "impregnable propositions"? Aunt Mary had seemingly tried to lead him to the Hindus before, possibly sensing the fact that they would afford him congenial answers to his probing questions. But she had aroused only a mild curiosity. When she wrote him of the Hindu books he had answered:

One is apt to lament over indolence and ignorance, when he reads some of those sanguine students of the Eastern antiquities, who seem to think that all the books of knowledge and all the wisdom of Europe twice-told lie hid in the treasures of the Bramins and the volumes of Zoroaster. When I lie dreaming on the possible contents of pages as dark to me as the characters on the seal of Solomon, I console myself with calling it learning's El Dorado.[5]

It was an uninitiated boy who spoke in these words. What a recantation was there in later years! At this youthful stage Emerson was even evangelical. Rammohun Roy was the probable source of Mary Emerson's Oriental enthusiasms. She had written to her nephew, we may infer, of the work of this unusual Hindu and the founding of Unitarian missionary work in India. The young Emerson's answer was that he knew nothing of the man save what he had read in *The Christian Register*,[6] but he was "truly rejoiced that Unitarians have one trophy to build up on the plain where the zealous Trinitarians have builded a thousand."[7] Such words sound strange to one who has forgotten that Emerson was not always a lover of the East.

Aunt Mary's enthusiasm and the lure inherent in the books of the Orientals eventually vanquished the boy's indifference, as well as his disdain of the sanguine hopes of the men of research. Once he understood the Orientals he never ceased to love them. There were periods when the more immediate problems of life, domestic and national, pushed the books aside, but Emerson always came back to them. And with them he bolstered his faith in transcendental religion.

II

The correspondence between Emerson and his aunt marked the real beginning of his serious study of the Orientals, but not the first signs of his being aware of them. The chronological record, as it may be exhumed from the published *Journals*, commences with January, 1820, when Emerson was a college junior and in his seventeenth year. The very first entry indicating his interest in the Orient is in significant connection with the Greeks: "The ostentatious ritual of India which worshipped God by outraging nature, though softened as it proceeded West, was still too harsh a discipline for Athenian manners to undergo."[8] This sentence stands on the page, solitary and undeveloped, indicating little save the subsequent life-long habit of speaking of both Greek and Oriental in the same breath with little concern for differences, but in youth recognizing the opposition between them. The second passage followed soon. Edward Everett in a lecture had mentioned the East, and the young Emerson, recording his impressions, wrote as follows:

. . . as we go back, before the light of tradition comes in, the veil drops. "All tends to the mysterious East." . . . From the time of the first dispersion of the human family to the time of Grecian rise, everything in the history of man is obscure, and we think ourselves sufficiently fortunate "if we can write in broad lines the fate of a dynasty".[9]

Then came the description of the curious attraction toward his class-mate Martin Gay. Making note of experience, Emerson recorded:

I begin to believe in the Indian doctrine of eye-fascination. The cold eye of ——— has so intimately connected him with my thoughts and visions that a dozen times a day, and as often by night, I find myself wholly wrapped up in conjectures of his character and inclinations. We have had already two or three long profound stares at each other. Be it wise or weak or super-stitutious, I must know him.[10]

Nothing more may be indicated by these words than the fact that somewhere the youth had picked up information of Oriental teaching. Nevertheless it is the first budding of another habit, that of deliberately turning to the East for a terminology. Emerson later describes this habit aptly: "Therefore it is that we fly to the pagans and use the name and relations of Socrates, of Confucius, Menu, Zoroaster . . . because they are good algebraic terms, not liable to confusion of thought like those we habitually use."[11]

Over a year passed after the experience with Martin

Gay before the leaves of the *Journals,* in their present in-
complete form, present more tangible evidence of an
Oriental interest. But the passage which next presents itself is amply rewarding. The youth had been transported
in imagination by some magic carpet, or whisked through
space by a token from Aladdin. What occurred his editors
entitled "A Venture in Romance":

I was the pampered child of the East. I was born where the
soft western gale breathed upon me the fragrance of cinnamon
groves, and through the seventy windows of my hall the eye
fell on the Arabian harvest. An hundred elephants, apparelled
in cloth of gold, carried my train to war, and the smile of the
Great King beamed upon Omar. But now—the broad Indian
moon looks through the broken arches of my tower, and the wind
of Desolation fans me with poisonous airs; the spider's threads
are the tapestry which adorns my walls, and the rain of the
night is heard in my halls for the music of the daughters of
Cashmere. Wail, wail for me, ye who put on honor as gay
drapery.[12]

What is to be said of such a venture in romance? It is
confused, to be sure. Cashmere is far removed from the
Arabian harvests; and in the usual sense of local color,
Omar does not belong so close to the beams of the Indian
moon. But these things should not matter. The boy's
Orientalism was not yet disciplined by many books. However, it was sending out venturesome feelers.

A few months later, Emerson tried to express his
thoughts on God. There were several diary pages of these,
containing a rather youthful, monistic faith, not yet full-
blown, but clearly indicating the course of his mind. Then
appeared the fact that the young person had been reading

Sir William Jones, for he appended the following words to his sentences on God:

I know nothing more fit to conclude the remarks which have been made in the last pages than certain fine pagan strains.
. . . "Of dew-bespangled leaves and blossoms bright
Hence! vanish from my sight,
Delusive pictures; unsubstantial shews!
My soul absorbed, one only Being knows,
Of all perceptions, one abundant source,
Hence every object, every moment flows,
Suns hence derive their force,
Hence planets learn their course;
But suns and fading worlds I view no more,
God only I perceive, God only I adore![13]

The passage had been taken from Sir William Jones's "Narayena." It is indeed significant that a boy of nineteen, gropingly trying to put into words his philosophy and religion, his feelings regarding the Divine, should have found in Oriental verse the lines which seemed best to conclude his thought. The passage also offers an interesting contrast between Emerson's romantic and intellectual uses of the East.

The quotations which have been given indicate well enough the nature of Emerson's early Oriental interests, so far as one can judge from available evidence. The year 1820 was the beginning—at any rate the available sources show that he had not advanced far into Eastern lore. Two years later he had read the works of Sir William Jones, the father of the Royal Asiatic Society. But there was little evidence in these early diary pages of other books, until Aunt Mary entered with her enthusiasm and advice. Even she could not at first break down the boy's Anglo-Saxon sense of superiority.

On one occasion he read an article on Hindu mythology in the *Edinburgh Review*.[14] It recorded among other things that the two distinguishing characteristics of Hindu religion were the number and absurdity of its gods, "in which there is nothing to match it that is, or ever was, upon the surface of the globe." The writer mentioned two other prominent characteristics of the religion: "its cruelty and its sensuality."[15] The temper reflected in the young Emerson's *Journals*, after the reading, was as biased and unfriendly as the article itself. For facts he recorded that "the Indian Pantheon is of prodigious size; 330 million Gods have in it their heaven, or rather each their parlor, in this immense 'goddery.' " And he also wrote of the "squalid and desperate ignorance of untold millions who breathe the breath of misery in Asia."[16]

Back and forth, between the romantic, or intellectual, and the actual East, swung the pendulum in those early years. In February, 1824, this was his mood: "Humanity finds it curious and good to leave the armchair of its old age and go back to the scenes of Auld Lang Syne, to the old mansion house of Asia, the playground of its childhood. . . . It brings the mind palpable relief, to withdraw it from the noisy and overgrown world to these peaceful, primeval solitudes."[17] And over a decade later, in 1837, the diary pages bear these sentences:

I read with great content in the August number of the *Asiatic Journal*. Herein is always the piquancy of the meeting of civilization and barbarism. Calcutta or Canton are twilights where Night and Day contend. A very good paper is the narrative of Lord Napier's mission to China. . . . There stand in close contrast the brief, wise English dispatches, with the mountainous nonsense of Chinese diplomacy. The "red permit" writ by the vermillion pencil of the Emperor, the super-African ignorance with which England is disdained as out of bounds of civilization, and her king called "reverently submissive," etc., etc.[18]

Nevertheless, tolerance for Oriental custom and thought developed with the growth of his idealism. It required time for him to become superior to human foibles and variance. "Religion, like metaphysics or physics," he wrote at the age of twenty-one, "hath its string of old wives' tales, told to its dishonor in every country; one tissue in Assyria, another at Memphis, another in Gaul, another by the Baltic."[19] And late in life he wrote: "In matters of religion, men eagerly fasten their eyes on the differences between their creed and yours, whilst the charm of the study is in finding the agreements and identities in all the religions of men."[20] The cause of his growing tolerance was his interest in eclecticism. This interest was crucial with him. Witness the words he gave to the theologians in the making in the "Divinity School Address":

Man fallen into superstition, into sensuality, is never quite without the visions of the moral sentiment. In like manner, all the expressions of this sentiment are sacred and permanent in proportion to their purity. The expressions of this sentiment affect us more than all other compositions. The sentences of the oldest time, which ejaculated this piety, are still fresh and fragrant. This thought dwelled always deepest in the minds of men in the devout and contemplative East; not alone in Palestine, where it reached its purest expression, but in Egypt, in

Persia, in India, in China. Europe has always owed to oriental genius its divine impulses. What these holy bards said, all sane men found agreeable and true.[21]

It was very natural that Emerson's firm belief in the universally prevalent instinct of veneration should lead him to find glimmers of divinity in all the world's scriptures. His own words in the *Journal* of 1839, best define his attitude toward the Bible:

The Bible.—The transcendent, I have said, is economy also. Literary accomplishments, skill in grammar, logic and rhetoric can never countervail the want of things that demand voice. Literature is but a poor trick when it busies itself to make words pass for things. The most original book in the world is the Bible. This old collection of the ejaculations of love and dread, of the supreme desires and contritions of men, proceeding out of the reign of the grand and eternal, by whatsoever different mouths spoken, and through a wide extent of times and countries, seems the alphabet of the nations, and all posterior literature either the chronicle of facts under very inferior Ideas, or, when it rises to sentiment, the combinations, analogies or degradations of this . . . I have used in the above remarks the *Bible* for the Ethical Revelation considered generally, including, that is, the Vedas, the Sacred writings of every nation, and not of the Hebrews alone; although these last, for the very reason I have given, precede all similar writings so far as to be commonly called *The Book,* or Bible, alone.[22]

These words were written when Emerson was a man of thirty-six. At the age of forty-three he wrote more briefly in his *Journals* but with the suggestion that an intimacy had arisen between himself and the Eastern bibles: "Yes, the Zoroastrian, the Indian, the Persian scriptures are majestic, and more to our daily purpose than this year's almanac or this day's newspaper."[23] And at the age of fifty-two, after all his study and observation of life, men, books, and the Over-Soul, he was convinced that "The Bible will not be ended until creation is."[24] He felt that the wisest investment of life was to occupy time in making up his own bible by hearkening to the voice within, to the sentences which in the nursery rhyme as well as the classics of the world thrilled him like a trumpet.[25] He himself loved all these spiritual log-books of other men, because "when the intervals of darkness come, as come they must,—when the sun is hid and the stars withdraw their shining,—we repair to the lamps which were kindled by their ray, to guide our steps to the East again, where the dawn is."[26] He did not bother about differences in names. He insisted that underneath them all was the Over-Soul.[27]

III

The analysis of the exotic literary adornment which Emerson found in the Orientals may well be left for later discussion. More important were the interesting ideas which he found, and the commentaries he wrote upon these ideas. He was fascinated with them and used them abundantly, sometimes with a purpose quite contradictory to that in the Oriental mind. But however they were used, they reflected his own moods, impulses, and spiritual experience. He turned to them as a religious psychologist, not as a metaphysician. This use of many of the cardinal doctrines of the Vedanta as an expression of his own beliefs is the most interesting feature of Emerson's Orientalism. And the first and most obvious parallel is that of Brahma and the Over-Soul.

Not long ago Mr. Gilbert K. Chesterton, an able spokesman for those who conceive of the universe as composed of three distinct and separate entities, God, man, and matter, attempted to impale all absolute idealists with a question that is as unanswerable on its own grounds as it is devastating. The poser was this: "Is Picadilly Circus God?" Picadilly Circus with all that it connotes of beauty and filth, virtue and crime, the embodiment of God!

Now the human mind has never produced an idealism as extreme as that of the Vedanta, which would insist that the Absolute God is as much in Picadilly Circus as in the most immaculate madonna. The introductory discussion of the *Upanishads* has partially shown how the Indian mind came to its conclusion. Curiously enough Emerson wrote as if he had anticipated Chesterton's question and wished to be listed with the Vedantists. "What is there of the divine in a load of bricks?" he asked in his *Journal* of 1834. "What is there of the divine in a barber's shop?" His answer was clear and definite. "Much. All."[28] Stark matter and the center of the village's ribaldry the home of divinity? The Vedantic mind answers with a strong affirmative. The negative view is familiar to all the Occident. It is necessary to turn to the *Upanishads* again to understand the extreme affirmative view, and perhaps even to understand Emerson.

There is a legendary dialogue in the *Chandogya Upanishad* which has become a classic in the literature of India.[29] In it is the concentrated monistic teaching of the East. With it, divinity in Picadilly Circus, bricks, and barber shops will become intelligible. There is probably no commentary which more clearly explains the Indian philosophy of identity and the premise on which the entire Vedanta system rests. It is a long dialogue, which, somewhat abridged and paraphrased, would be as follows:

Now, there was Svetaketu, whose father said to him, "Live the life of a student of sacred knowledge. Verily, my son, from our family there is no one unlearned in the Vedas, a Brahman by connection, as it were." So Svetaketu became a pupil at the age of twelve. He studied diligently until his twenty-fourth year, became conceited, immensely learned and exceedingly proud.

Then his father said to him, "Svetaketu, since you are conceited, think yourself learned, and are proud, did you also ask for that teaching whereby what has not been heard of becomes heard of, what has not been thought of becomes thought of, what has not been understood becomes understood?"

"How, pray, Sir, is that teaching?"

With this request the father commences to instruct his son in the essentials which twelve years of schooling have not taught him.

"Bring hither a fig from there."

"Here it is, Sir."

"Divide it."

"It is divided, Sir."

"What do you see there?"

"These rather fine seeds, Sir."

"Of these, please divide one."

"It is divided, Sir."

"What do you see there?"

"Nothing at all, Sir."

Then the father said to him: "Verily, my son, that finest essence which you do not perceive—verily, from that finest essence this great Nyagrodha tree thus arises. Believe me, that which is the finest essence—this whole world has that as its soul. That is Reality. That is Atman. That art thou, Svetaketu."

"Do you, Sir, cause me to understand even more."

"So be it, my son," said the father.

"Place this salt in the water. In the morning come unto me."

The son does so and the next morning Svetaketu receives a new lesson in the mystery of Reality.

"That salt you placed in the water last evening—please bring it hither."

Svetaketu grasped for it, but did not find it, as it was completely dissolved. The father continues his commands, asking his son to drink of the water.

"Please, take a sip of it from this end. How is it?"
"Salt."

"Take a sip from the middle," said he. "How is it?"
"Salt."

"Take a sip from that end," said he. "How is it?"
"Salt."

"Set it aside, then come unto me."

Svetaketu did so, saying to himself, "It is always the same."

Then the father presents the moral. "Verily, indeed, my son, do you not perceive Being here? Verily indeed, it is here. That which is the finest essence—this whole world has that as its soul. That is Reality. That is Atman. That art thou, Svetaketu."

A number of philosophical implications are in this dialogue: transcendence, immanence, pantheism. Yet as it stands, it is but a vague parallel to Emerson's thought. He must speak for himself if any clear parallel is to be seen. "Wherever is life, wherever is God, there the Universe evolves itself as from a center to its boundless irradiation," he wrote in his *Journals*. Then he added even more provoking nouns to his bricks and barber shop: "Whosoever therefore apprehends the infinite,—and every man can,— brings all worth and significance into that spot of space where he stands, though it be a *ditch, a potato-field, a work-bench. . . .*"[30] The higher pantheism of Tennyson's flower in the crannied wall is not so sweeping as Emerson's thought. "God is the substratum of all souls. Is not that the solution of the riddle. . . .?"[31] These sentences surely suggest the *Tat t'vam asi—That art thou* doctrine of the Vedanta.[32]

The occasions when Emerson wrote of the Over-Soul as the substrate of the soul and universe are not as numerous as those on which he pointed out the heartening moral effects of his doctrine. He once wore the cloth of the Church; the effects never left him. In formulating his doctrine of the Over-Soul he paralleled the Vedanta, but in the application of his doctrine he was Christian. His own self-reliance, and that which he advocated for American youth, was a personal God-reliance, a trusting of the Substrate, expressed in a curious synthesis of Christian beatitude and Oriental monism. "Blessed is the day when the youth discovers that Within and Above are synonymous."[33]

It is no difficult task to cull from Emerson's work more passages to illustrate his doctrine. A few, in other applications, will be sufficient:

A wise old proverb says, "God comes to see us without bell"; that is, as there is no screen or ceiling between our heads and the infinite heavens, so is there no bar or wall in the soul, where man, the effect, ceases, and God, the cause, begins. The walls are taken away. We lie open on one side to the deeps of spiritual nature, to the attributes of God. Justice we see and know, Love, Freedom, Power.[34]

His theories of friendship and love are also inherent in the doctrine of the Atman which transcends and yet pervades men. "Every friend whom not thy fantastic will but the great and tender heart in thee craveth, shall lock thee in his embrace. And this because the heart in thee is the heart of all; not a valve, not a wall, not an intersection is there anywhere in nature, but one blood rolls uninterruptedly in endless circulation through all men, as the water of the globe is all one sea, and, truly seen, its tide is one."[35] This union of all seas, all tides, all beings, of man and God is ineffable. Yet the simplest person who lovingly and with integrity worships God, becomes God.[36] Forever is the influx of this better and universal self into man new and unsearchable. Emerson could only explain it by the Over-Soul. He read his doctrine into Christ's words, "I and the Father are one." He saw that man's life was unfortunately in succession and division, in parts and particles,[37] but the redeeming fact for him was that "within man is the soul of the whole; the wise silence; the universal beauty, to which every part and particle is equally related; the eternal One."[38]

Emerson would have agreed with the father of Svetaketu in every essential of the moral he wished to teach his son. His was a philosophy to which he had been driven by personal spiritual needs. He was an order-loving individual. Without the Over-Soul nothing held meaning for him. "Without identity at base," he wrote, "chaos must be forever."[39] A falling back upon his experiences and intuitions had produced the belief in the *One Bottom,* to use his own phrase. The Hindus did not give it to him; rather, it led him to the Hindus, for he held that because of it "the eminent men of each church . . . think and say the same thing."[40] The chief difference between Emerson's Over-Soul and the Hindu Brahma was that there was a Christian flavor in the former that was not in the latter, a beatitude accessible to all in earnest active moral endeavor, sufficing and perfect in every hour.

IV

The kinship of the Brahma and the Over-Soul must be qualified in one sense, however. No impartial critic can ignore the question of the nature of Emerson's God, a question not easily solved. It is obvious that the road he had taken led him far from the Judaic theology of his clergyman forebears. But the disciplines of youth were not easily discarded, and the training in Divinity at Harvard must have been an influence he never completely escaped. Also, Emerson was as difficult to pin down as a wraith. In his own lifetime he was often asked whether his was a personal or impersonal God, but he was ever reluctant to grant a definite answer. Like the Hindus, he never struggled after an exactitude of formulation or concerned himself with the meticulous correctness of his statements. And like them, he was driven by an irresistible logic to consider a negation of the personal attributes of God.

The issue became very acute after he turned theological New England topsy-turvy with the "Divinity School Address." Students persistently came to him for help. Exploring the problem himself, and still unsettled, his answer to them was anything but definite:

What shall I answer to these friendly youths who ask of me an account of Theism, and think the views I have expressed on the impersonality of God desolating and ghastly? I say, that I cannot find, when I explore my own consciousness, any truth in stating that God is a person, but the reverse. I feel that there is some profanation in saying, He is personal. To represent Him as an individual is to shut Him out of my consciousness. He is then but a great man such as the crowd worships Yet, yet, *Cor purgat oratio*.[41]

And when a friend wrote to him on the subject he answered: "Personality, too, and impersonality, might each be affirmed of the Absolute Being; and what may not be affirmed of it, in our own mind? And when we have heaped a mountain of speeches, we have still to begin again, having nowise expressed the simple unalterable fact."[42] It was a similar vein that Emerson probably answered the youths who came to him from the Divinity School before and after his famous address. The advocate of either side of the question may take assurance from such an answer, if assurance is to be got. Not so from the sole occasion which seems to be on record when Emerson stated succinctly, "I deny personality to God because it is too little, not too much."[43] If it could be completely demonstrated that his answer is to be accepted as the ground on which he stood, Emerson would be very much of a Hindu indeed. It is easy to see how in this temper he came to "the soul knows no persons" phase of his thought from which Andrews Norton reacted so violently. God could not exist, he argued, as other objects exist, a unit in an indefinite multiplicity of objects, distinct from them all as they are distinct from each other, each knowable. To think of God thus was to bring him down to the level of the finite.

Cabot attempted to temper the austerity of Emerson's thought for contemporary laymen with the explanation that he did not deny self-consciousness to God.[44] But this hardly solves the problem; nor does it dispel the force of Emerson's own words. The issue is important. Men could see clearly that Emerson's God was an indifferent God, indifferent to the praise or curses of mankind, ruling the world with a cold, inexorable law called Compensation. He was the God of the poem "Brahma," a concept very foreign in a predominantly Calvinistic land, and hardly to be called comfortable. He was not the Father of Christ.

V

More light may be thrown on the problem of Emerson's God by considering a few minor points that are inherent in his belief in the Over-Soul. The first and probably the most obvious is the doctrine of polarity and law. "The laws above are the sisters of the laws below," he writes. "Shall we study the mathematics of the sphere, and not its causal essence also?"[45] Even a superficial introduction to Hindu thought will obviate the necessity of a detailed explanation of this sentence. Throughout the universe there is a mystic affinity of the positive for the negative. In chemistry the negative valence combines with the positive. In algebra the school boy computes with positive and negative signs, with positive and negative quantities, all the while assuming that the minus quantity is as real as the plus. Emerson found everything, in all worlds, on all planes, bi-polar.[46] For positive Essence rolled through all. The laws of physics and the moral laws are one, he says:

The first quality we know in matter is centrality,—we call it gravity,—which holds the universe together, which remains pure and indestructible in each note as in masses and planets, and from each atom rays out illimitable influence. To this material essence answers Truth, in the intellectual world,—Truth, whose centre is everywhere and its circumference nowhere, whose existence we cannot disimagine; the soundness and health of things, against which no blow can be struck but it recoils on the striker; Truth, on whose side we always heartily are. And the first measure of a mind is its centrality, its capacity of truth, and its adhesion to it.[47]

The ideal of the intellect is to discover the unifying principle which comprehends and governs both the subject and object. That there is such a unity is the working principle of logic and life for both Emerson and the Hindus.[48] Emerson's doctrine of polarity is but the attempt of a Massachusetts man to state the law by which Brahma governs itself.

Take another inherent doctrine. There is a passage in the essay "Demonology" which, surprising as it may seem, has escaped the attention of students. Emerson writes: "My dreams are not me; they are not Nature, or the Not-me: they are both. They have a double consciousness, at once sub- and ob- jective. We call the phantoms that rise, the creation of our fancy, but they act like mutineers, and fire on their commander," by which Emerson means to say that every act, thought and cause is bi-polar, and "in the act is contained the counteraction." He concludes with his own expression of the familiar "Brahma" motif: "If I strike, I am struck; if I chase, I am pursued."[49]

It is not reading too much into these sentences to find in them a hint of the *neti, neti* ratiocination of the Hindus, and the *asat,* or non-being doctrine,[50] a doctrine most peculiar to the Hindu mind. The Brahman cannot be understood in terms of finite experience, they say. To indicate it, one can only point out that it is not any of the concepts found in ordinary knowledge. It is not whatever one knows as this and that. *Neti, neti.* In it is no *meum* or *tuum.*

Professor James gives a very apposite description of this feature of Hindu thinking in his *Varieties of Religious Experience:*

Their very denial of every adjective you may propose as applicable to the ultimate truth,—He, the Self, the Atman, is to be described by "No! no!" only, say the Upanishads,—though it seems on the surface to be a no-function, is a denial made on behalf of a deeper yes. Whoso calls the Absolute anything in particular, or says that it is this, seems implicitly to shut it off from being that—it is as if he lessened it. So we deny the "this," negating the negation which it seems to us to imply, in the interests of the higher affirmative attitude by which we are possessed.[51]

James then goes on to say that Dionysius the Areopagite, the fountain-head of Christian mysticism, described Absolute Truth in negative terms exclusively, for the cause of all things is neither soul nor intellect, nor can it be spoken or thought. The Absolute is without number, order, and magnitude; in it is no littleness, equality, inequality, similarity, or dissimilarity. It neither stands, nor moves, nor rests. It cannot be defined as essence, eternity, or time. Intellectual contacts do not belong to it. It is not any of the things man can postulate *ad libitum*. Dionysius denies these qualifications not because the truth falls short of them, but because they are all excelled. Truth must be above them. It must be *super*-lucent, *super*-essential, *super*-everything that can be named.[52] Mystics of this type travel toward the positive pole of truth by the "Methode der Absoluten Negativitat." Witness the thoughts of the German mystic Eckhart in this connection:

God is nameless, for no man can either say or understand aught about him. If I say, God is good, it is not true; nay more; I am good, God is not good. I may even say, I am better than God: for whatever is good, may become better, and whatever may become better, may become best. Now God is not good, for He cannot become better. And if He cannot become better, He cannot become best. For these three things, good, better, and best, are far from God, since He is above all. If I also say, God is wise, it is not true; I am wiser than He. If I also say, God is a Being, it is not true; He is transcendent Being, and superessential nothingness.[53]

At this point, in view of the fact that the argument which would establish a semblance between the Over-Soul and Brahma is by mere similarity, it might be questioned whether Emerson was not largely influenced by Eckhart or at least that part of Western mysticism which is represented by Eckhart and Boehme. Western mysticism emphatically did influence Emerson. But it also paved the way to Hinduism, making him receptive to it, for when a thinker has reached the *neti, neti* stage he is above many of the frontiers and divisive boundaries of human thought. Occidental or Oriental, he feels that his limited powers cannot compass the transcendent vastness of God, yet he is humanly impelled to describe him in his own small way. The pictures he frames of the sublime, inscrutable source of the universe are necessarily inadequate. This he knows. He knows too that personality implies a distinction of the self and not-self, and hence is inapplicable to the Being which includes and embraces all that is. The moment he reduces the Absolute to an object of worship, it becomes something less than the Absolute, for the formless is given form, the universal is made personal, the omnipresent is fixed to a local habitation, and the eternal is given a temporal setting. He therefore, as a philosopher, says God is not this, God is not that—*neti, neti.* Thus far there is no difference between Eastern and Western thinkers of this type.

The difference appears not in what men like Emerson and Thoreau think about the phenomenal, but in their attitude toward it. They insist on the power of the spirit to build this world. They look upon this world, like the Creator of *Genesis,* and find it good. The typical Hindu, on the other hand, sees in this world the absence of good, darkness, and evil. He insists on the power of the mind to get rid of it for him, to negate the phenomenal life he is obliged to live; and so he turns from it. These two attitudes are totally incompatible. Up to this point the speculative journeys of the American Transcendentalists and the Hindus are parallel. Beyond it, they part. But before the separation, the Americans took freely of the hoary wisdom of India. It is necessary to recognize the common ground of both the Over-Soul and Brahma, for very similar results followed.

Edward Emerson disclosed one manner in which his father came to think of the world as unreal. Daily the Concord seer went from the confines of his library to a larger study in the woods, regarding what he saw, not as a final fact "with a pin through it," but as an appearance, a suggestion or parable of the wisdom behind all. He saw light and flowers and shadows on solid rock; but he saw also that the light glanced, the flower unfolded, and the shadow passed. Even the solid substance of the rock was crumbling and vanishing under the tooth of the air and the erosion of natural elements, to pass into soil, seed, and man. He came to feel that all life was flowing and new each moment, that the world was in endless creation. Shadows as well as mountains were present one day and gone the next. But the Real could not so change—or be both unity and multiplicity.[54] So he probed for the Universal Fact, like the Hindus. Emerson called this Fact the Over-Soul; the Hindus called it Brahma.

VI

It was quite natural that one of the first principles in Hindu thought to attract Emerson was that of Maya. Much in his own philosophy approximated the Hindu concept. He called his own thoughts the doctrine of Illusion, but he recognized their resemblance to Maya, and he admitted that the Hindus had treated the subject with the greatest catholicity. Whether he was right or not, Emerson accepted the doctrine as fundamental.

In the *Journal* of 1861, under the date of February 18, is the following:

The doctrine of the Imagination can only be rightly opened by treating it in connection with the subject of Illusions. And the Hindoos alone have treated this last with sufficient breadth in their legends of the successive Maias of Vishnu. With them, youth, age, property, condition, events, persons, self, are only successive Maias, through which Vishnu mocks and instructs the soul.[55]

Immediately following these sentences was a quotation from the *Brihadaranyaka Upanishad:* "When he sleeps, then becomes this Purusha unmingled light. No chariots are there, no horses, no roads; then he creates chariots, horses, roads; no pleasures are there, no tanks, no lakes, or rivers; then he creates joys, tanks, lakes, rivers; for he is the agent."[56]

The *Journals* afford another passage which places superlative value on the Hindu concept of Maya:

In the history of intellect no more important fact than the Hindu theology, teaching that the beatitude or supreme good is to be attained through science: namely, by the perception of the real and the unreal, setting aside matter, and qualities and affections or emotions and persons, and actions, as Maias or illusions, and thus arriving at the contemplation of the one eternal Life and Cause, and a perpetual approach and assimilation to Him, thus escaping new births or transmigration.[57]

Emerson did not ignore the Greeks in his thinking on the subject, but he did not give them the most honored place. This emphatically went to the Hindus.

The early Greek philosophers Heraclitus and Xenophanes measured their force on this problem of identity. Diogenes of Apollonia said that unless the atoms were one stuff, they could never blend and act with one another. *But the Hindoos, in their sacred writings, express the liveliest feeling, both of the essential identity and of that illusion which they conceive variety to be.* "The notions, 'I am,' and, 'This is mine,' which influence mankind, are but delusions of the mother of the world. Dispel, O Lord of all creatures! the conceit of knowledge which proceeds from ignorance." And the beatitude of man they hold to lie in being freed from fascination.[58]

It is easy to mass quotations to show Emerson's thinking on the subject of Maya, for this Hindu doctrine found a large place in his thought. Yoganidra, the Hindu goddess of illusion, receives first mention in a passage in which Hindu, Greek, and Scandinavian mythology are eclectically merged: "I find men victims of illusion in all parts of life. Children, youths, adults and old men, all are led by one bawble or another. Yoganidra, the goddess of illusion, Proteus, or Momus, of Gylfi's Mocking,—for the Power has many names,—is stronger than the Titans, stronger than Apollo."[59] The concept is so close, so native to all his thinking that it seems to him to be a fixed rule and theory of life. "In fact we may come to accept it as a fixed rule and theory of our state of education, that God is substance, and his method is illusion. The Eastern sages owned the goddess Yoganidra, the great illusory energy of Vishnu, by whom, as utter ignorance, the whole world is beguiled."[60]

What Emerson has written of Maya compels a discussion of the Hindu doctrine. It is one of the most important, yet evasive, Oriental parallels in his thought and deserves extensive study. Space, however, prohibits an exhaustive treatment of all the conceptions the Hindus have of Maya, or an interpretation of its implications. In general, the latitude of the term is indicated by the fact that an able Hindu expositor has himself attempted to disclose the nature of Maya by comparing it with the Nous of Anaxagoras and Plotinus, with the Logos which became flesh in the Johanine Gospel, and the Logos which is the Second Person of the Trinity in the teaching of St. Paul.[61] In quite a different sense this expositor even viewed Maya in the light of the infinite modes of Spinoza—a connecting link between the phenomenal world and Brahma, between the Absolute and Being.[62] It is a principle on which the Hindus themselves differ greatly in interpretation. There is hardly an adequate definition for a term which permits such varying comparisons as have been indicated. Perhaps the best and most suggestive exposition will be found in Sankara's illustration which attributes the phenomenal world to Brahma as a snake is likened to an innocuous rope:

A man may in the dark mistake a piece of rope for a snake and run from it, frightened and trembling. Thereupon another man may tell him, "Be not afraid, it is only a rope, not a snake," and he may then dismiss the fear caused by the imagined snake and stop running. But all the while the presence and the subsequent absence of his erroneous notion as to the rope being a snake make no difference whatever to the rope itself.[63]

The riddle of Sankara's rope is the riddle of the universe, as the Hindu sees it. The reason why the rope appeared a snake is a question which, in Radhakrishnan's words, "schoolboys raise and philosophers fail to answer."[64]

So the Hindus say that Maya registers man's finiteness and sets the limit to his knowledge. It is the name of the dividing force, the finitising principle, and that which measures out the immeasurable and creates form in the formless. It is a quality of the Real, but in itself it must be unreal, never identical with nor different from the Central Reality, else the world is dualistic. Maya cannot exist, for if it did, it would constitute a limit to Brahma. Still, if it does not exist the world cannot be accounted for. It is real enough to produce a world, but not real enough to limit Brahma. When men see trees it is because the trees *are* there. The Hindu's logic would say that the trees are not the Real, though this same logic cannot fully explain their presence. The trees are therefore called Maya, which term loosely accounts for all phenomenal life. Maya is accepted as the *modus operandi* of the universe, concealing the eternal Brahma under an aggregate of names and forms. Browning expressed a thought closely akin to the Hindu concept in "Bishop Blougram's Apology":

> Some think Creation's meant to show him forth,
> I say it's meant to hide him all it can.

Of course it all seems a paradox. Men live in a world of matter whose metaphysical properties Boswell says Doctor Johnson thought he had determined by striking his foot with mighty force against a large stone. Doctor Johnson demonstrated the materialistic view; Sankara, with his symbols of the rope and snake, the purely idealistic. The Hindu would say that the root of the problem is logical and psychological, that the pluralistic universe is the result of an error in judgment.[65] When men intuit Brahma, the question of the nature of the world never rises, for a principle which disarms all discussion is seen as a fact. Standing on logic, they will see that the pure Brahma needs not to be related to the world, which is but an imaginary difficulty. The finite is the infinite hidden through certain barriers. There is no real solution for an imaginary difficulty. Men have but failed to discriminate between Reality and its appearance. The sole end of the Vedanta is to lead men to recognize the Real. And realization is like the restoring of eyesight to a blind man by the grace of God.

The words of a Hindu will show in other ways the difference between the Unreal, or Maya, and the Real:

Brahma is without attribute, and form, Maya is endowed with both; Brahma is infinite, Maya finite; Brahma is immaculate and serene, Maya fleeting and restless; Brahma is without adjuncts, Maya is full of them; Maya is visible, Brahma invisible; Maya perceptible, Brahma imperceptible; Maya perishable, Brahma imperishable; Maya groweth, Brahma waxeth not; Maya diminisheth, Brahma waneth not; Maya appealeth to the ignorant, Brahma attracts him not; Maya is born, Brahma is birthless; Maya dieth, Brahma is deathless; Maya descendeth into cognition, Brahma is beyond cognition; Maya fructifieth, Brahma doth not; Maya dissolveth, Brahma is indissoluble; Maya palleth, Brahma is a joy forever; Maya changeth, Brahma is immutable; Maya acteth, Brahma is beyond all activity; Maya assumeth various forms, Brahma is formless; Maya is of the five elements, manifold, Brahma is one and eternal. . . . Maya is spread everywhere enveloping the Brahma, the sage alone can pierce through the mist.[66]

It cannot therefore be strictly said that the phenomenal world is nothing. Emerson and the Hindus do not deny the existence of so-called matter.[67] But as idealists, believing the infinite to be Absolute, they faced the necessity of somehow preventing the finite world from becoming. So they say that matter itself is the veil, the Maya, through which men see only glimpses, like glints of gold in a lump of ore, of the Beauty and Perfection which is God. But God is not to be seen by finite eyes; and men err when they think that the ephemeral forms He assumes in the process of creation are real. The highest beatitude which the mystic can seek is the perfection of the spiritual sense which will enable him to see and know nothing but God as the Essence interpenetrating all matter. In the supreme moment of illumination the oneness of subject and object, of substance and shadow, the relativity of all objects in the world, and the non-ultimate nature of oppositions is realized. In the words of St. Paul, "When that which is perfect is come, that which is in part shall be done away."

The belief touched Emerson closely. How vital it was to him, how inseparably a part of the entire man, was never better shown than in the essay "Experience." Even after the death of his own son, he could say that affections, emotions and persons were all to be set aside as illusions. "Grief too will make us idealists," although the true realization comes "with the costly price of sons and lovers."[68] The sentence suggests that even Ellen Tucker had become unreal. Again Emerson writes in the same essay:

In the death of my son, now more than two years ago, I seem to have lost a beautiful estate,—no more. I cannot get it nearer to me . . . it does not touch me; something which I fancied was part of me, which could not be torn away without tearing me nor enlarged without enriching me, falls off from me and leaves no scar.[69]

Emerson also distilled the belief into his poetry. The following brief lines which are quoted from "Illusions" were probably as much of an enigma to the men who first

read them as was the poem "Brahma." In the light of the
doctrine of Maya they offer no difficulty at all.

> Sleep is not, death is not;
> Who seem to die live.
> House you were born in,
> Friends of your spring-time,
> Old man and young maid,
> Day's toil and its guerdon,
> They are all vanishing,
> Fleeing to fables,
> Cannot be moored.
> See the stars through them,
> Through treacherous marbles.
> Know the stars yonder,
> The stars everlasting,
> Are fugitive also,
> And emulate, vaulted,
> The lambent heat lightning
> And fire-fly's flight.[70]

There is another short poem to which Emerson has given
as title the very Hindu word "Maya." Such a title cannot
be insignificant, and the lines themselves have images and
suggestions which an Oriental might easily parallel from
his scriptures:

> Illusion works impenetrable,
> Weaving webs innumerable,
> Her gay pictures never fail,
> Crowds each other, veil on veil,
> Charmer who will be believed
> By man who thirsts to be deceived.
>
> Illusions like the tints of pearl,
> Or changing colors of the sky,

Or ribbons of a dancing girl
That mend her beauty to the eye.[71]

Our discussion of Maya may be summed up with the
words which Emerson's editor wrote as introduction to the
essay "Illusions": "As a boy in college, Emerson probably
owed to Plato his first notion of the shadowy and deceptive
character of events and experiences, especially to the image
of the Cave in the *Republic*. The thoughts of Plato led him
in later years to their remote source in the Hindoo Scriptures, whose influence threw new light for him upon the
Bible of his youth, widening its significance."[72] To this it
is justifiable to add, that the Hindu books gave more than
a larger significance to the Greek. The Hindus gave a
terminology, a poetic imagery, and a deeper insight.

VII

The Vedanta teaches that Maya as concealment has no
power over the liberated soul.[73] When the mirage has been
dissipated by true knowledge, the illusory appearance of
the world remains, but it no longer deceives. The same appearance is seen, but a different value is given to it. And
so the emancipated man may logically set about to develop a cosmogony from appearances.

The theory of emanation which is to be found in the
Vedanta is not unique. It may be found in Neo-Platonism
and in the systems of some of the most eminent Christian
philosophers and German mystics. Kirtikar claims as kinsmen for the system such thinkers as Thomas Aquinas,
Eckhart and Tauler.[74] Plotinus and Emerson may be
added to this group. Certainly the latter's cosmogony is
inconsistent with the Hebraic. Neither is it Aristotelian

with its distinctions of the first mover and the first matter.
When he writes,

> Ever fresh the broad creation,
> A divine improvisation,
> From the heart of God proceeds,
> A single will, a million deeds,[75]

his thought can be explained only in the light of a theory
of emanation from some Transcendent Immanence that
comprises all things. "What are these thoughts we utter,"
he asks in his *Journals*, "but the reason of our incarnation? To utter these thoughts we took flesh, missionaries
of the everlasting Word which will be spoken."[76]

The Vedanta repudiates as an unscientific conception
of creation whatever implies, first, a creation out of nothing; and, secondly, the concept of the *deus ex machina*,
the separation of the Creator from His creation; and
thirdly, in this implication, the leaving unexplained the
organic growth and development of all the life in the universe.[77] "Matter," writes Radhkrishnan, "cannot develop
life or consciousness unless it had the potentialities of them
in its nature. No amount of shocks from the external en-
vironment can extort life out of mere matter."[78] There
must be an identity of existence in the effect and its cause,
between *causa* and the *causatum*. The effect is ever latent
in the cause; the cause is identical with effect. In the words
of the *Aitareya Aranyaka*, "Whatever there is belonging
to the son belongs to the father; whatever there is belonging to the father belongs to the son."[79]

The metaphors with which the Vedanta illustrates this
endless creative chain of cause and effect are indeed apt
and eloquent. The figure of the spider and its web, of hair

and nails growing on an animate body, of the sea and its
waves and the foam which comes from the sea, seeming to
finite eyes different but in reality not, and eventually returning to its kindred source—with such figures do Hindus
explain their conception.[80] To these may be added the mystery of the bearing of a child by its mother, and the melody
which flows from a flute merely because of a breath which
passes through the reed.[81] The breath is a symbol of
Brahma flowing through a universal flute. The notes seem
different, but they all come from and are of the mystic
breath of life pervading all things, even all matter, as salt
pervades the water in which it is dissolved. In thus giving
of itself, Brahma is not diminished, for all the virtue that
thus passes out, any more than the light coming from the
sun leaves the sun changed. How all this can be the *Upanishads* do not explain save in the language of symbols and
similes, some of which have been given.

The seeming blindness of Emerson to the difference between the scientific principle of evolution and the moralis-
tic laws of compensation disappears when his thought is
taken in conjunction with the Vedanta.[82] The Indian doctrine, and the Emersonian, is that the Over-Soul, through
the laws of its own being throws itself into manifestations
on itself. Emerson, however, contrary to the Vedanta, erects
the principle of law into a doctrine of causal agency, or
free will, as a basis for his Western doctrine of Self-reliance. His theory, expressed in the lecture on "Human Culture," is this:

Man drinks of that nature whose property it is to be
Cause. With the first surge of that ocean he affirms, *I am*. Only

Cause can say I. But as soon as he has uttered this word he transfers this *me* from that which it really is to the frontier region of effects, to his body and its appurtenances, to place and time. Yet is he continually wooed to abstract himself from effects and dwell with causes; to ascend into the region of law. Few men enter it, but all men belong there.[83]

The comment which Professor Gray makes on this passage is illuminating. "This is the most impossible of compromises," he writes. "Man cannot 'belong' in one kind of existence and 'be' in another . . . for it leaves an impossible dualism in the nature of man."[84] Had Professor Gray realized that Emerson used Oriental thought, what seems an impossible compromise would not have occurred to him, for it would have been explained by the doctrine of Maya. It is the veil before all mortal eyes which creates the seeming paradox of man *belonging* to one realm and *being* in another.

In the world of nature which is imbedded in the Universal Mind,[85] then, the method of advance is "perpetual transformation. Be ready to emerge from the chrysalis of today, its thoughts and institutions, as thou hast comes out of the chrysalis of yesterday."[86] The poetic expression of this phase of Emerson's thought will be found in "The Three Dimensions," which was printed in the *Dial* but never in the published poems. In this poem Emerson presents the thought of the One entering into variety, just as Brahma projects itself into the various world of Maya:

> Room! cried the spheres when first they shined,
> And dived into the ample sky:
> Room! room! cried the new mankind,

And took the oath of Liberty:
Room! room! willed the opening mind,
And found it in Variety.[87]

Emerson shared with Thoreau an impatience for the conventional interpretation of science. "Science was false by being unpoetical. It assumed to explain a reptile or mollusk, and isolated it,—which is hunting for life in graveyards. Reptile or mollusk or man or angel only exist in system, in relation. The metaphysician, the poet, only sees each animal form as an inevitable step in the path of the creating mind."[88] Of course what might be construed as possible theological evolutionism is not Oriental emanation. But Emerson's idealistic thought, as it includes nineteenth-century science, is hardly to be called theological evolutionism in the usually understood Occidental sense. There is as close a parallel between his view of the method of the world's becoming as exists between any of the other broad resemblances with the Vedanta that he has himself suggested.[89]

VIII

In Hindu thought the doctrine of Karma is of equal importance with that of Maya. It finds its reflection in Emerson in his doctrine of Compensation.

The charge of amateurishness, of playing the ostrich and hiding from the winds and weather of fact in a relentless world, has been leveled at Emerson more because of this law than any other element in his Transcendental system. The layman scoffs because he sees little evidence of the law in his work-a-day world. The affluent are not always the guileless; the afflicted are not always the sinful. Gray, in the dissertation that has already been mentioned, speaks of the flat absurdities of the over-praised essay; and John Erskine, writing in *The Cambridge History of American Literature,* attempts to impale Emerson's thought by reducing it to absurdity. "The thief is punished," he writes, "though the police never find him, for the price of theft is loss of innocence, fear of arrest, suspicion of other men. What compensation is destined for the victim of the thief, optimistic Transcendentalism preferred not to investigate."[90] Thus laymen and scholars have ridiculed the doctrine of Compensation.[91] It has fared worse than any other tenet in Transcendentalism.

A complete study of the place of Fate in Emerson's thought must take into account the Hindu, Greek, and Mohammedan aspects. Emerson himself disposes of the Greek with little ceremony, in a passage of the *Journals* in which his dependence on the Hindu Karma emphasizes itself:

The Indian system is full of fate, the Greek not. The Greek uses the word, indeed, but in his mind the Fates are three respectable old women who spin and shear a symbolic thread, —so narrow, so limitary is the sphere allowed them, and it is with music. We are only at a more beautiful opera, or at private theatricals. But in India, it is the dread reality, it is the cropping-out in our planted gardens of the core of the world: it is the abysmal Force, untameable and immense. They who wrestle with Hari, see their doom in his eye before the fight begins.[92]

In such a passage Emerson's insight into the Hindu books he read is clearly seen. He was deeply impressed with the Hindu doctrine, else how account for the following from his essay on "Fate"?

It was a poetic attempt to lift this mountain of Fate, to reconcile this despotism of race with liberty, which led the Hindoos to say, "Fate is nothing but the deeds committed in a prior state of existence" . . . To say it less sublimely,—in the history of the individual is always an account of his condition, and he knows himself to be a party to his present estate.[93]

A possible source of confusion in thinking of this Oriental aspect of Fate must be clearly pointed out. Emerson's wide reading of the Persian Mohammedans, particularly Hafiz and Saadi, brought characteristically into his verse and prose a deluge of quotation and allusion to a form of fate far removed from the Hindu law of Karma which is similar to the basis of his doctrine of Compensation. The Kismet of the Mohammedan is not the Karma of the Hindu. Kismet is the decree of Allah, an autocratic god whose word is never questioned, whose dictates are irrevocable, whose word is a law unto itself. Karma can be transcended by a man's will, if he devotes all his energies to the good and by good deeds accumulates the merit which will advance him upward on the tortuous road to Brahma; the Kismet of the Mohammedan was the decree of Michael Wigglesworth's God in *The Day of Doom*. Struggle against Kismet was as useless as it was for any one who was not elect.

When Emerson quotes, in the essay on "Self-Reliance": " 'Thy lot or portion of life,' said Caliph Ali, 'is seeking after thee; therefore be at rest from seeking after it,' "[94] he is inconsistently using the fatalism of the Mohammedan, which is incompatible with that of the Hindu. There are other baffling passages which show Emerson's confusion. Take as an instance one from the *Journals* of 1834: "The

Mussulman is right, by virtue of the law of Compensation, in supposing the scraps of paper he saves will be a carpet under his feet over the bridge of Purgatory. He has learned the lesson of reverence to the name of Allah."[95] The Mohammedan might enter paradise on a carpet of paper or by rushing on his enemy's sabre in a holy war,[96] but not the Hindu. Such fate is not the compensation to which man "knows himself to be a party." Emerson had a love for the poetry of the Persians which seems to have grafted upon his mind love's characteristic blindness. As will be seen in the discussion of Persian poetry, he read into the Mohammedans what he wished to find, and ignored that against which he had inherent prejudice. He seems never to have realized that Mohammedanism had far more affinity with the Hebraic thought in which he himself had been schooled as a clergyman, than with Hindu thought.

Against the autocratic decrees of Allah and Calvin's God, the Hindus asserted the principle that whatsoever a man reaps, that must he have sowed. All that he suffers or enjoys is the fruit of his own deed, a harvest sprung from the actions of a previous life. No one, according to the Vedanta, inherits the good or evil deed of another.[97] And the Hindu argues that the facts of life are on the side of the believer in Karma. Sin does lead to suffering. Men do reap what they sow. Experience testifies to the truth of the principle. Its logic is verified in life.

The doctrine is obviously counter to much in Christian ethics, particularly vicarious suffering, such as is exemplified in the bearing of one another's burdens and seen in sublime form in the Cross of Christ. And it may be argued that life also demonstrates conclusively that men do suffer the good and ill effects of others' deeds, for human society is so linked together that any act may touch with pleasure or pain an indefinite number who have no responsibility for it. Christian ethics approves of the doctrine of Karma in so far as it states the principle that the wage of sin is death. But it goes further, and considers the individual in society, whereas the Hindu considered the individual alone.

Emerson gave intellectual assent to the Hindu doctrine and practical expression to the Christian ethic. His law of Compensation seems to have had a native growth in his mind. In the memorable letter written to Aunt Mary with which this book commenced, he expressed an early aspect of his doctrine. There he had asked what became of the slave, born in chains, beaten and starved, toiling incessantly, ignorant of virtue and never practicing it, dying with curses upon God and men. And what, he asked his aunt, of the millions of worldly and impure, born generation after generation upon earth, never coming up to the best rules of human virtue? He felt they could not possibly find favor in the spiritual world toward which they were travelling. Why, then, did God persist in introducing upon the state of existence the millions who in incessant series pursued the same wrong road and consummated the same fate? Neither Calvinism, nor Unitarianism, nor any other theology of Emerson's time gave such an answer as the Hindus offered in Karma. The alternatives were between Michael Wigglesworth's God, who might have assigned the easiest room in hell to the ignorant slave, or some diluted, modified form of Protestant theology, and a doctrine akin to the rigorous logic of the Hindu which stated that each man's fate was in his own hand.

So as the youthful Emerson pondered life, he formulated his own doctrine of Compensation. We have his own words for it. In a reminiscent talk on the two years spent with his brother William in teaching school, the years when still in his teens his sensitive spirit shrank from the uncongenial work and he wrote the youthful "Good Bye, Proud World," he told how his leisure hours were employed. "I was at the very time already writing every night, in my chamber, my first thoughts on morals and the beautiful laws of compensation and of individual genius, which to observe and illustrate have given sweetness to many years of my life."[98] And as Emerson grew older he rejected the Greek interpretation of Fate as too easy-going, found that the *Bhagavadgita* and the *Upanishads* approved of his own theory, found in fact that Karma and Compensation were practically two coins of the same mintage, until coming upon the Mohammedan Kismet he mistook it for Karma because it was Oriental.

No uncongenial response could have come to Emerson's thoughts of Compensation even from his mother. One almost gets the impression that it was she who first planted the seed in his mind. There was a note of austerity that is not wholly maternal in the conclusion of the mother's letters to her sons:

Wishing you all the happiness consistent with a life of progressive knowledge, piety and heavenly wisdom, I remain,
Your truly affectionate friend and mother,
RUTH EMERSON.[99]

It is of course true that Compensation may also have had its roots in other creeds, and parallels for it may be found in other systems. The very eclectic aspects of Emerson's thought would almost presuppose this. What he wrote of Karma and admitted of its worth are the important things for the student of his Orientalism to remember. Both Karma and Compensation were the consequences of very similar attitudes toward the world and the Over-Soul. Emerson argues that either Chaos or Law is at the base of things. If Law, then God is not mocked. The familiar identification of all law, moral and physical, is the logical outcome. Both Karma and Compensation represent the counterpart of the physical law of uniformity in the moral world. They are the laws of the conservation of moral energy as well as of physical energy in a world where there is nothing uncertain or capricious. The process of moral evolution, or devolution, is no more to be arrested than the sweep of the tides or the course of the stars. As futile is it to attempt the evasion of the Karmic process as it is to evade one's shadow. Emerson wrote:

You think me the child of my circumstances: I make my circumstance. Let any thought or motive of mine be different from that they are, the difference will transform my condition and economy. I—this thought which is called I—is the mould into which the world is poured like melted wax. This mould is invisible, but the world betrays the shape of the mould. You call it the power of circumstance, but it is the power of me. Am I in harmony with myself? my position will seem to you just and commanding. Am I vicious and insane? my fortunes will seem to you obscure and descending. As I am, so shall I associate, and so shall I act.[100]

Emerson's essay "Compensation" and all that he ever wrote in his diaries on the doctrine, indicate how far he had travelled from the theism of his time. Both Karma and

Compensation are utterly inconsistent with theism, for they are unconscious principles which control the universe, a drag-net in which even God could conceivably be caught. Emerson never wrote of escaping from one's sin through the grace and atonement of Christ. He always thought in terms of absolutes. He insisted that a mechanical law would administer itself. If Law, and not Chaos, controlled the universe, it would work itself out. In writing of this Law in the affairs of men, he was very partial to the Hindu expression of it, practically ignoring its reflection in other systems of thought.

IX

In the Hindu mind Karma is inseparable from an elaborate eschatology and the doctrine of Transmigration. Transmigration is the method of recompensing good and bad merit. This doctrine cannot be regarded as a matter of belief with Emerson, but he played with it, both seriously and humorously. It may be well to note some of these occasions, in order to determine how the doctrine fitted into his thought.

The essay "Swedenborg" offers one of the most interesting passages in this light:

The Arabians say, that Abul Khain, the mystic, and Abu Ali Seena, the philosopher, conferred together; and, on parting, the philosopher said, "All that he sees, I know"; and the mystic said, "All that he knows, I see." If one should ask the reason of this intuition, the solution would lead us into that property which Plato denoted as Reminiscence, and which is implied by the Brahmins in the tenet of Transmigration. The soul having been often born, or, as the Hindoos say, "travelling the path of existence through thousands of birth," having beheld the things which are here, those which are in heaven and those which are beneath, there is nothing of which she has not gained the knowledge: no wonder that she is able to recollect, in regard to any one thing, what formerly she knew.[101]

In the same essay Emerson later offers a more provoking passage, indicating that he had examined both the Hindu and Greek aspects of the doctrine:

That metempsychosis which is familiar in the old mythology of the Greeks, collected in Ovid and in the Indian Transmigration, and is there *objective*, or really takes place in bodies by alien will,—in Swedenborg's mind has a more philosophic character. It is subjective, or depends entirely upon the thought of the person.[102]

Emerson's last words on Swedenborg are that he thinks of him as a "transmigrating votary" from an Indian legend who said, "Though I be dog, or jackal, or pismire, in the last rudiments of nature, under what integument or ferocity, I cleave to right, as the sure ladder that leads up to man and to God."[103]

The pages of the *Journals* also give instances of Emerson's use of the doctrine. Most interesting is probably what he wrote in 1845:

For this Indian doctrine of transmigration, it seems easy of reception where the mind is not preoccupied. Not more wonderful than other methods which are in use, and so readily suggested, not only by the manners of insects, but by the manners of men. Here is a gentleman who abused his privileges when in the flesh as a gentleman, and curtailed therefore his amount of vital force. We cannot kill him, for souls will not die. This punishment, self-imposed, is, that he take such form as his diminished vital force can maintain. Now it takes, to make a good dog, say, half a grain; to make a peacock, a quarter grain; to make a great general, a pennyweight; a philosopher, two; a poet, ten; and a good and wise man, a thousand pounds. Now our ill-behaved man, on emerging from his rotten body, and a candidate for a new birth, has not capital enough to maintain himself as a man, and, with his diminished means, nothing is left for it but that he should take a turn through nature, this time as monkey. That costs very little, and by careful governance in the monkey form, he shall have saved something and be ready at his turn to begin the world again more decently, say, as a dog. There he saves again, and, at the end of that period, may drop his tail, and come out Hottentot. Good Hottentot, he will rise, and one of these ages will be a Massachusetts man.[104]

Of course such sentences are not convincing. If one could have heard Emerson read them aloud, he probably would have detected a baffling chuckle and good humor in the voice. Yet after suggesting the rise of the Hottentot into the Massachusetts man, he becomes more sober and writes, "What other account is to be given to these superfluous triflers who whisk through nature, whom we are sure we have seen before, and who answer no purpose to the eye while they are above the horizon? They are passing through their grub state, or are expiating their ill economy of long ago. 'Travelling the path of life through thousands of births!' "[105] Furthermore he writes in all literalness of the suttee, the custom of the Indian widow who

. . . burns herself on her husband's funeral pile, because she believes in Transmigration; and being born again, if faithful, in a form not less than the last, retains enough memory to find her husband in his new form, though a dog, or a jackal, or a wolf, and, by affectionate speech, recalls to him also his memory and exhorts him to divest his present unworthy weeds. In the long rotation by fidelity they meet again in worthy forms. The flame of the funeral pile is cool to the widow.[106]

And as an afterthought he adds that the Occident has nothing to correspond to this practical doctrine of Transmigration. All its theories were sentimental and literary.[107]

The facts of life presented a sad spectacle for him. "The transmigration of souls," he writes in "History," "is no fable. I would it were; but men and women are only half human. Every animal of the barn-yard, the field and the forest, of the earth and of the waters that are under the earth, has contrived to get a footing and to leave the print of its features and form in some one or other of these upright, heaven-facing speakers. Ah! brother, stop the ebb of thy soul,—ebbing downward into the forms into whose habits thou hast now for many years slid."[108]

It is probably true that Emerson is merely figurative in these words. Cheap people are animal-like. But it is worthwhile to note other instances in which the doctrine is reflected in his work. At the mellow age of sixty-six he thought of infinite time as belonging to God, who could have given man, had He willed, "one immense track of a lazy millenium."[109] Instead, "He cut it up into a neat succession of new mornings," and with each granted man a new lease on life, and new ideas, inventions and applications. There is no definite suggestion of Transmigration here, but a quarter of a century before, he had written prophetically of his sense of the cosmic vitality within, significantly apostrophizing Indur: "Life itself is an interim and a transition; this, O Indur, is my one and twenty thousandth form, and already I feel old Life sprouting underneath in the twenty thousand and first, and I know well that he builds no new world but by tearing down the old for materials."[110] He saw reason for nothing but optimism. Self-reliantly, he asked nothing of men, believing that in the endless mutation, the firm column must presently appear king of all men, seated on the throne.[111]

What, finally, can be said of Emerson's belief in Transmigration? It is clear that he was not hostile to the doctrine. His premises and his sympathy with the Hindus forbade that. The materialistic view that the soul was annihilated at death was untenable for him. He was strong in the conviction of the eternality of the soul. At the same time he probably never accepted the theological theory that God creates a new soul every time a child is born. The sexual act creates a new life in the human sense, but it does not adequately explain the new life itself. It was easier for Emerson to think of a deathless soul as a portion of God, manifesting or emanating itself in the germ and assuming the shape it was destined to take. The one qualification he would probably have placed on an acceptance of the Hindu doctrine was that it be subjective, depending entirely on the thought of the individual, which obeys, or strictly speaking, manifests the Over-Soul.

There is much of poetry in the language with which the Hindu scriptures describe the release of the soul from one body and its reincarnation into a new form. Some of the most beautiful figures appear in the *Brihadaranyaka Upanishad,* from which Emerson quoted in his *Journals.* In this *Upanishad* man approaching the portal of death is described as a caterpillar that has come to the end of a blade of grass, whence it draws itself over to a new blade. Just so man, having put aside one body, draws himself over to a new existence.[112] Again the mutation of the soul is likened to the work of a goldsmith. "As a goldsmith, taking a piece of gold, reduces it to another newer and more beautiful form, just so this soul, striking down this body and dispelling its ignorance, makes for itself another newer and more beautiful form."[113] Emerson the poet, reading such sentences would not have quarrelled with them, for he was free to interpret them as he wished.

But he probably had more difficulty with another passage of the same *Upanishad*, which tells of those who in the forest truly worship and strive for realization of the Brahman. After death they pass into the flame of the cremation-fire; "from the flame, into day; from the day, into the half month of the waxing moon; from the half month of the waxing moon, into the six months during which the sun moves northward; from these months, into the world of the gods; from the world of the gods, into the sun; from the sun, into the lightning-fire."[114] They return to earth in the form of rain; from rain they take the form of grain and vegetable foods and are eaten by animal life. The bridge between the vegetable and animal kingdoms is seminal. "Again they are offered in the fire of man. Thence they are born in the fire of woman. Rising up into the world, they cycle round again thus."[115] By no stretch of the imagination is it possible to accept this mythology as one in which Emerson believed. The *Katha Upanishad*, which had come to his hand through Thoreau's bequest, presented the future life in less fantastic terms: "Look how it was with those who came before, look forward how it will be with those who come hereafter. A mortal ripens like grain, like grain he springs up again."[116] Emerson could have accepted such a simile.

His belief in personal immortality waned as did his belief in a personal God. At the age of twenty-four he felt himself immortal. His *Journal* demonstrates this: "I believe myself immortal. The beam of the balance trembles, to be sure, but settles always on the right side. For otherwise all things look so silly."[117] But as the years advance his certitude fades. In the essay on "Immortality" he experiences difficulty in finding a place for personal immortality in his system. "I confess that everything connected with our personality fails. Nature never spares the individual."[118] At times his optimism and faith rise and he believes that "if it be best that conscious personal life shall continue, it will continue."[119] But at last this impulse of personal faith also vanishes and he tells us that an

... individual body is the momentary arrest or fixation of certain atoms, which, after performing compulsory duty to this enchanted statue, are released again to flow in the currents of the world. An individual mind in like manner is a fixation or momentary eddy in which certain services and powers are taken up and minister in petty niches and localities, and then, being released, return to the unbounded soul of the world.[120]

In conclusion, Emerson's eschatology was a very composite affair, made up of Greek, Hindu and modern concepts, among the last—evolution. In 1833, after seeing the ascending steps of animal forms in the Jardin des Plantes of Paris, he wrote in his *Journals:* "We feel that there is an occult relation between the very worm, the crawling scorpion and man."[121] In "Bacchus" appear the lines

> And the poor grass shall plot and plan
> What it will do when it is man.[122]

And in 1836, while lecturing on "The Humanity of Science," Emerson spoke on Lamarck's theories and quoted him: "He says to the caterpillar, How dost thou, brother? Please God you shall yet be a philosopher."[123] It is with such instances of his interest in scientific theory that his interest in Transmigration must be considered.[124]

Emerson had very definitely discarded his past and current New England theology. His premises of the Over-Soul and Compensation forced him to reckon with some theory of a future life. As he himself said, it was impossible to kill a deathless soul, so the doctrine of annihilation was definitely counted out. His youthful correspondence with Aunt Mary indicated that neither Calvinism nor Unitarianism had satisfied him. No vague Universalist conception, even, could quite explain the end of the millions of triflers who appeared in incessant series, or the slave who died in complete ignorance with bitter curses. Compensation, with some modified form of Transmigration, seemed the only logical and impartial interpretation of the future. When the soul went home to the Over-Soul, Compensation followed after. This Emerson believed. His published work, however, does not indicate that he ever considered the exact manner in which the soul is reincarnated into new forms. Evolution probably became for him a symbol of the upward march of the soul, and the mutations of animal qualities the emanations of the Over-Soul. If the issue is pressed to a nicety, it must be admitted transmigration was for Emerson probably more a metaphor of the spiritual career of the soul than the full career of the Hindu's karmic body. Nevertheless he clearly believed that in petty niches or in great, as justice warranted and the universal law of Compensation decreed, the momentary fixation of life served its allotted time.

X

As a result of Emerson's pains to punctuate his writings with the language and symbolism of the Hindu scriptures, numerous similarities have appeared between his thought and the Vedanta. The correspondence of the Over-Soul and Brahma as the only Reality has been suggested, as well as the extensive use which Emerson made of the doctrine of Maya to describe the illusory nature of the phenomenal world. Similarly he considered Karma and Compensation to be corresponding forces regulating the affairs of men here and hereafter. There is reason to expect, therefore, that echoes of the Hindus will be heard when Emerson's thoughts on the origin of sin and evil are examined.

A quaint conceit of Freud's lends itself aptly as an introduction to this subject. It is one of his cynicisms that the child in its mother's womb is the happiest of all creatures. He has been aware of no conflict. He knows no limitation of desire; his needs are satisfied before he knows of them. His universe is exactly as it ought to be. The discomfort of being born is the first evil that enters his existence, the first stab of pain which mars what had been an all-enfolding, all-sufficing existence in which he was unconscious of good or evil. In Emerson's thought, man's coming to consciousness, his projection into a world from the unconscious source, was his fall.[125] Spirit no longer functioned according to its own perfect laws. When the intellect and will wished, like the Prodigal Son, to leave their native place and become something of themselves, then came the lapse. The moral will was attained at the expense of innocence. "The men, though young, having tasted the first drop from the cup of thought, are already dissipated; the maples and ferns are still uncorrupt; yet no doubt when they come to consciousness they too will curse and swear."[126] It is this separation from God, the being born into a world of sense where Maya rules supreme, that presents the problems of redemption. Why men were born they do not know. The unalterable fact is that they are here and must get back home. The following is Emerson's view of how the return is to be effected:

The problem of restoring to the world original and eternal beauty is solved by the redemption of the soul. The ruin or blank that we see when we look at nature, is in our own eye. . . . The reason why the world lacks unity, and lies broken and in heaps, is because man is disunited with himself. He cannot be a naturalist until he satisfies all the demands of the spirit. . . . We make fables to hide the baldness of the fact and conform it, as we say, to the higher law of the mind. But when the fact is seen under the light of an idea, the gaudy fable fades and shrivels. We behold the real higher law.[127]

Now there is nothing essentially Hindu in this passage when it is considered by itself. The context of *Nature* is decidedly that of Western idealism. Yet when Emerson's predilection for the Vedanta is considered, it is not necessarily far-fetched to read into these words the rishi's method of salvation by *recognition*. The thought that a seeming lack of harmony without is the result of a lack of harmony within, is probably to be found in all systems. This must be admitted. But the point is that the Vedanta,

and the Hindus who practice its asceticism, insist that
salvation means to be led from the unreal to the real, from
materialism to idealism, until all illusions fade and the
devotee recognizes the highest in Brahma as in himself
and all matter. He continually strives for this stage of
enlightenment. The superb prayer of the *Brihadaranyaka
Upanishad,*

> From the unreal lead me to the real!
> From darkness lead me to light!
> From death lead me to immortality!

expresses the Salvation he yearns for. Though Emerson
may not have considered the Hindus when he wrote of his
view of redemption, he assuredly said the same essential
thing.

In his consideration of evil Emerson pushed his monism
to its logical ultimate. "Good is positive," he wrote. "Evil
is merely privative, not absolute: it is like cold, which is
the privation of heat. All evil is so much death or non-
entity."[128] He fortifies his argument with other examples:
"To science there is no poison; to botany no weed; to
chemistry no dirt."[129] In the realm of consciousness into
which men have fallen, it is the obstructed that calls the
obstructor evil. Men often raise a standard of good, and
whatever is contrary to it is pronounced bad. To a mouse,
the cat is the greatest evil; to man, the cat may be a bene-
faction; the same object serving in both cases as good and
evil. Thus in the absolute sense evil must be relative.

But reasoning evil out of existence does not solve man's
conflict with it. Once in a great while Emerson came down
from the thin air of his Olympus and faced the problems
which confronted men, showing that there were moments

of awareness. He realized that a real and formidable doubt menaces men when they face fate, destiny, luck and fortune, and realize that the

. . . laws of the world do not always befriend, but often hurt and crush us. . . . We have too little power of resistance against this ferocity which champs us up. What front can we make against these unavoidable, victorious, maleficent forces? What can I do against the influence of Race, in my history? What can I do against hereditary and constitutional habits; against scrofula, lymph, impotence? against climate, against barbarism, in my country? *I can reason down or deny everything, except this perpetual Belly: feed he must and will, and I cannot make him respectable.*[130]

But such moods of despondency were rare. Emerson retreats quickly to his Ivory Tower. What he does there John Morley has described: "The courses of nature and the prodigious injustices of man in society affect him with neither horror nor awe. He will see no monster if he can help it. For the Nemesis or terrible Erinnyes, daughters of Erebus and Night, Emerson substitutes a fair-weather abstraction named Compensation."[131] He had no eye like Dante's, for the vileness and cruelty, the utter despicableness to which humanity may be moulded. But his son Edward defends him with these words: "It is now imputed as a shortcoming that he did not do justice to the prevailing power of evil in the world. Fortunately he did not. It was not the message given to him. He could not. For that which made him live and serve and love and be loved was—a good Hope."[132]

In 1847, while Emerson was in England he wrote home to his family, describing some of the things he had seen.

Dear Lidian, . . . Ah! perhaps you should see the tragic specta-
cles which these streets show—these Manchester and those
Liverpool streets, day by day and by night,—to know how
much of happiest circumstance, how much of safety, of dignity,
and of opportunity, belongs to us so easily, that is ravished from
this population. Woman is cheap and vile in England, it is tragi-
cal to see; childhood, too, I see oftenest in the state of absolute beggary. My dearest little Edie, to tell you the truth,
costs me many a penny, day by day. I cannot go up the street
but I shall see some woman in rags, with a little creature just of
Edie's size and age, but in coarsest ragged clothes and barefooted, stepping beside her; and I look curiously into *her*
Edie's face, with some terror lest it should resemble *mine,* and
the far-off Edie wins from me the half a pence for this near
one. Bid Ellen and Edie thank God they were born in New
England, and bid them speak the truth, and do the right forever and ever, and I hope they and theirs will not stand barefooted in the mud on a bridge in the rain all day to beg of
passengers. But beggary is only the beginning and the sign of
sorrow and evil here.[133]

Men will easily understand Emerson's terror that it
might have been his own little Edie standing barefooted
all day in the rain and mud. They will understand and
sympathize. But when Emerson has returned to his own
complacent Concord and found his little Edie snug and
warm he writes in a different tenor: "I cannot look without
seeing splendor and grace. How idle to choose a random
sparkle here and there, when the indwelling necessity
plants the rose of beauty on the brow of Chaos and discloses the intention of Nature to be harmony and joy."[134]
Many will say that it was a sad thing that the only word
Emerson had for the forlorn mother in that stark Man-

chester scene was a vague, "Hear what the Morning says and believe that."[135] There were many who could not tolerate such a blind optimism. Carlyle was among them.

Carlyle contrasted himself with his friend in a conversation with Charles Eliot Norton:

"There's a great contrast between Emerson and myself. He seems verra content with life, and takes much satisfaction in the world, especially in your country. One would suppose to hear him talk that ye had no troubles there, and no share in the darkness that hangs over these old lands. It's a verra strikin' and curious spectacle to behold a man so confidently cheerful as Emerson in these days.

"Well, it may be as you say. I'm not such a verra bloody-minded villain after all" (here a cordial laugh,) "not quite so horrid an ogre as some good people imagine. But the warld is verra black to me; and I see nothin' to be content with in this brand new, patent society of ours. There's nothing to hope for from it but confusion. I agree with ye in thinkin' that the times that are comin' will be warse than ours, and that by and by men may, through long pain and distress, learn to obey the law eternal of order, without which there can be neither justice nor real happiness in this warld or in any other." . . .[136]

The worst of the matter, some would say, is that Emerson is deliberate in the turning of his eyes toward the bright. Men who feel like Carlyle have difficulty in forgiving him for this, at least for saying that evil is not positive, and for attempting to reason it out of existence. One last passage to illustrate Emerson's thought and the bluntness with which he stated it will be sufficient:

A philosophy which sees only the worst; believes neither in virtue nor in genius; which says 'tis all of no use, life is eating

us up, 'tis only question who shall be last devoured,—dispirits
us; the sky shuts down before us. A Schopenhauer, with logic
and learning and wit, teaching pessimism,—teaching that this
is the worst of all possible worlds, and inferring that sleep is
better than waking, and death than sleep,—all the talent in the
world cannot save him from being odious. But if instead of these
negatives you give me affirmatives; if you tell me that there is
always life for the living; that what man has done man can do;
that this world belongs to the energetic; that there is always a
way to every thing desirable; that every man is provided, in the
new bias of his faculty, with a key to Nature, and that man only
rightly knows himself as far as he has experimented on things,
—I am invigorated, put into genial and working temper; the
horizon opens, and we are full of good will and gratitude to the
Cause of Causes.[137]

Nowhere is there a more illuminating evaluation of Emerson and his belief than Charles Eliot Norton's penetrating
analysis of the man as he came to know him through the
intimacy bred on shipboard during a trans-Atlantic crossing:

His serene sweetness, the pure whiteness of his soul, the reflection of his soul in his face, were never more apparent to me;
but never before in intercourse with him had I been so impressed
with the limits of his mind. . . . He can accept nothing as a fact
that tells against his dogma. His optimism becomes a bigotry,
and, though a nobler type than the common American conceit
of the preeminent excellence of American things as they are,
has hardly less of the quality of fatalism. To him this is the
best of all possible worlds, and the best of all possible times. He
refuses to believe in disorder or evil. Order is the absolute law;
disorder is but a phenomenon; good is absolute, evil but good in
the making. . . . He is the most innocent, the most inexperi-

enced of men who have lived in and reflected on the world; he is also the most cheerful and the most hopeful. . . . He has not allowed himself to doubt the supremacy of the best in the moral order. He is never weary of declaring the superiority of assertion and faith over negation.[138]

Norton finally concludes by stating that whatever the limitations Emerson's creed may have put to his intelligence, it served as the foundation of a large and beautiful morality. "He would find no difficulty," Norton writes, "in entering any kingdom of heaven; his sympathies will be perfect with its denizens. If by any mistake he were to visit Hell he would deny its existence, or find it what he believes it, still the abode of good and the realm of order."[139]

One is impelled to explain Emerson's optimism if he can. It may be well, however, to take into account some of the explanations that have already been made.[140] Few have come to write on Emerson without feeling an urge to tackle the problem. Most of the views have been divergent, and yet all have found warrant in the essays. Francis Grierson states that "the explanation of Emerson's optimism lies in his intellectual aloofness, his mental indifference to the things beneath the plane on which he lived." With this opinion most laymen will agree. William F. Dana denies that the source is to be found in Christian dogma, and W. Robertson Nicoll finds it to be a "direct inference" from some of Emerson's "propositions." Augustine Birrell is sure that it "rests on his theory of compensation." Professor William James, likewise, has attached himself to the company of investigators and finds the source of Emerson's optimism in the philosophical directions of his states of mystical ecstasy. And finally, Henry David Gray sees the source "only in his evolution doctrine." This is a notable list of men who have written of the problem Emerson has presented. To attempt a new explanation from the Oriental basis is not to indulge in the ungrateful and uncongenial task of disproving what these men have said. It is rather to see whether new light might not be thrown on the problem, by virtue of the fact that it has never been fully attempted before.

All Emerson's Hindu-like premises converge to explain his optimism. Temperament and the sequestered life of Concord probably had much to do with determining his point of view; they conspired with and abetted his love for the mystics and idealists. He saw evil and he suffered pain, but they could not touch him. His faith in the reality of the ideal world was so fundamental that even the loss of a bride and his first-born in a brief time left no deep scar. When he could thus rise above the cruelest evils that death could deal him personally, it was no blindness to pain and suffering that made him forget the rain-soaked, barefooted Manchester child. His optimism, instead of being blindness or indifference, is a most persistent type of therapeutics.

Emerson neither placed the responsibility of evil on God, nor did he relieve him of it, by accepting something like the mythology of Persia which made Satan responsible for it. Had he done so, he would have been traitor to his belief in the Universal Oneness of the Over-Soul. To reinstate a dualism between God and Satan was but to escape from the problem. The religion of his forefathers had done that, but their theology failed to meet his needs. It did not meet all the facts consistently and logically. It needed an apologia, like Milton's effort to justify the ways of God to men. Even as a boy in the teens he groped for a religious philosophy which should say that the moral universe was run by undeviating Law and not an arbitrary Calvinistic deity.

Whatever the devious routes were by which Emerson, an eclectic, came to a creed of Transcendental absolutes, he arrived eventually at a position where he could view good and evil as opposite only from the point of view of ignorance or Illusion. This idealism is represented among all peoples. Failings and sin belong to the unreal phenomenal world and cannot possess metaphysical significance. To reason thus is not to deny their existence; it is but to say that they do not touch the Absolute. God must be beyond our little goods and ills, relative as they are to individual human tastes and ends that are ephemeral. All difficulty was overcome for Emerson by the doctrine of Compensation, as it is overcome for the Hindu by Karma. God's acts, he argued, were not arbitrary but with reference to the deeds of men. The creation men live in is the result of deeds, the scene of atonement for past works. God's rôle is that of the Gardener who gives rain and life and the opportunity for growth. It is unjust to attribute to him what is due to the vital forces of a plant and the nature of the seed. This is a just summary of the essays "Illusion" and "Compensation" and the tenor of all Emerson's work.[141]

The manner in which Deussen, one of the ablest expositors of the Vedanta, sums up the difference between the Brahman and Christian points of view will show with which side Emerson is in closer agreement. "Christianity sees the essence of man in will, Brahmanism in knowledge; there-

fore for the former, salvation consists in a transformation of the will, a new birth, whereby the old becomes
the new man; for the latter in a transformation of knowledge, in the dawning of the consciousness that one is
not an individual but Brahman, the totality of all Being."[142] Words which Emerson himself wrote may well be
quoted again to show where he stood: "The problem of
restoring to the world original and eternal beauty is solved
by the redemption of the soul. The ruin or the blank that we
see when we look at nature, is in *our own eye.* . . . The reason why the world lacks unity, and lies broken and in
heaps, is because man is disunited with himself."[143] The
veil of Maya must be pierced. Men must be shown that
they are one, part and parcel, with the Over-Soul. For both
Emerson and the Vedantist, salvation is in the spiritual
eye which is not deluded by the mirage of phenomena.
Their seeming blindness to pain, and indifference to many
of the material provocations of men, rise from their ir-
repressible idealism and the universal law by which it
acts. The difference, essentially, between Emerson and the
Hindus is that, being Occidental, Emerson probably had
a much more positive conception of how unity was to be
restored. Also, his *knowledge* was undoubtedly permeated
with *will.* Emerson, as the world knows, was not a passive
ascetic. These facts reflect his heritage and his environ-
ment, but they do not destroy the broad Oriental likeness
in his conception of how man is to be saved from evil or his
place in the universe.

XI

The Confucian, or Chinese, parallel is to be found in
Emerson's ethical writings.[144] Obviously his ethics cannot

be taken as the mere talk of a cultured gentleman. It is a consistent part of his idealism, as spontaneous as it is eclectic, a fusion of all that he had read.[145] "There is no more in Emerson's ethics," wrote Professor Gray, "than the translation and elaboration of his philosophical dicta in ethical terms; indeed the ethics implies the philosophy just as the philosophy entails the ethics."[146]

Emerson's broad, eclectic premises may be stated in brief review. Man innocent was man unconscious. After he became aware of himself and an objective world, the insidious work of Maya commenced, and like the prodigal son of Christ's parable, he sought to be something of himself. Thus came the lapse, and the moral will was attained at the great expense of innocence. But although man is morally free, the laws of fate are back of what seems to be individual freedom. In the largest sense it is fate that keeps the universe law-abiding, fate synonymous with the controlling forces or laws, the highest and most inclusive of which is the moral law. This moral law—in man the moral sentiment—is the substrate and ground-work of the human being. For this reason man is moral. And since man is part and parcel of nature, it, too, must be moral. From these principles Emersonian ethics are evolved. Man's duty is to find his center. When he has found that, Deity will shine through him. The essay on the Over-Soul is primarily a discussion to this end.

The tie that bound Emerson to Confucius was their common belief in the goodness of man. Their differences—if they have not already been suggested—may be passed over. Emerson's speech in honor of the Chinese embassy at the banquet in Boston in 1868 will best express that for which he valued the Chinese:

Confucius has not yet gathered all his fame. When Socrates heard that the oracle declared that he was the wisest of men, he said, it must mean that other men held that they were wise, but that he knew that he knew nothing. Confucius had already affirmed this of himself: and what we call the GOLDEN RULE of Jesus, Confucius had uttered in the same terms five hundred years before. His morals, though addressed to a state of society unlike ours, we read with profit today. His rare perception appears in his GOLDEN MEAN, his doctrine of Reciprocity, his unerring insight,—putting always the blame of our misfortunes on ourselves; as when to the governor who complained of thieves, he said, "If you, sir, were not covetous, though you should reward them for it, they would not steal." His ideal of greatness predicts Marcus Antoninus. At the same time, he abstained from paradox, and met the ingrained prudence of his nation by saying always, "Bend one cubit to straighten eight."[147]

One may well question whether Socrates, Jesus, and Marcus Antoninus were as Confucian as Emerson thought. As always, his mind was a composite of many things he had eclectically brought together and interpreted in his own way. His reading of the doctrine of Karma into the incident of the governor and the thieves is an excellent example. He seems not to realize that a person's Karma is his very private problem, whereas the Confucian doctrine of reciprocity is social in a very broad sense. His Confucianism will best be examined in his own uses of it.

First of all, it must be noted that Emerson had scorned the Chinese in his youth. As a young man, writing in 1824, he sounded a note of independence from the past and wrote:

> I laugh at those who, while they gape and gaze,
> The bald antiquity of China praise.[148]

When the responsibilities of manhood were on his shoulders and when he faced economic necessities, he found, after browsing among his books, that Confucius could speak to his condition. It was probably at a time when the exchequer of the family needed healthy replenishing and he was in doubt whether he should not leave the comfortable isolation of his Concord study and sally out into the larger world and gain his share of wealth that Emerson wrote:

Every one must seek to secure his independence; but he need not be rich. The old Confucius in China admitted the benefit, but stated the limitation: "If the search for riches were sure to be successful, though I should become a groom with a whip in hand to get them, I will do so. As the search may not be successful, I will follow after that which I love."[149]

And so he stayed in Concord.

But even there were disturbing nudges from friends, such as possible calls and appeals from Brook Farm and the fantastic *isms* of the new day. Alcott might have begged him to enter the ill-fated Fruitlands venture. Thoreau was considering Walden about this time. Emerson must have been tried and tempted. I imagine, in reading the following passage, that he thought of himself in the rôle of Confucius, with Alcott and Thoreau as Chang Tsoo and Kee Neih, when he wrote in his *Journal* of 1843:

Reform. Chang Tsoo and Kee Neih retired from the state to the fields on account of misrule, and showed their displeasure at Confucius who remained in the world. Confucius sighed and said, "I cannot associate with birds and beasts. If I follow not man, whom shall I follow? If the world were in possession of right principles, I should not seek to change it!"[150]

Such a passage, written during the momentous years of American pantisocracies and phalanxes, shows what a moral staff Confucius was in helping him to stand on his own feet, braced against the examples and appeals of his own spiritual brethren. But the passage is not isolated. Emerson was too intimate with Alcott to venture employing Carlyle's stern words when he told the Fruitlands farmer that his was a "damned potato-philosophy" which would never solve the evils of the world. His answer to the agrarian principles which governed the management of Fruitlands and Brook Farm were the words of Mencius. He copied them into his *Journal* of 1843. They were a sop to his conscience or his common sense, his answer to his contemporaries and the apologia for his own conduct. For these reasons, the words may well be presented in entirety here:

Chin Seang praised Heu Tsze to Mencius as a prince who taught and exemplified a righteous life. A truly virtuous prince, he added, will plough along with his people, and while he rules will cook his own food.

Mencius. Does Heu Tsze sow the grain which he eats?

Seang. Yes.

M. Does Heu Tsze weave the cloth and then wear it?

S. No: Heu Tsze wears coarse hair-cloth.

M. Does Heu Tsze wear a cap?

S. Yes.

M. What sort of a cap?

S. A coarse cap.

M. Does he make it himself?

S. No: he gives grain in exchange for it.

M. Why doesn't he make it himself?

S. It would be injurious to his farming.

M. Does he use earthenware in cooking his victuals, or iron utensils in tilling his farm?

S. Yes.

M. Does he make them himself?

S. No, he gives grain in barter for them.

M. Why does not Heu Tsze act the potter, and make everything from his own shop he wants to use? Why should he be in the confused bustle exchanging articles with the mechanics? He is not afraid of labor, surely?

S. The work of the mechanic and that of the husbandman ought not to be united.

M. Oh, then the government of the Empire and the labor of the husbandman are the only employments that ought to be united. Were everyman to do all kinds of work, it would be necessary that he should first make his implements, and then use them: thus all men would constantly crowd the roads. Some men labor with their minds, and some with bodily strength. Those who labor with their strength are ruled by men. Those who are governed by others, feed others. This is a general rule under the whole heavens.

Mencius proceeds to instance Yu, who, after the deluge, was eighty years abroad directing the opening of the channels to let off the inundation into the sea, and the burning of forests and marshes to clear the land of beasts of prey, so that he had no time to go home even, but passed his own door repeatedly without entering; and asks if he had leisure for husbandry if he had been inclined? Yu and Shun employed their minds in governing the Empire, yet they did not plow the fields. . . .[151]

Emerson employed all his energies in the labors of his study and the lyceum, and, like the Chinese, found no time to plow the fields with Alcott or Ripley. It seems improbable that the significance of the two passages from Confucius and Mencius, written into the *Journal* for the year

1843, can be over-emphasized. It was the *urbane* Emerson that was Confucian. "Confucius, glory of the nations, Confucius, sage of the Absolute East, was a *middle* man. He is the *Washington* of philosophy, the *Moderator* . . . of modern history."[152] In many ways this is also a picture of Emerson.

The simplest and clearest exposition of further influence from the reading of the Confucian books is to note the most significant instances in the essays in which Confucian thought is apparent. It is now obvious that what Confucius gave Emerson was moral corroboration of his observations on men—not the universe. The parallels which appear are therefore totally different from those to be found in the Vedanta.

In the passages of the essay "Spiritual Laws" which deal with character and its self-evident nature, Emerson made use of a Confucian quotation which he had previously copied into his *Journals*. "No man need be deceived who will study the changes of expression," he wrote. "When a man speaks the truth in the spirit of truth, his eye is as clear as the heavens. When he has base ends and speaks falsely, the eye is muddy and sometimes asquint."[153] The emphasis on the eye finds a curious analogy in similar words from Mencius: "Of all parts of the body there is none more excellent than the pupil of the eye. The pupil cannot be used to hide a man's wickedness." Mencius continues: "If within the breast, all be correct, the pupil is bright. If within the breast all be not correct, the pupil is dull. Listen to a man's words and look at the pupil of his eye. How can a man conceal his character?" More of Emerson's words from the same context will show the relation between these sentences. "A man passes for what he is worth." This is quite Emersonian. "What he is engraves itself on his face, on his form, on his fortunes, in letters of light. Concealment avails him nothing, boasting nothing. . . . Confucius exclaimed,—'How can a man be concealed?' "[154] This quotation was, of course, the previously quoted *Journal* passage[155] which in the original was: "Chee says, observe what a man does. Observe whence his actions proceed. How can a man remain concealed! How can a man remain concealed!"[156]

There is another parallel to be found in "Spiritual Laws." When Emerson wrote, "Very idle is all curiosity concerning other people's estimate of us, and all fear of remaining unknown is not less so,"[157] he approximated Confucius' thought in the *Analects* on the same theme. The Chinese sage had said: "Be not grieved that you are not known, but seek to be worthy of being known."[158] And again, closer to Emerson's thought: "I will not be concerned at men's not knowing me; I will be concerned at my own want of ability."[159]

The essay "Friendship" also contains a very Confucian sentiment: "Set the highest value on faithfulness and sincerity. Have no friend unlike yourself"[160] was the laconic advice of the Chinese sage. Emerson but expanded this maxim when he wrote, "There can never be deep peace between two spirits, never mutual respect, until in their dialogue each stands for the whole world. . . . You shall not come nearer a man by getting into his house. If *unlike*, his soul only flees the faster from you, and you shall never catch a true glance of his eye."[161]

And there are parallels in "The Poet" which offer room

for conjecture regarding a verbal dependence, particularly in view of the fact that Confucius' words were transcribed into the *Journal* of 1836. He had remarked, "The accomplished scholar is not a utensil."[162] When Emerson wrote, "For we are not pans and barrows, nor even porters of the fire and torch-bearers, but children of the fire, made of it,"[163] was he conceivably enlarging upon the Confucian thought?

The essay on "Character" also offers an extraordinary parallelism in metaphor, which, like beauty, has its own ample excuse for being regarded. The metaphors seem too closely related to be accidental. In this essay Emerson wrote: "The reason why we feel one man's presence and do not feel another's is as simple as gravity. Truth is the summit of being; justice is the application of it to affairs. All individual natures stand in a scale, according to the purity of this element in them. *The will of the pure runs down from them into other natures, as water runs from a higher into a lower vessel.*"[164] Now note the same use of the water-metaphor by the Chinese, this time Mencius: "Water indeed will flow indifferently to the east or to the west, but will it flow indifferently up or down? *The tendency of man's nature to good is like the tendency of water to flow downwards.* There are none but have this tendency to good, just as all water flows downward."[165]

Whether Emerson consciously or unconsciously borrowed this unusual simile from Mencius cannot, of course, be proved, but the evidence seems to point to a conscious borrowing. Both sages were discussing the same thing—the essential moral nature of man. And later in the essay Emerson quoted directly from the *Doctrine of the Mean:*

"I find it more credible," he wrote, "that one man should *know heaven,* as the Chinese say, than that so many men should know the world." Then came the quotation from Mencius:

The virtuous prince confronts the gods, without any misgiving. He waits a hundred ages till a sage comes, and does not doubt. He who confronts the gods, without any misgiving, knows heaven; he who waits a hundred ages until a sage comes, without doubting, knows men. Hence the virtuous prince moves, and for ages shows empire the way.[166]

"For a philosopher," wrote Walt Whitman, "Emerson possesses a singularly dandified theory of Manners."[167] This criticism came from a super-democrat who naturally would have been impatient with Emerson's fondness for gentility on any score. Emerson consistently kept insisting that the outward man was an expression of the inward, nevertheless. He was perfectly aware that he went further than his countrymen in his insistence on courtesy and manners. Consider such a sentence as this from the essay on "Manners": "It is easy to push this deference to a *Chinese etiquette;* but coolness and absence of heat and haste indicate fine qualities. A gentleman makes no noise; a lady is serene."[168] Chinese etiquette in its finest form would have been most acceptable to him. The one reservation he would have insisted upon he found in the *Doctrine of the Mean.* Such words as these give the high moral note in both the Chinese and Emerson:

It is only he who is possessed of the most complete sincerity that can exist under heaven, who can give its full development to his own nature. Able to give full development to his own nature, he can do the same to the nature of other men. Able to give its full development to the nature of other men, he can give their full development to the natures of animals and things. Able to give their full development to the natures of creatures and things, he can assist the transforming and nourishing powers of Heaven and Earth. Able to assist the transforming and nourishing powers of Heaven and Earth, he may with Heaven and Earth form a ternion.[169]

The influence of this powerful passage on Emerson's thought is to be felt rather than demonstrated. A gentleman, to him, was "a man of truth, lord of his own actions, and expressing that lordship in his behavior";[170] to Confucius, "he who possesses complete sincerity, is he who, without effort, hits what is right, and apprehends, without exercise of thought;—he is the sage who naturally and easily embodies the right way."[171] Emerson's gentleman possesses more virtues than sincerity and truth: "Beyond this fact of truth and real force, the word denotes good nature or benevolence."[172] The character of Confucius' superior man was "to be cultivated by his treading in the ways of duty. And the treading those ways of duty is to be cultivated by the cherishing of benevolence. Benevolence is the characteristic element of humanity."[173] Finally Emerson made a frank avowal of his ideal social group: "A circle of men completely well-bred would be a company of sensible persons in which every man's native manners and character appeared."[174] The earmarks of a Chinese gentleman were not essentially different from Emerson's. In China, "That whereby the superior man is distinguished from other men is what he perceives in his heart;—namely benevolence and propriety. The benevolent man loves others. The man of propriety shows respect to others. He who loves others is **constantly loved by them**."[175]

There is no danger of reading too much into Emerson's insistence on propriety, and drawing a parallel between it and the Chinese emphasis on etiquette and an elaborate ceremonial courtesy. Emerson defended his own emphasis stoutly:

We may easily seem ridiculous in our eulogy of courtesy, whenever we insist on benevolence as its foundation. The painted phantasm Fashion rises to cast a species of derision on what we say. But I will neither be driven from some allowance to Fashion as a symbolic institution, nor from the belief that love is the basis of courtesy. We must obtain *that*, if we can; but by all means we must affirm *this*."[176]

The reason for Emerson's eulogy of courtesy, and its flowering in the Confucian, was the belief that man can only become inwardly perfect by expressing himself perfectly in outward manner.

Morality has sometimes been regarded by Westerners as the result of an external law imposed by an external force, be it God or some other authority. In both Confucian and Emersonian thought, however, the moral principle was that by which the individual acted necessarily and naturally. It is in the nature of things. If all men show each other benevolence and faithfulness, morality is the result of its own accord. The emphasis must be laid on human nature. Confucianists did not attempt, as did Emerson, to live in touch with an Over-Soul. However, they regulated their social order on the basis of a profound social and moral concept. Actual living by it produced very similar results.

Also, both Emerson and Confucius took it as a matter of course that the organism of the state rested on a moral basis. Politics was the external expression of ethics and justice the normal emanation of good intentions. The ultimate value of every man in the commonwealth, potentially and actually, was the aim of all government. It is in this individualism that the Oriental nature of Emerson is farthest removed from the Hindu and closest to the Chinese. Both Emerson and the Chinese thought of each individual as responsible to the other, not in any loose sense, but in the sense of the mechanism of a watch. If the watch goes badly, the fault is apparent.

No words will illustrate Emerson's whole theory of government better than the following from "Politics": "For, according to the order of nature, which is quite superior to our will, it stands thus; there will always be a government of force where men are selfish; and when they are pure enough to abjure the code of force they will be wise enough to see how these public ends . . . can be answered."[177] The following from the Chinese *Great Learning* does not need elucidation. Its affinity with Emerson's thought will be apparent. "Their thoughts being sincere, their hearts were rectified. Their hearts being rectified, their persons were cultivated. Their persons being cultivated, their families were regulated. Their families being regulated, their States were rightly governed. Their States being rightly governed, the whole empire was made tranquil and happy."[178] Not quite as close as parallels, but still important, are the following passages which emphasize the same thing. "When we do not, by what we do, realize what we desire," said Mencius, "we must turn inwards, and examine ourselves in every point. When a man's person is correct, the whole empire will turn to him with recognition and submission."[179] Emerson also placed the whole emphasis on the individual, though he never found a man to meet Mencius' ideal: "What is strange too, there never was in any man sufficient faith in the power of rectitude to inspire him with the broad design of renovating the State on the principle of right and love."[180]

If the correspondence of the preceding passages has not been self-evident, the following will be clear. There can be no misinterpretation or doubt regarding such words of Emerson as these: "that the highest end of government is the culture of men; and that if men can be educated, the institutions will share their improvement and the moral sentiment will write the law of the land."[181] Confucius but expressed the same principle in his own way: "Let there be men and the government will flourish; but without men, their government decays and ceases. . . . Therefore the administration of government lies in getting proper men."[182] The crucial identity of both the Emersonian and Confucian theories of the state can finally be stated with the utmost brevity. Emerson's was this: "The appearance of character makes the State unnecessary. The wise man is the State."[183] And the Chinese point of view will be found in these well known words: "The root of the empire is the State. The root of the State is the family. The root of the family is the person of its head."[184]

In the essays on "Politics" and "Character" will be found Emerson's chief debt to China. These essays should not be studied separately, for the interdependence of the thought is close. Direct Chinese quotations appear in them as well as allusions and parallels. If one remembers Emerson's vigorous defense of extensive quotations as justifiable when they express his thought to better advantage than his own words, one may well find more than suggestive parallels in those which appeared. Emerson was very Confucian in his theories of government. He believed implicitly in the power of the moral sentiment to renovate society. It must be granted that this is too universal a concept to be strictly confined to Confucian and Emersonian thought. The significant thing, however, which cannot be ignored, is that the Yankee Emerson is very partial to Confucian words as an expression of his own thoughts. It would be difficult to reject all the implications of such a telling passage as the following from the essay on "Character":

Confucius said one day to Ke Kang, "Sir, in carrying on your government, why should you use killing at all? Let your evinced desires be for what is good, and the people will be good. The grass must bend, when the wind blows across it." Ke Kang, distressed about the number of thieves in the state, inquired of Confucius how to do away with them. Confucius said, "If you, sir, were not covetous, although you should reward them to do it, they would not steal."[185]

Emerson thus found himself reflected in the Confucian books as well as the Indian.

XII

But there was neither a Hindu nor a Chinese monopoly on the minds of the Concord Transcendentalists. This has already been clearly shown in Emerson. It will be just as clearly seen in Thoreau and Alcott. Their eclectic bias made them cordial to all things Oriental, even the practical ethics of the Chinese. The Brahmanism of the Hindu, being transcendental, was naturally the most congenial, and therefore the most effective. But the Mohammedanism of the Persians also exerted its own peculiar influence. That this should have been, is as much an anomaly as the influence of the Chinese. Except for the Sufi sect within its fold, Mohammedanism was historically and essentially allied to the dualism of the Hebraic mind. It offered little which the *Old Testament* had not already given to the Puritan tradition of New England. For this reason an attempt to find a philosophic or religious affinity between American Transcendentalism and Mohammedanism is useless.

The Persian contribution to Emerson, therefore, is to be found only in the realm of poetry. Emerson was of course totally committed to the doctrine that Beauty is Truth, the root of which doctrine goes back to Plato. Probably all Christian mystics have been familiar with it in some form, especially in the peculiar aspect that divine love lives within every one. The mystics of Persia, accepting this thought, emphasized the manifestation of this love as dependent on externals, whether love of woman, appropriate surroundings, or a hard fate. The soul is subject to change. Ideally, it is attuned to God, who plays upon it through the externals, reminding it of its true nature. This is the fundamental principle in Sufi poetry. It should not be forgotten.

That Emerson was influenced to some degree by Persian poetry can never be doubted. The only question is that of degree. He coined the name *Seyd*, a kind of anagram from Saadi, for his ideal poet. He was asked to write the preface for the first American edition of Gladwin's translation of Saadi's *Gulistan*,[186] and not without reason. He had published an essay on Persian poetry in the *Atlantic Monthly* of April, 1858, which Holmes thought "should be studied by all readers who are curious in tracing the influence of Oriental poetry on Emerson's verse."[187] And after Von Hammer-Purgstall's translations[188] came into his hands in 1841, he experimented widely in the Persian forms, so widely that Holmes was convinced that "in many of the shorter poems and fragments published since 'May-Day,' as well as in the 'Quatrains' and others of the later poems in that volume, it is sometimes hard to tell what is from the Persian from what is original."[189] These words of half-truth must be qualified. Emerson approximated something of the general flavor of Persian poetry, it is true, but he was unable to condone the traditional and generally accepted interpretation of that poetry.

Now Mohammedanism with its dualism, and philosophic Hinduism with its monism, might seem incompatible in Emerson's mind, but he would not have considered the objects of either the Yogi or the Sufi essentially different. Nor was his own. The purpose of the Hindu was absorption into Brahma; of the Sufi, union with the Beloved; of Emerson, uninterrupted fellowship with the Over-Soul. Emerson appreciated the Hindu and wrote sympathetically in dealing with his literature. The Sufi should have fared equally well, when Emerson considered his work. But that was not his fate.

The essay "Persian Poetry" commences with a general comment on the work of Von Hammer-Purgstall as a translator. Then, of the specimens of the two hundred Persian poets which this German translator had given to the Western world, Emerson writes: "That for which mainly books exist is communicated in these rich extracts . . . there are many virtues in books, but the essential value is the adding of knowledge to our stock by the record of new facts, and, better, by the record of intuitions which distribute facts, and are the formulas which supersede all histories."[190] If one comes to the essay with foreknowledge of the essential nature of Persian poetry, the turn of the page is disappointing. Emerson enters, among numerous topics, what might be called a semi-geographical discussion, interspersed with wide-ranging quotations from sources dealing with Cyrus and Xenophon. The climate also comes in for mention, but this subject with typical inconsecutiveness merges into the influence of the amatory ditties of native girls upon a young Bedouin chief's excitement in war time, an excitement which exceeds that of the grape. And suddenly, without any sort of transition, we read: "Persian poetry rests on a mythology whose few legends are connected with the Jewish history and the anterior traditions of the Pentateuch. The principal figure in the allusions of Eastern poetry is Solomon."[191] Whereupon follow legends of Solomon's methods of travelling on his magic carpet, of Solomon learning the language of the birds "so that he heard secrets whenever he went into his gardens,"[192] and others, until we read that "It is related that when the Queen of Sheba came to visit Solomon, he had built, against her arrival, a palace, of which the floor or pavement was of glass, laid over running water, in which fish were swimming. The Queen of Sheba was deceived thereby, and raised her robes, thinking she was to pass through water."[193] Immediately after, one reads that "On the occasion of Solomon's marriage, all the beasts, laden with presents, appeared before his throne. Behind them all came the ant, with a blade of grass: Solomon did not despise the gift of the ant." As good as any in Aesop—but the informed reader is impatient, feeling that the author is very much on the surface of Sufi thought. In this essay one gets the impression that Emerson is a sailor who has been to the tropics and brought home the proverbial trinkets—say, a parrot, a sandal wood fan, silk brocades, some curios bought at a bazaar, innumerable objects of no particular consequence other than that they charmed his fancy, and a few precious gems. All these he displays.

After several other myths about Solomon, Emerson switches to Firdousi, whom he calls the Persian Homer, and tells the story of the *Shah Nameh* as he might have told a nursery tale. The résumé of the epic, in which he deals with events and characters, ends with an account

. . . of Afrasiyab, strong as an elephant, whose shadow extended for miles, whose heart was bounteous as the ocean and his hands like the clouds when rain falls to gladden the earth. The crocodile in the rolling stream had no safety from Afrasiyab. Yet when he came to fight against the generals of Kaus, he was but an insect in the grasp of Rustem, who seized him by the girdle and dragged him from his horse. Rustem felt such anger at the arrogance of the King of Mazinderan that every hair on his body started up like a spear. The gripe of his hand cracked the sinews of an enemy.[194]

But the paragraph immediately following this poetic account of Rustem is the most telling of all:

These legends, with Chiser, the fountain of life, Tuba, the tree of life; the romances of the loves of Leila and Medschnun, of Chosru and Schirin, and those of the nightingale for the rose; pearl-diving, and the virtues of gems; the cohol, a cosmetic by which pearls and eyebrows are indelibly stained black, the bladder in which musk is brought, the down of the lip, the mole on the cheek, the eyelash; lilies, roses, tulips and jasmines,—make the staple imagery of Persian odes.[195]

In this passage is revealed Emerson's broad reading in Persian poetry, and the limitations of his treatment of the subject. It shows him much impressed with the imagery, so much so that the catalogue which he gives is far more complete than one would ever have expected from a layman in the field. Secondly, it is the pivot on which an evaluation of his Persian Orientalism must turn. With such emphasis laid on the images, one wonders why he does not say more about them, especially as they are crucial in the interpretation of Sufi thought.[196]

He candidly confessed the reason: "We do not wish to strew sugar on bottled spiders, or try to make mystical divinity out of the Song of Solomon, much less out of the erotic and bacchanalian songs of Hafiz."[197] In other words, there was the venom of the scorpion in the subtle eroticism of Persian poetry. To interpret its symbols as a large section of the Christian Church has interpreted the *Song of Solomon*[198]—in terms of Christ and his Bride—was to gild the bestial. It seems paradoxical indeed that Emerson could excuse the popular perversions of Hinduism but not accept the license in Sufi imagery, especially when he writes of Persian poetry as "proof of the identity of mysticism in all periods." His Puritan heritage was poor preparation for the poetry of the Sufis.

Emerson is probably better known for his preface to Gladwin's translation of Saadi's *Gulistan*. In the essay Emerson concentrated his attention on Hafiz; in the preface, on Saadi. The two poets he compared in a Yankee manner:

Saadi, though he has not the lyric flights of Hafiz, has wit, practical sense, and just moral sentiments. He has the instinct to teach, and from every occurrence must draw the moral, like Franklin. He is the poet of friendship, love, self-devotion, and serenity. There is a uniform force in his page, and, conspicuously, a tone of cheerfulness, which has almost made his name a synonyme for this grace.[199]

It is necessary only to present choice portions of the preface to observe what Emerson would have the American audience note regarding the man he was introducing. First, he warned his readers that Oriental rhetoric might not please the Western taste, since life in the East wanted the complexity of European and American existence, and a certain monotony betrayed the poverty of landscape and social conditions:

We fancy we are soon familiar with all their images . . . rose and nightingale, parrots and tulips; mosques and dervishes; desert, caravan, and robbers; peeps at the harem; bags of gold dinars; slaves, horses, camels, sabres, shawls, pearls, amber, cohol, and henna; insane compliments to the Sultan, borrowed from the language of prayer. . . . I do not know but, at first encounter, many readers take also an impression of tawdry rhetoric, an exaggeration, and a taste for scarlet, running to the borders of the negrofine,—or, if not, yet a pushing of the luxury of ear and eye where it does not belong.[200]

The Oriental had a taste for the superlative, he noted, but the superlative, vivacious as it may be in Eastern speech, is nevertheless "distasteful in the temperate region."[201]

Proceeding, we find Emerson reading into the Persians his pet doctrines: "The poet or thinker must always be, in a rude nation, the chief *authority on religion*. All questions touching its truth and obligation will come home to him, at last, for their answer."[202] And then he tells why Saadi became his ideal poet:

I find in him a pure theism. He asserts the universality of moral laws, and the perpetual retributions. He celebrates the omnipotence of a virtuous soul. A certain intimate and avowed piety, obviously in sympathy with the feeling of his nation, is habitual to him.[203]

While no one can say that this is not a portrait of Saadi, it is decidedly a portrait painted by Emerson's hand, which was directed by numerous preconceptions of what Saadi— or Seyd—should be in order to qualify as his ideal.

There is another sense in which the preface to the *Gulistan* is a self-portrayal of Emerson. In writing of the style of the Persian poets, he notes the absence of the unity of a beautiful whole which Western criticism demanded, pointing out that "not only the story is short, but no two sentences are joined." Then comes the most paradoxical statement of all: "Wonderful is the inconsecutiveness of the Persian poets."[204] It is easy to see why Emerson, his style traditionally charged with the fault of striding the world with seven-league boots and ranging the whole gamut of his thought with so little concern for sequence that many a reader is bewildered, would have found in Persian inconsecutiveness a virtue. He explained that in a country where there were no libraries and printing, wisdom must necessarily be carried in sentences. These sentences—*lustres* he called them—entranced him. And he in turn composed lustres, with no particular thought for sequence. Herein, perhaps, lies a close affinity with the Persians, and one reason he read them so extensively. Holmes was so impressed by his pre-occupation with them that he thought it was Persian poetry that had been the most effectual of the Oriental readings. But he was wrong in the surmise. The Brahman was an intellectual ascetic; the Sufi was an epicure. Emerson was incapable of loving both equally well. Had the Sufis not written such choice, quotable and memorable sentences, packed with wisdom, Emerson might have shunned them entirely.

If, then, there is a conceivable influence of the Persians on Emerson's *lustrous* prose style, it is more than probable that a link can be found between his poetry and that of Hafiz and Saadi, his favorites. But such a connection must be different from that of "Brahma" and "Hamatreya." These poems were paraphrases of definite Vedantic models, whereas in the "Quatrains" it would probably be well-nigh impossible to show that Emerson did more than write in what he conceived to be the Persian manner.

Emerson's biographers and critics early recognized that there was such a connection. Joel Benton, writing on the quatrains and supposed translations from Hafiz, concluded that if the translation seems "a little more like Emerson than it does like Hafiz, the balance is more than preserved by his steeping his own original quatrain in a little tincture of the wine and spirit of Oriental thought. When he translated Hafiz, he was probably thinking of his own workmanship; when he described him, he was simply absorbed in the milieu of the Persian poet."[205] In another instance

Benton compares a quatrain from Hafiz with Emerson's adaptation, and finds that

. . . the kinship of the mintage is, in some respects, curious. Shall we say on account of this homogeneity that the Oriental is but another Yankee? Or is it that the Yankee is merely the Oriental moved farther west. At any rate, what Hafiz addresses to himself, and what Emerson says of him are wondrously alike in mood, texture, and tune.[206]

The instance which Benton had in mind when he wrote of Hafiz addressing himself was the following:

> Thou foolish Hafiz! do churls
> Know the worth of Omar's pearls?
> Give the sun which dims the moon
> To the noblest, or to none.[207]

And this is Emerson's portraiture of Hafiz which Benton found close in texture to the Persian:

> Her passions the shy violet
> From Hafiz never hides;
> Love-longings of the raptured bird
> The bird to him confides.[208]

It is probably unnecessary to discuss the basis on which Benton saw the kinship between Emerson and Hafiz in these quatrains.

But there were writers besides Joel Benton who sensed the "kinship of the mintage." Emerson's own son wrote: "Another influence now came in on the side of grace and finish, the Oriental poetry, in which he took very great interest, especially the poems of Hafiz."[209] And Holmes observed: "Of course his Persian and Indian models betray themselves in many of his poems, some of which, called translations, sound as if they were original."[210] Most telling of all, however, is the letter Emerson himself wrote in July, 1846, to Elizabeth Hoar, whom he always considered a sister and confidante. He had been working on some poems, he wrote, which he felt impatient to show her, "especially some verses called Bacchus—not, however, translated from Hafiz."[211] Such a confession of conscious similarity in method is revealing. William Sloane Kennedy early detected the similarity. In no manner aware, so far as it is known, of the letter to Elizabeth Hoar, Kennedy writes:

In his fine lyric cry "Bacchus", in which he calls for a wine of life, a cup of divine soma or amrita, that shall sinew his brain and exalt all his powers of thought he gives his lines, I think, the outward form of some verses by Hafiz, in which that singer intimates that, give him the right kind of wine, and he can perform wonders as if with Solomon's ring or Jemschid's wine-cup mirror.[212]

Pertinent lines from the poem itself will show better the nature of Emerson's work:

> Bring me wine, but wine which never grew
> In the belly of the grape,
> Or grew on vine whose tap-roots, reaching through
> Under the Andes to the Cape,
> Suffer no savor of the earth to escape.
>
> .   .   .   .
>
> That I intoxicated,
> And by the draught assimilated,
> May float at pleasure through all natures;
> The bird-language rightly spell,
> And that which roses say so well.
>
> .   .   .   .

> Quickened so, will I unlock
> Every crypt of every rock.[213]

What grounds there might have been for the warning to Elizabeth Hoar that the poem was not to be taken as a translation will appear when Emerson's lines are compared with those of Hafiz as presented by William Rounseville Alger in the *Specimens of Oriental Poetry*. Wine in the symbolism of the Sufis, it will be remembered, stood for the intoxication of God. Thus intoxicated, both Emerson and Hafiz write of their mystical sense of oneness with the worlds añd divine omnipotence. A sample of Emerson's lines has been given; the following is from Hafiz, as translated in Alger's anthology:

> Bring me wine! By my puissant arm
> The thick net of deceit and of harm,
> Which the priests have spread over the world,
> Shall be rent and in laughter be hurled.
> Bring me wine! I the earth will subdue.
> Bring me wine! I the heaven will storm through.
> Bring me wine, bring it quick, make no halt!
> To the throne of both worlds will I vault.
> All is in the red streamlet divine.
> Bring me wine! O my host, bring me wine![214]

It is Joel Benton who is most prolific in comments on Emerson's affinity with the style of the Persians. There are lines even from a poem on as Anglo-Saxon a theme as "Merlin" in which he finds an "almost playful Persian touch."[215] Here are the lines:

> He shall not seek to weave,
> In weak, unhappy times,

> Efficacious rhymes;
> Wait his returning stength.
> Bird that from the nadir's floor
> To the zenith's top can soar,—
> The soaring orbit of the muse
>   exceeds that journey's length.[216]

And here Benton's comment:

> I detect an almost playful Persian touch in the final cadences of this extract, as if the author were mounting to his purpose "by the stairway of surprise"—or, as if Hafiz or Firdousi himself were speaking. It is said that Persian poetry, and, in fact, all Oriental verse—admits of endless license in the matter of rhythm and versification, there being no less than three systems of metre, marked by different rules, which need not be kept separate, and which are often allowably made to coalesce in a single piece. But Emerson not only takes an Oriental freedom in his measures; he employs as the Asiatic bards do, all the machinery of subtle, unexpected and fantastic conceit. His sensitive harp catches in the air many tones.[217]

Since Emerson's information regarding all things Oriental was always second-hand, reading as he did through translations, it is obviously doubtful whether he ever could have attempted anything like an imitation of the original Oriental meters. He may have wondered about them, guessing at them in the translations he read. At best it is only safe to assume a fortunate coincidence in his love of epigram and the inconsecutive terseness of the Persians, together with a general playing with the movement of some Persian poems. An example of this will be found in a stanza from the "Song of Seyd Nimetollah of Kuhistan."[218]

Emerson prefixed a prose introduction in which he explained the thought:

> Among the religious customs of the dervishes is an astronomical dance, in which the dervish imitates the movements of the heavenly bodies, by spinning on his own axis, whilst at the same time he revolves round the Sheikh in the centre, representing the sun; and, as he spins, he sings the song of Seyd Nimetollah of Kuhistan.

The first stanza was as follows:

> Spin the ball! I reel, I burn,
> Nor head from foot can I discern,
> Nor my heart from love of mine,
> Nor the wine-cup from the wine.
> All my doing, all my leaving,
> Reaches not to my perceiving;
> Lost in whirling spheres I rove
> And know only that I love.

In the words of Joel Benton again, this is "one of his draughts on the Persian muse, which is so alive and fluent that it fairly sings and dances itself in the reader's brain."[219]

Although Benton saw the Persian muse in these lines, they are more distinctly an echo of the Emersonian muse. The poem is not a description of a primitive dance alone, with its gyrating, spinning dervishes. The exhilaration of the dance may have transported the dizzy dervish into the whirling spheres, but the identity of head and foot, heart and love, wine-cup and wine, is more evidently an echo of the familiar "Brahma" motif and Emerson's idealism, with its doctrines of illusion and substance and shadow. Such doctrines belong more to his own form of Vedantism than Sufi poetry.

Some concept of the poetics which he distilled into the word *Seyd* may be gained from such lines as,

> Was never form and never face
> So sweet to SEYD as only grace
> Which did not slumber like a stone,
> But hovered gleaming and was gone.
> Beauty chased he everywhere,
> In flame, in storm, in clouds of air.
> He smote the lake to feed his eye
> With the beryl beam of the broken wave;
> He flung in pebbles well to hear
> The moment's music which they gave.
>
> . . . .
>
> While thus to love he gave his days
> In loyal worship, scorning praise,
> How spread their lures for him in vain
> Thieving Ambition and paltering Gain!
> He thought it happier to be dead,
> To die for Beauty, than live for bread.[220]

Emerson's notebooks were full of verses about the joyful Seyd,[221] who without optimism, could not have been his ideal. These may be found in the "Fragments on a Poet," which commences with the lines,

> There are beggars in Iran and Araby,
> Said was hungrier than all;
> Hafiz said he was a fly
> That came to every festival.

The fifteen pages which these fragments occupy give a remarkably true picture of Emerson himself:

> God only knew how Saadi dined;
> Roses he ate, and drank the wind;[222]

He freelier breathed beside the pine,
In cities he was low and mean.[223]

Picture Emerson in his fondness for rural Concord, strolling under his pines or by Walden, repeating his lines in soliloquy as he composed, and it is easy to see how Saadi became Seyd.

Suggestive as may be these lines of the Seyd-Emersonian variety, they offer warrant for nothing save general surmise. They are not so faithful to the Oriental spirit as the paraphrases from Hindu models and adaptations of Vedantic imagery. There is more of the personal Emerson in them. It is probably best to accept them in the same manner as Elizabeth Hoar was advised to accept "Bacchus."[224]

The similarities which comparison has shown between certain lines of "Bacchus" and those of Hafiz of course raise a persistent question which cannot be ignored.[225] To what extent can these near-Persian poems be taken as translations? And if they are in any way translations, how faithful are they to the original? The answer has already been suggested by Holmes: it is almost impossible to distinguish between Emerson and many translations of Persian poetry. He may have occasionally modeled his own lines after poems he read in the German of Von Hammer-Purgstall or from the work of a friend like William Rounseville Alger, but under no circumstances were his lines direct translations from the Persians. Emerson knew no Oriental languages.

A specific example will serve best to indicate Emerson's workmanship as a translator. In his personal copy of Von Hammer-Purgstall's rendering of Hafiz, which I was privi-

leged to examine in his Concord library, is inserted a small
sheet of time-yellowed paper, approximately the size of an
ordinary envelope. On this paper were inscribed two unpublished renderings of lines from the German. The original poem was as follows:

In das Ohr des Verstand's ist ein Ruf von oben gekommen,
Von dem einzigen Gott: Sage; kein Gott ist als Gott.
Freunde! wem Erniedrigung ist vom Loose gefallen,
Kommt auch selbst mit Gewalt niemals zu Ehren und Rang.
Durch die Fluthen Semsems und Kewsers wird nicht gewaschen
Deines Glückes Tuch, schwarz von dem Schicksal gewebt.[226]

Appended to the fifth line was a note which Emerson used
in his rendering, and for that reason it may be well to include it also:

Semsen der Quell bei Mecca, der unter Hagars Füszen em-
porsprudelte, als sie auf der Flucht aus dem Hause Abrahams
sich in der Müste niederliesz. Kewser eine der Quellen des
Paradieses.[227]

The first rendering, with Emerson's italics for the Mohammedan *La ilaha illa 'llahu* was:

To the ear of the mind is a cry come from above.
From the only God, *Say, there is no God but God.*
O Friend he to whom low estate is from the lot appointed
Comes also himself never to honor & rank
Though the web of thy fortune were washed in the floods
Of Semsem and Kewser fountain of Mecca, fountain of Paradise
It remains woven by fate black.

Whether because he was unsatisfied with his rendering, or
because he wished to give it more grace, I cannot say,
Emerson recast his first draft into the following:

To the ear of the mind a cry has come from high heaven,
Saying there is no God but God.
O friend! he to whom low estate is by lot appointed
Strive as he may, comes never to honor & rank.
Though the web of thy life were washed
In the brook of Mecca or the brook of Paradise,
It remains woven by Fate black.

This sample translation may be taken to serve in several important ways: as an instance of Emerson's proficiency in German, as an example of his free manner in translating, and as an indication of the type of Persian poetry to which his Puritan austerity lead him. The conclusion must be that he liked the Persians because he sensed in them that which he called "the expansiveness which is the essence of the poetic element," and the corroboration of some of his own doctrines. Particularly was he enamored of their proverbs, their pithy, epigrammatic statements of age-old wisdom. What the Persians eventually gave to Emerson is best suggested by lines from Lowell's *A Fable for Critics:*

There comes Emerson first, whose rich words, every one,
Are like gold nails in temples to hang trophies on,
Whose prose is grand verse, and whose verse, the Lord knows,
Is some of it pr—— No, 'tis not even prose;
I'm speaking of meters; some poems have welled
From those rare depths of soul that have ne'er been excelled;
They're not epics, but that doesn't matter a pin,
In creating, the only hard thing's to begin;

. . . .

Now it is not one thing nor another alone
Makes a poem, but rather the *general tone,*

and in tone and expansiveness both the poetry and prose of Emerson owe a great deal to the Persians.

XIII

Early in our analysis of the various Oriental influences on Emerson's thought, it was suggested that there were philosophic doctrines which logically demanded to be examined before the purely literary effects of his wide reading. The reason will now be apparent. It lies in such differences as exist between Emerson's pseudo-Persian verse and the poems "Brahma" and "Hamatreya," differences which could never have been revealed without an understanding of the basic principles of Emerson's thought. The relation between the craftsman's play with form and his inmost thoughts is subtle. To have attempted, therefore, a deduction of Emerson's philosophy from the mere adornment of his pages would have been a dangerous thing. But to examine that adornment, both of the verse and prose, now that his beliefs are understood, is to see the former in a clearer light. Emerson used strange Oriental ornamentation in almost everything he wrote. One finds it even in the least Oriental of his *Representative Men*. A few typical examples will show his method.

Taking down a volume of Emerson's *Journals*, we see him at work. It is 1836 and he is thirty-three, preparing one of the addresses that made his fame. He is thinking of what it should contain, collecting the stuff which inflamed his audiences and brought about the declaration of independence for contemporary intellectuals. As he writes he remembers the inspiration Manu had been to him, and so he jots down:

Put into the Sermon to Scholars the brave maxim of the Code of Menu: "A teacher of the Veda should rather die with his learning than sow it in sterile soil, even though he be in grievous distress for subsistence."(Approved by C. C. E.).[228]

That he should have sought the approval of his brother Charles for this passage is interesting. But more interesting is his conscious searching for sentence and figure.

Even when he wrote to his American friends he found occasion to refer to the Orientals. He found his beloved Hafiz in a Massachusetts clergyman: "Everett's genius is Persian. The poetry of his sermons in his youth, his delight in Destiny, the elements, the colors and forms of things, and the mixture he made of physical and metaphysical, strongly recalls the genius to Hafiz."[229] When he turned to Goethe it was the same: "If we try Goethe by the ordinary canons of criticism, we should say that his thinking is of great altitude, and all level; not a succession of summits, but a high Asiatic table-land."[230] And then Carlyle, the man with whom he corresponded for long years, whose *Sartor Resartus* he launched in America, to see whom he made a pilgrimage all the way to Scotland.

Carlyle, with his unimitable ways of saying the thing, is next best to the inventor of the thing, and I think of him when I read the famous inscription on the pyramid, "I King Saib built this pyramid. I, when I had built it, covered it with satin. Let him who cometh after me, and says he is equal to me, cover it with mats."[231]

In thus writing of Everett, Goethe, and Carlyle, Emerson forced nothing strange into his style. It was natural. His theory had become a habit. There was for him no gift more welcome than a new symbol, for it "satiates, transports, converts."[232] Because of their happiest figures were the Vedas, the Edda, and the Koran remembered.

A fine-combing of Emerson's prose for samples of these symbols reveals how far he journeyed for similes and metaphors. The use of war was "to shatter your porcelain dolls; to break up in a nation Chinese conservatism, death in life."[233] When Lafayette died, the bells of America tolled. But Emerson felt that the bells of the world should toll for such a man, "the bells in all the earth, in church, monastery, and pagoda."[234] Contemporary society, he thought, was encumbered by ponderous machinery which could be likened to the endless aqueducts which the Romans built over hill and dale, but which were destined to be superseded by the discovery of the law that water rises to the level of its source. These laws and conventions of society were nothing but "a Chinese wall which any nimble Tartar can leap over."[235] He could even find a Chinese simile in his domestic, Concord life. Thinking of what he called his day-labor, probably in the garden which Thoreau helped him to cultivate, he found that it had "a certain emblematic air, like the annual ploughing and sowing of the Emperor of China."[236]

The Arabs and Persians contributed as many symbols to his thought as did the Chinese. Writing of his quiet, rural life and meditative strolls in wood and meadow, he remembered that Allah in his allotment of life "does not count the time which the Arab spends in the chase."[237] In this Emerson found comfort and justification for his woodland idling. In the essay "Over-Soul" he deplored the descent of men from their native nobility, when they are in the habitual service of the world, for "they resemble those Arabian sheiks who dwell in mean houses and affect an external poverty, to escape the rapacity of the Pacha, and reserve all their display of wealth for their interior and guarded retirements."[238] It would not be far from the mundane world of the present to the golden age, if men would eschew injustice and adorn their spiritual houses externally, he thought. This golden age he described in the "Sovereignty of Ethics": "An Eastern poet, in describing the golden age, said that God had made justice so dear to the heart of Nature that, if any injustice lurked anywhere under the sky, the blue vault would shrivel to a snake-skin and cast it out by spasms."[239] There was a salutary effect in nature. Emerson had discovered it for himself. Nature killed egotism and conceit. It dealt strictly with men; it gave sanity. This was the reason, he had read somewhere, that the Persians "let insane persons wander at their own will out of the towns, into the desert, and, if they liked, to associate with wild animals."[240]

Even some of his humor did the many-sided Emerson draw from the Orientals. His essay on "Eloquence" contains a borrowing from Saadi over which he probably often chuckled to himself and applied to the throaty preachers of his own day:

The Persian poet Saadi tells us that a person with a disagreeable voice was reading the Koran aloud, when a holy man, passing by, asked what was his monthly stipend. He answered, "Nothing at all." "But why then do you take so much trouble?" He replied, "I read for the sake of God." The other rejoined, "For God's sake, do not read; for if you read the Koran in this manner you will destroy the splendor of Islamism."[241]

Many of Emerson's readers may have wondered whether there might not have been more of an Oriental influence on his style than the mere importation of allusions and symbols. His laconisms, his terseness, his epigrammatic flavor, all suggest a larger indebtedness. This is no idle query that will fail of support. It is most probable that the growth of his mature style was abetted by his Oriental readings, which, for the most part were extremely aphoristic. Furthermore, it should be noted that he more than once experimented, playing the sedulous Stevensonian ape to his models. As a boy he wrote the fantastic and brief "Venture in Romance";[242] as a man of forty, he left the realm of romance and concerned himself with men and virtue, in a paragraph which he entitled "The Reformer." Far more important than the content is the fact that he labeled it *after the Chinese*. Those who know Confucius, his content and style, will find in the following significant purport. It was only 1843, and Emerson had many creative writing years ahead of him when he experimented thus:

There is a class whom I call the thieves of virtue. They are those who mock the simple and sincere endeavorers after a better way of life, and say, These are pompous talkers; but when they come to act they are weak, nor do they regard what they have said. These mockers are continually appealing to the ancients, and they say, Why make ourselves singular? Let those who are born in this age, act as men of this age. Thus they secretly obtain the flattery of the age.[243]

The transition from mere figures and experiments in style to allegories which suggest Emerson's philosophy is best effected by noting three sentences from the *Journals*. They are: "All science is transcendental, or else passes away. Botany is now acquiring a right theory. . . . The Avatars of Brahma will presently be text books of natural history."[244] How rich the connotation of these words is, only those with an insight into Hinduism can appreciate. If only one could know exactly what Emerson meant by them! Parallel with these words another passage may be placed. It is a diary record of a dream. As paraphrase would weaken it, it is presented in entirety:

I walked in my dream with a pundit who said, . . . he could not speak with me many words, for the life of incarnate natures was short, but that the vice of men was old age, which they ought never to know; for, though they should see ten centuries, yet would they be younger than the waters, which,—hearken unto their sound! how young is it, and yet how old! Neither, said he, ought men ever to accept grief from any external event; for, poverty, death, deluges, fires, are flaws of cold wind or a passing vapor which do not affect a constant soul. He added, that, as a river flows, and the plant flows (or emits odours), and the sun flows (or radiates), and the mind is a stream of thoughts, so was the universe the emanation of God. . . . Therefore, he added, they mistake who seek to find only one meaning in sacred words and images, in the name of gods, as Jove, Apollo, Osiris, Vishnu, Odin: or in the sacred names of Western Europe and its colonies, as Jesus and the Holy Ghost: for these symbols are like coins of different countries, adopted from local proximity or convenience, and getting their cipher from some forgotten accident, the name of a consul, or the whim of a goldsmith; but they all represent the value of corn, wool, and labor, and are readily convertible into each other, or into the coin of any new country. That sense which is conveyed to one man by the name and rites of Pan or Jehovah, is found by another in the study of earthquakes and floods, by another in the forms and habits of animals; by a third in trade, or in politics; by a fourth in electro-magnetism. Let a man not resist the law of his mind and he will be filled with the divinity which flows through all things. He must emanate; he must give all he takes, nor desire to appropriate and to stand still.

He also said, that the doctrine of Pantheism or the Omnipresence of God would avail to abolish the respect of circumstance, or the treating all things after the laws of time and place, and would accustom men to a profounder insight.[245]

In this record of a dream, in which he held philosophic converse with a pundit, Emerson has assuredly stated, with commendable insight, what he considered to be the essentials of Hindu thought. We have already attempted to qualify his acceptance of some specific doctrines. This dream-account is to be taken as an indication of how isolated paragraphs could well lead one to believe Emerson very much of a Vedantist.

The last three pages of the essay "Immortality" are, in many minds, among the most purple to be found in Emerson's writings. There the author of the "Threnody," who was struggling with despair after the death of a beautiful child, had emerged from the cloud-shadowed valley. Through the years which followed little Waldo's death that father had immersed himself in Hindu thought. At the age of fifty-three he confided to his diary, "A grander legend than Western literature contains, is the story of Nachiketas."[246] And when at last he came to write his essay on death and immortality, it was natural that the story of the boons which the death-god Yama granted to Nachiketas, with all the meaning of the tale, should be the sum of his own thought on the subject. The story has a double significance. It is the most beautiful of the ornaments for his prose which Emerson borrowed from India, and it indicates how naturally a Hindu myth expressed the conclusions to which he himself had come.

Those who remember the essay will recall that Emerson tells of Yama, the lord of Death, promising to grant three boons to Nachiketas. The youth, knowing that his father had been offended at him, asked first that the mind of his father might be appeased and anger forgotten. This boon Yama granted. For the second boon, Nachiketas asks that the fire by which heaven is gained be made known to him. Yama allows this also and urges the youth to ask the third, whereupon the youth broaches the deep question of the existence of the soul after death. He had heard some say that the soul did exist; others, that it did not. The word of Yama, the god of Death, was his last boon. Yama was perturbed. He assured the youth that the gods had asked the same question of old. The answer even they found difficult to understand, so subtle was its nature. "Choose another boon, O Nachiketas! Do not compel me to this." Nachiketas' answer was, "Even by the gods was it inquired. And as to what thou sayest, O Death, that it is not easy to understand it, there is no other speaker to be found like thee. There is no other boon like this." Yama continued in his attempts to evade the answer, offering in lieu sons and grandsons who would live a hundred years, herds of cattle, elephants and gold and horses. He adjured Nachiketas to choose the wide expanded earth, to receive the boon of living as long as he listed. Yama offered to grant anything the youth could think of, a kingdom, the gratification of all the desires of earth, even the companionship of the fair nymphs of heaven with their music, which had never yet been gained by man. All these things Yama offered, begging to be excused from telling of the state of the soul after death. Nachiketas' answer was eloquent. "All those enjoyments are of yesterday. With thee remain thy horses and elephants, with thee the dance and song. If we should obtain wealth, we live as long as thou pleasest. The boon which I choose I have said." There was no escape for Yama; there was no alternative but to grant the boon. The heart of Hinduism is in his words:

One thing is good, another is pleasant. Blessed is he who takes the good, but he who chooses the pleasant loses the object of man. But thou, considering the objects of desire, hast abandoned them. These two, ignorance (whose object is what is pleasant) and knowledge (whose object is what is good), are known to be far asunder, and to lead to different goals. Believing this world exists, and not the other, the careless youth is subject to my sway. That knowledge for which thou hast asked is not to be obtained by argument. I know worldly happiness is transient, for that firm one is not to be obtained by what is not firm. The wise, by means of the union of the intellect with the soul, thinking him whom it is hard to behold, leaves both grief and joy. Thee, O Nachiketas! I believe a house whose door is open to Brahma. Brahma the supreme, whoever knows him obtains whatever he wishes. The soul is not born; it does not die; it was not produced from any one. Nor was any produced from it. Unborn, eternal, it is not slain, though the body is slain; subtler than what is subtle, greater than what is great, sitting it goes far, sleeping it goes everywhere. Thinking the soul as unbodily among bodies, firm among fleeting things, the wise man casts off all grief. The soul cannot be gained by knowledge, not by understanding, not by manifold science. It cannot be obtained by the soul by which it is desired. It reveals its own truths.[247]

This was the answer which Yama gave to Nachiketas. This was the comfort which Emerson offered his fellows through his essay. In the Over-Soul was no death. What seems so was, as Longfellow said, but transition to the life Elysian. As Yama had promised, the answer was subtle, but Emerson grasped it. It was a happy boon to receive, because it gave him assurance of his immortality here.

XIV

In the poetry also of Emerson one finds evidence of borrowed figures and models for paraphrase. The poem "Brahma" is, of course, the outstanding instance. No single poem ever mystified its readers more. Probably no poem ever will. It will always remain an enigma to the Western mind. Oliver Wendell Holmes writes of it as "the nearest approach to a Torricellian vacuum of intelligibility that language can pump out of itself," and in his own discussion unwittingly discloses his failure to grasp its essential significance.[248]

Even Emerson's publishers plead with him to omit the poem when they were about to publish the *Selected Poems* in 1876, because of the ridicule it invoked. Emerson insisted that "Brahma" was to be retained, whatever else went by the board.[249] In this poem, if ever it can be found, is the Kipling sense of the incompatibility of the East and West. When it came to "Brahma," Emerson and Holmes, both Massachusetts men and sons of Harvard, utterly failed to find common ground.

The poem is rightly understood to be the crystallization of Emerson's Oriental interests. It will clarify discussion to present all the verses here:

If the red slayer think he slays,
   Or if the slain think he is slain,
They know not well the subtle ways
   I keep, and pass, and turn again.

Far or forgot to me is near;
   Shadow and sunlight are the same;
The vanished gods to me appear;[250]
   And one to me are shame and fame.

They reckon ill who leave me out;
   When me they fly, I am the wings;
I am the doubter and the doubt,
   And I the hymn the Brahmin sings.

The strong gods pine for my abode,
   And pine in vain the sacred Seven;
But thou, meek lover of the good!
   Find me, and turn thy back on heaven.

What must have been the confusion of the readers of the *Atlantic Monthly* when this poem appeared! And with what readiness the parody-makers went to work! Here is a sample:

If the gray tom-cat thinks he sings,
   Or if the song think it be sung,
He little knows who boot-jacks flings
   How many bricks at him I've flung.[251]

Emerson should not have fared so ill. Even Swinburne wrote verse of a similar mystical nature. The first stanza of "Hertha," it will be remembered, ran as follows:

I am that which began;
   Out of me the years roll;

> Out of me God and man;
>   I am equal and whole;
> God changes, and man, and form of them
>   bodily; I am the soul.

In essence such lines are no more intelligible than "Brahma."

The first appearance of the central philosophy of the poem appears in the *Journal* of 1830.[252] In notes made upon Parmenides, after reading Degérando's *Histoire comparée des systémes de philosophie,* Emerson had quoted: "Thought and the object of thought are but one." During these years he was reading widely in Hindu works, particularly in the *Vishnu Purana,* and numerous extracts were being recorded in the notebooks. Among these is one which he paraphrased. It seems to contain the thought of the first stanza of "Brahma" in a modified form. The extract was, "What living creature slays or is slain? What living creature preserves or is preserved? Each is his own destroyer or preserver, as he follows evil or good."[253] This passage was later rendered into

> What creature slayeth or is slain?
> What creature saves or saved is?
> His life will either lose or gain
> And he shall follow harm or bliss.

Studies of "Brahma" have been made by William T. Harris,[254] Emerson's intimate friend, David Lee Maulsby,[255] William Sloane Kennedy,[256] and, more recently, in summary, by Frederic Ives Carpenter in *Emerson and Asia.* The work of these writers is so complete that another detailed discussion of the poem is unnecessary. But there is value in briefly restating some of their conclusions, if only to suggest the wide interest in the poem, as well as the perfectly understandable variance in conclusions as to the source.

Dr. Harris found the source of Emerson's lines in the *Bhagavadgita,* concluding that they seemed "a wholly admirable epitome, or condensed statement, of that wonderful book."[257] This is a fair statement. The sentiments of "Brahma" are to be found in the *Gita.*[258] As has already been shown, it may even be said that the roots of the idealism of the poem can be traced in the *Rigveda.* Assuredly it is the essence of the *Upanishads.* The theme of "Brahma" is to be found in all Hindu literature.

It was, therefore, not disproof of Harris, but a closer approach to Emerson's exact source, when Maulsby arrived at the conclusion that the model for the famous paraphrase was to be found in the *Laws of Menu* and the *Katha Upanishad.* Maulsby erred only in suggesting that Emerson read the *Katha Upanishad* in the *Sacred Books of the East,* a chronological impossibility since no volumes in Max Müller's series appeared before 1879, over two decades after the printing of Emerson's poem in the *Atlantic Monthly.* Kennedy determined the exact source in a rendering of the *Katha* which appeared in a volume of the *Bibliotheca Indica,* published in Calcutta in 1853. Had he known that this was one of the books in the Cholmondeley collection which Emerson later inherited, he would have practically concluded the whole hunt for the sources of the poem.

As one compares Emerson's opening lines,

> If the red slayer think he slays,
> Or if the slain think he is slain,

with Röer's rendering of a passage in the *Katha,* "If the slayer thinks I slay, if the slain thinks I am slain, then both of them do not know well. It (the soul) does not slay, nor is it slain,"[259] the identity is too close to be doubted. The evidence of the diction seems conclusive.

It is interesting to note the identification of other phrases and deities in the poem. Dr. Harris finds the "strong gods" of the final stanza in Indra, the god of the sky and fire, the wielder of the thunderbolt; and Yama, the god of death and judgment. The "sacred seven" are the seven Maharishis or highest saints. "The seven Maharishis . . . were born of my mind, and from them these inhabitants of the world are sprung."[260] Finally, the concluding line of the poem, "Find me, and turn thy back on heaven," is identified in the *Bhagavadgita.* There the passage appears: "The high-souled ones, who achieve the highest perfection, attaining to me, do not come again to life. . . . All worlds, O Arjuna! Up to the world of Brahman, are destined to return. But . . . after attaining to me, there is no birth again."[261]

Into his poem "Brahma" Emerson distilled the heart of his Hindu readings. For years the quotations he culled from the Orientals played on his fancy; for years they tinged his innermost thoughts. As he lived with them on such intimate terms, it would be singular did one not hear reverberations, sometimes faint, sometimes clear, of this thunder which was the best remedy for "musty self-conceited English life made up of fictions, hating ideas."[262] An echo of the thought of "Brahma" is heard in the little poem "Rex."

> I was the trustee of the hand-cart man,
> The brother of the fisher, porter, swain,

And these from the crowd's edge well pleased beheld
The service done to me as done to them.[263]

The doubter and the doubt must be one when "the laws
and powers of the Intellect have . . . a stupendous peculiar-
ity, of being at once observers and observed."[264]

In this instance, Greek and Hindu thought is in no way
separated in Emerson's mind. Even in a detailed study of
Plato[265] as a representative man, Emerson weaves in passage after passage from the Hindus and exclaims, "The
Same, the Same: friend and foe are of one stuff; the plough-
man, the plough and the furrow are of one stuff; and the
stuff is such and so much that the variations of form are
unimportant." Then he continues with quotation: " 'You
are fit' (says the supreme Krishna to a sage) 'to appre-
hend that you are not distinct from me. That which I am,
thou art, and that also is this world, with its gods and
heroes and mankind. Men contemplate distinctions, because they are stupefied with ignorance.' 'The words *I* and
mine constitute ignorance. What is the great end of all,
you shall now learn from me. It is soul,—one in all bodies,
pervading, uniform, perfect, pre-eminent over nature, ex-
empt from birth, growth and decay, omnipresent, made up
of true knowledge, independent, unconnected with unreali-
ties, with name, species and the rest, in time past, present
and to come. The knowledge that this spirit, which is essentially one, is in one's own and in all other bodies, is the wisdom of one who knows the unity of things. As one diffusive
air, passing through the perforations of a flute, is distinguished as the notes of a scale, so the nature of the Great
Spirit is single, though its forms be manifold, arising from
the consequences of acts. When the difference of the in-

vesting form, as that of God or the rest, is destroyed, there is no distinction.' 'The whole world is but a manifestation of Vishnu, who is identical with all things, and is to be regarded by the wise as not differing from, but as the same as themselves. I neither am going nor coming; nor is my dwelling in any other place; nor art thou, thou; nor are others, others; nor am I, I.' " As if he had said, " 'All is for the soul, and the soul is Vishnu; and animals and stars are transient paintings; and light is whitewash; and durations are deceptive; and form is imprisonment; and heaven itself is a decoy.' "[266]

But Emerson is writing of Plato. Why, then, so much of Vishnu, and Maya and Karma and even transmigration —when one writes of Plato?

The poem "Brahma" may well be considered the high water mark of that flood of Orientalism which inundated Concord during the second quarter of the last century and baffled the practical Yankee villagers. But another poem from Emerson's pen is scarcely less significant. This was "Hamatreya."[267] It, too, is based on lustres culled from the Hindus, and it has lines which are directly modeled from the *Vishnu Purana;* but unlike "Brahma" it has characters, Yankee farmers, Bulkeley, Hunt, Willard, Hosmer, Merriam and Flint. They are undeniably necessary to the thought, for they illustrate the main idea, namely, that "the words *I* and *mine* constitute ignorance." This is a sentiment common in Hindu scriptures and Emerson's later thought. It may be found frequently through all his work. In his essay "Illusions" he uses it:

But the Hindoos in their sacred writings, express the liveliest feeling, both of the essential identity and of that illusion which they conceive variety to be. "The notions, '*I am*,' and '*This is mine*,' which influence mankind, are but delusions of the mother of the world."[268]

A passage from the *Journal* of 1845, long as it is, properly belongs here further to illustrate the emphasis which Emerson placed on the thought. It is not the immediate source of Emerson's lines, but it is a valuable instance of how Emerson toyed with the same thought in prose:

Brahma descended from the highest heaven which decayeth not, and with the light of his own body illumined the dark abyss which now constitutes this world, and walking in the heavens, joyed in the possession of his glory.

One Brahma and then another from time to time descended and dwelt in the heavens, and from the self-inherent virtue of the said Brahmas this world below became sweet as the honey of the honey-bee.

One of the Brahmas, beholding the earth, said to himself, What thing is this?—and with one of his fingers having touched the earth put it to the tip of his tongue and perceived the same to be deliciously sweet: from which time all the Brahmas ate of the sweet earth for the space of sixty thousand years. In the mean time having coveted in their hearts the enjoyment of this world, they began to say one to another, This part is mine; that is thine, and so, fixing boundaries, divided the earth between them. On this account the earth lost its sweetness; then grew a mushroom; then a creeping plant; then a tree; then a grain of rice; then rice grain; then later, because of the sons of the Brahmas having used substantial food, the light which once shone in their bodies was extinguished.[269]

There is charm, a lilt, and a readableness in Emerson's poem and the passage from the *Vishnu Purana* which served as its model. A fairly complete presentation of both is necessary in order to indicate their closeness in imagery, sentiment and form, but these passages, if only by their beauty, will, in the Emersonian manner, be compensation enough for the space they occupy. The following selection will serve to indicate the source from which Emerson probably secured his title and theme:

The words "*I* and *mine*" constitute ignorance.

I have now given you a summary account of the sovereigns of the earth.—These, and other kings who with perishable frames have possessed this ever-enduring world, and who, blinded with deceptive notions of individual occupation, have indulged the feeling that suggests "This earth is mine,—it is my son's,—it belongs to my dynasty,"—have all passed away. So, many who reigned before them, many who succeeded them, and many who are yet to come, have ceased or will cease to be. Earth laughs, as if smiling with autumnal flowers to behold her kings unable to effect the subjugation of themselves. I will repeat to you, Maitreya, the stanzas that were chanted by Earth, and which the Muni Asita communicated to Janaka, whose banner was virtue:—

"How great is the folly of princes who are endowed with the faculty of reason, to cherish the confidence of ambition when they themselves are but foam upon the wave. Before they have subdued themselves, they seek to reduce their ministers, their servants, their subjects, under their authority; they then endeavor to overcome their foes. 'Thus,' say they, 'will we conquer the ocean-circled earth'; and intent upon their project, behold not death, which is not far off. But what mighty matter is the subjugation of the sea-girt earth, to one who can subdue himself? Emancipation from existence is the fruit of self-control. It is through infatuation that kings desire to possess me, whom their predecessors have been forced to leave, whom their fathers have not retained. Beguiled by the selfish love of

sway, fathers contend with their sons, and brothers with brothers, for my possession. Foolishness has been the character of
every king who has boasted, 'All this earth is mine—everything
is mine—it will be in my house forever';—for he is dead. How
is it possible that such vain desires should survive in the hearts
of his descendants, who have seen their progenitor, absorbed
by the thirst of dominion, compelled to relinquish me whom he
called his own, and tread the path of dissolution? When I hear
a king sending word to another by his ambassador, 'This earth
is mine; resign your pretentions to it'—I am at first moved to
violent laughter; but it soon subsides to pity for the infatuated
fool."

These were the verses, Maitreya, which Earth recited and
by listening to which ambitions fade away like snow before the
sun.[270]

On this quotation, which, as I have indicated, Emerson
copied into his *Journal,* the poem "Hamatreya" is based.
The central thoughts are identical; there is no difference
between the Hindu kings and the six Yankee farmers who
were Emerson's neighbors and acquaintances. There is in
the poem no indication, philosophically, of Yankee *difference* and Hindu *identity*. There probably was none in
Emerson's mind when it came to the pretensions of the
Yankees to their fields of hay and hemp and the Indian
potentates to their imperial realms. Emerson rose above all
difference and saw avarice and ambitions as common to
all men. The poem is as universal in its scope and application as Shelley's "Ozymandias." Nothing withstands the
erosion of Time and Death.

The lines quoted below do not indicate the complete
poem, but they are all that is essential to illuminate parallels with the model:

Bulkeley, Hunt, Willard, Hosmer, Merriam, Flint,
Possessed the land which rendered to their toil
Hay, corn, roots, hemp, flax, apples, wool, and wood.
Each of these landlords walked amidst his farm,
Saying, " 'Tis mine, my children's, and my name's.
How sweet the west wind sounds in my own trees!
How graceful climb those shadows on my hill!
I fancy these pure waters and the flags
Know me, as does my dog: we sympathize;
And, I affirm, my actions smack of the soil."
Where are these men? Asleep beneath their grounds:
And strangers, fond as they, their furrows plough.
Earth laughs in flowers, to see her boastful boys
Earth-proud, proud of the earth which is not theirs;
Who steer the plough, but cannot steer their feet
Clear of the grave.

. . . .

EARTH-SONG

"Mine and yours;
Mine, not yours.
Earth endures;
Stars abide—
Shine down in the old sea;
Old are the shores;
But where are old men?
I who have seen much,
Such have I never seen.

. . . .

They called me theirs,
Who so controlled me;
Yet every one
Wished to stay, and is gone,
How am I theirs,

If they cannot hold me,
But I hold them?"

When I heard the Earth-song
I was no longer brave;
My avarice cooled
Like lust in the chill of the grave.[271]

The most obvious similarities between these long quotations may be noted in summary. In both it is the Earth which recites the song telling of the futility of human pride and avarice. In both appears the figure of lust or ambition vanishing at the sound of the Earth-song, save that one is "like snow before the sun" and the other is "like lust in the chill of the grave." Finally, Emerson was so captivated by the Hindu metaphor—"Earth laughs, as if smiling with autumnal flowers," that he rendered the line as

Earth laughs in flowers, to see her boastful boys
Earth-proud, proud of the earth which is not theirs;

and in another poem entitled "Solution" as follows:

Earth smiled with flowers, and man was born.
Then Asia yeaned her shepherd race,
And Nile substructs her granite base.[272]

There is little of value to be gained from comparing "Brahma" and "Hamatreya" merely as poems. They have separate significance. In both poems Emerson's hand is clearly seen. "Hamatreya" possesses the virtue of being the most intelligible to those uninitiated in Oriental idealism; "Brahma" on the other hand, has no peer, in prose or verse, as a crystallization into the English language of that age-old body of thought which may be denominated Vedic. But the significance of these poems does not end here. They are based on direct Oriental models. They reflect unerringly Oriental thought. They borrow and beautifully portray Oriental imagery and figures of speech. They may be taken, except for the few Yankee names, without hesitation, as pure Hinduism. So far as I am aware, they may be accepted as pure Emersonianism. We find them in a context dealing with Plato and Plotinus, of Swedenborg and the English deists. We may accept them as evidence of the many-sidedness of Emerson's thought, and of the lightning rapidity with which the habiliments of his mind take on the aspect of the Greek and Hindu, the German and Yankee. His mind is almost chameleon-like as it plays upon the old faiths of the world.

There remain smaller portions of Emerson's poetic output which show traces of his wide reading in the Orientals, exclusive of the Persians. They do not suggest the Brahmanism in his mind, but they give telling testimony of his method of work, of his genius in taking a foreign figure or image and reclothing it for his own purposes and thought.

In this connection are lines from "Celestial Love" whose symbolism will afford a close analogy, if not proof, that they had at one time a Hindu model:

> In a region where the wheel
> On which all beings ride
> Visibly revolves;
> Where the starred, eternal worm
> Girds the world with bound and term;
> Where unlike things are like;
> Where good and ill,
> And joy and moan,
> Melt into one.[273]

The wheel is a symbol often used by Hindu writers. They speak of the First Cause in terms of a wheel, and not infrequently the births and rebirths of individual souls. The figure of the "starred eternal worm" hardly sounds native to New England. But it could easily have been taken from Wilson's translation of the *Vishnu Purana*,[274] which Emerson received from Thoreau. There we read that Sesha, a serpent, supports Vishnu while he sleeps during the intervals of creation.

Sesha . . . has a thousand heads, which are embellished with the pure and visible mystic sign; and the thousand jewels in his crests give light to all regions. . . . Sesha bears the entire world, like a diadem, upon his head, and he is the foundation on which the seven Patalas [regions below the earth] rest. His power, his glory, his form, his nature, cannot be described, cannot be comprehended by the gods themselves. Who shall recount his might, who wears this whole earth, like a garland of flowers, tinged of a purple dye by the radiance of the jewels of his crest.[275]

After having watched the workmanship of Emerson's hand in "Brahma" and "Hamatreya," no one should be reluctant to concede that the *Vishnu Purana* may have supplied him with another image.

But there are other baffling lines in "Celestial Love":

> There Past, Present, Future, shoot
> Triple blossoms from one root;
> Substances at base divided,
> In their summits are united;
> There the holy essence rolls
> One through separated souls.[276]

The lines might escape notice save by a careful reader of the *Journals,* that jumble of the pure gems of Emerson's thought and the slag of a work-a-day world. There one may read that

The doctrine of the Triform came from India, as did the poetic horror that the demons in hell had that tremendous power of vision that they saw through all intermediate regions and worlds, the great and happy gods moving in heaven; whilst the heavenly souls were also made to know their own felicity by discovering the infernal spaces.[277]

And again in another passage one reads that "Vishnu traversed this world; three times he planted his foot, and the whole world was collected in the dust of his footsteps."[278] Still another passage shows Emerson's mind playing with this thought of the trimurti or triform, finding in his out-of-the-way readings, as well as the homely things of domesticity, corroborating proof: "The mystery of triangulation, of the Trinity in theology, and in philosophy, runs through Nature. The father, mother, and child are a single example."[279]

There is a curious affinity in these passages. The first passage quoted, in which Emerson speaks of the Triform coming from India, is the best clue. India with its rigorous monism and the Triform? It cannot be theology here. What of the "triple blossoms from one root"? There seems to be a close analogy between the one root and the Atman, between the triple blossoms and the Triform. But what do they mean?

In the same volume from which Emerson took the main lines on which he modeled his poem "Brahma," that is, from Röer's "Katha Upanishad" in the *Bibliotheca Indica*,[280] we read:

It (the world) is like an eternal fig-tree, whose root is up-
wards, and whose branches go downwards. This is called even
pure, this is called Brahma (all comprehensive); this is called
even immortal; upon this all the worlds are founded; none
becomes different from it. This is that.

And this Brahma is that root, at base divided into the
Past, Present, and Future, but in their summits united;
for in their heights where Brahma absorbs all, Time is also
absorbed.

One continues to find these Oriental images in the least
expected places in Emerson's poetry. There is an uncer-
tainty to the quest which lends exhilaration, particularly
if one cares at all about these mutations of poetic images
from Indian into American literature. In a writer to whom
Hindu lore was entirely an objective entity, a curio, or
something bizarre with which he adorned his work, there
would be less difficulty in recognizing what was native and
what foreign. But Emerson seems saturated with Orientalism. It tinged his philosophy, lent beauty to his prose,
afforded undulled images to many of his verses, and models
for entire poems. There is never a surety that the startling
image which so springs the reader's imagination may not
be a conscious adaptation for Emerson's own purpose of a
Hindu image. In illustration take the following lines from
"Woodnotes":

> Ever fresh and broad creation,
> A divine improvisation,
> From the heart of God proceeds,
> A single will, a million deeds.
> Once slept the world an egg of stone,
> And pulse, and sound, and light were none;

> And God said, "Throb!" and there was motion
> And the vast mass became vast ocean.[281]

To a reader acquainted with the scriptures of Indian thought, the line, "A single will, a million deeds" will sound familiar. But this is not the most intriguing line of the passage. The image of the world sleeping as an egg is the most provoking. It has as foreign a flavor as have all the parallels already presented.

Other ancient mythologies may speak of the world in its unformed state as an egg of stone. It is, of course, conceivable that Emerson found the figure elsewhere, but it does not seem probable when the figure is compared with a passage from Wilson's translation of the *Vishnu Purana,* particularly the first two chapters of first book, which deals with Hindu cosmogonal myths:

Then, ether, air, light, water, and earth, severally united with the properties of sound and the rest, existed as distinguishable according to their qualities. . . . Having combined, therefore, with one another, they assumed, through their mutual association, the character of one mass of entire unity; and from the direction of spirit, with the acquiescence of the indiscrete Principle, Intellect and the rest, to the gross elements inclusive, formed an egg. . . . This vast egg, O sage, compounded of the elements, and resting on the waters, was the excellent natural abode of Vishnu in the form of Brahma; and there Vishnu, the lord of the universe, whose essence is inscrutable, assumed a perceptible form, and even he himself abided in it in the character of Brahma. Its womb, vast as the mountain Meru, was composed of the mountains; and the mighty oceans were the waters that filled its cavity. In that egg, O Brahman, were the continents and seas and mountains, the planets and divisions of the universe, the gods, the demons, and mankind.[282]

One cannot but regret that Emerson did not make use of more equally vivid passages from Thoreau's Hindu books. But it is compensation enough to have found what seems to be the source of some of his most vivid metaphors.

It seems hardly appropriate to leave the literary aspects of Emerson's Orientalism without mentioning an unusual phase of his work. He is rarely thought of as an anthologist, yet one of the most noteworthy anthologies of the last century came of his editing. *Parnassus* was published in Boston in 1875. It was a volume which grew, as Emerson himself confesses in his preface, from the old habit of copying any poem or lines that interested him into a note-book. Through the years first one volume became filled, then another, until finally the convenience of having all his favorites in one volume suggested the anthology. It is a noteworthy book which seems to have escaped the attention of scholars and critics. The confidential way in which Emerson discloses the origin of the book, the likes and dislikes which are his, and essays of critical opinion on the great masters and his contemporaries, opinions which he has not expressed in his essays, make his volume most important.

The book is of importance here because of the translations from the Orientals which he included, not his own, but translations from the pen of Sir William Jones and Horace Hayman Wilson. A close reader of the excerpts in Emerson's *Journals* and the translations themselves will notice that the selections are entirely different from Emerson's own work. There is a homely appeal in the *Parnassus* selections, indicative of that softer, less intellectualized man, whom his neighbors loved so well. In an anthology for public use, Emerson undoubtedly realized that the austerities of "Brahma" were too severe. So we find the first selection to be "The Babe," from Sir William Jones's translation of Kalidasa's work:

> Naked on parents' knees, a newborn child,
> Weeping thou sat'st when all around thee smiled:
> So live, that, sinking to thy last long sleep,
> Thou then mayst smile while all around thee weep.[283]

The selection from Wilson's translations, again of the work of Kalidasa, is entitled "Woman":

> There in the fane a beauteous creature stands,
> The first best work of the Creator's hands,
> Whose slender limbs inadequately bear
> A full-orbed bosom and a weight of care;
> Whose teeth like pearls, whose lips like cherries, show,
> And fawn-like eyes still tremble as they glow.[284]

The selections are not numerous,[285] but those which Emerson used in his anthology fully carry out the impressions we have already formed of the breadth of his Oriental interests, which started with God and reached even to man's most domestic interests.

XV

But to have shown that Emerson was preoccupied with Oriental thought and that he possessed certain temperamental affinities with it, is far from proving that he accepted the organized Vedanta system *in toto*. There was much in the system of which he remained ignorant. He took only that which he could accept and mix successfully with his inhibitions and preconceptions. His writings do not contain an expanded and finished exposition of a complete system. Instead he wrote informal essays and verse, possibly the very reason why he was so successful in influencing the instinctive idealism of the rank and file of American life in his time. The law of the informal essay—whose province was the limitless world of fancy and the writer's every interest—was Emerson's only restraint. This is the master secret of his writings, which are as a mirror set before other mirrors, each reflecting the other. That there is an Oriental reflection in his work is proof only of the fact that he had seen himself in Oriental literature, projected himself into it, used it as an illustration of his own theory of how to treat books and history, and from the foreign store, borrowed forms of expression.

PART THREE

THOREAU AND ORIENTAL ASCETICISM

Depend upon it that, rude and careless as I am, I would fain
practice the yoga faithfully. . . . To some extent, and at rare intervals, even I am a yogi.

—Thoreau, *Writings,* VI, 175.

THOREAU AND ORIENTAL ASCETICISM

I

As we approach the Orientalism of Thoreau and Alcott, we are confronted by two alternatives in our treatment of the subject. Both have their disadvantages. One
is to repeat the method of our study of Emerson, to analyze ideas. But this method would lead to a monotonous
repetition and to anticlimax, for we may safely assume
that Thoreau and Alcott were in essential agreement with
Emersonian doctrine, and that Emerson was a far more
comprehensive thinker than they. The other method,
which has been elected, is to study the application by
Thoreau and Alcott of their Orientalism to their individual conduct of life. This method may result in an impression of having set too narrow a limit to the study, but
it will have the advantage of intensifying our insight into
the reason why Orientalism played an important part in
the lives of the Concordians. So, as we leave Emerson,
we rhetorically go down hill, but it is for the purpose of
closer study.

Franklin Benjamin Sanborn, friend and biographer of
the men of this study, was of the opinion that Emerson
and Thoreau became acquainted in 1837, and that it was
Emerson who first drew Thoreau's attention to the literature of the Orient.[1] Sanborn was probably correct. The first
comment on this subject in Thoreau's published diary is

under date of August 22, 1838. It discloses more maturity and wider reading than Emerson's early entries:

How thrilling a noble sentiment in the oldest books,—in Homer, the Zendavesta, or Confucius! It is a strain of music wafted down to us on the breeze of time, through the aisles of innumerable ages. By its very nobleness it is made near and audible to us.[2]

It is a singular fact that not a single Oriental volume appeared on the record of Thoreau's reading as an undergraduate at the Harvard College Library.[3] He probably contracted the enthusiasm from Emerson. It was during the residence in his friend's home in the year 1841 that Thoreau's extravagant outpouring of praise for the Eastern books commenced. His *Journal* of 1841 marks that as a red letter year in his reading. It is not difficult to guess the reason; he probably had access to all of Emerson's books. On May 31, 1841, after reading Manu, he wrote thus:

That title, "The Laws of Menu with the Gloss of Culluca," comes to me with such a volume of sound as if it had swept unobstructed over the plains of Hindostan; and when my eye rests on yonder birches, or the sun in the water, or the shadows of the trees, it seems to signify the laws of them all. They are the laws of you and me, a fragrance wafted down from those old times, and no more to be refuted than the wind.

When my imagination travels eastward and backward to those remote years of the gods, I seem to draw near to the habitation of the morning, and the dawn at length has a place. I remember the book as an hour before sunrise.[4]

And on August 6, Thoreau was still reading the Hindus. He was not chary of words in telling how they affected him:

I cannot read a sentence in the book of the Hindoos without

being elevated as upon the table-land of the Ghauts. It has such a rhythm as the winds of the desert, such a tide as the Ganges, and seems as superior to criticism as the Himmaleh Mounts. Even at this late hour, unworn by time, with a native and inherent dignity it wears the English dress as indifferently as the Sanscrit. The great tone of the book is of such fibre and such severe tension that no time nor accident can relax it. The great thought is never found in a mean dress, but is of virtue to ennoble any language.[5]

What the book was that could not be read without elevating him to "the table-land of the Ghauts" is disclosed in the diary of the next day, August 7, 1841:

The impression which those sublime sentences made on me last night has awakened me before any cock crowing. Their influence lingers around me like a fragrance, or as the fog hangs over the earth late into the day.

The very locusts and crickets of a summer day are but later or older glosses on the Dherma Sastra of the Hindoos, a continuation of the sacred code.[6]

Two days later the spell was still on him. Any book of great authority, he wrote, seemed to permeate and pervade all space. "Its spirit, like a more subtle ether, sweeps along with the prevailing winds of the country. Its influence conveys a new gloss to the meadows and the depths of the wood, and bathes the huckleberries on the hills, as sometimes a new influence in the sky washes in waves over the fields and seems to break on some invisible beach in the air. All things confirm it. It spends the mornings and the evenings."[7]

But one more passage need be quoted from the diary of 1841. It found its way into the *Week* and readers of that book may have become familiar with it there. Particularly is it interesting because of the kind of criticism which it discloses Thoreau applied to the Orientals:

It is now easy to apply to this ancient scripture such a catholic criticism as it will become the part of some future age to apply to the Christian,—wherein the design and idea which underlies it is considered, and not the narrow and partial fulfillment.

These verses are so eminently textual, that it seems as if those old sages had concentrated all their wisdom in little fascicles, of which future times were to be the commentary; as the light of this lower world is only the dissipated rays of the sun and stars. They seem to have been uttered with a sober morning prescience, in the dawn of time. There is a sort of holding back, or withdrawal of the full meaning, that the ages may follow after and explore the whole. The sentence opens unexpensively and almost unmeaningly, as the petals of a flower.[8]

Thus one could go through Thoreau's *Journal*, culling passage after passage to illustrate his fondness for Oriental books. What has been presented, however, is sufficient. The main point to be remembered is that Thoreau's interests commenced later than Emerson's. So far as information of specific volumes goes, there seems no evidence of his having read from the Hindu scriptures during his college years. Temperamentally, his needs were much the same as Emerson's. It may have been that he did not discover the Orientals before his friend introduced him to them because he had no aunt like Mary Moody Emerson. When at last he was free to live in Emerson's library, he was like a thirst-tortured man who had found an oasis in the desert. Through the two remaining decades of his life Thoreau read avidly from these books and his comments on them became more penetrating. The delighted ejaculations of the first discovery turned into commentary which disclosed his insight into what the books taught, commentary that is remarkably suggestive of the later trend of Thoreau's own life and gives ample warrant for believing that it was not curiosity alone that lead him Eastward. The *Journal* of 1850 offers an example:

What extracts from the Vedas I have read fall on me like light of a higher and purer luminary, which describes a loftier course through a purer stratum,—free from particulars, simple, universal. It rises on me like the full moon after the stars have come out, wading through some far summer stratum of the sky.[9]

This is pure impressionism. In the same manner there were such sentences as "The Vedas contain a sensible account of God" and "One wise sentence [from the *Vedas*] is worth the state of Massachusetts many times over."[10] But he wrote comments showing an acute insight. When he compared the religion and philosophy of the Hebrews with that of the Hindus, he declared that the former represented a "wilder and ruder tribe," while the latter reflected "civility and intellectual refinements and subtlety."[11] "With the Hindoos virtue is an intellectual exercise, not a social and practical one. It is a knowing, not a doing."[12] Such sentences suggest the reasons why the East appealed to Thoreau.

II

The difference between Emerson's and Thoreau's literary use of Oriental imagery was in kind. Natural objects were what appealed to Thoreau. It was a willow, with its branches curving outward that suggested "not a New England but an Oriental character, reminding us of trim Persian gardens."[13] It was a large toadstool that made him "think of parasols of Chinese mandarins."[14] The sulphur-like pollen of the pitch pine covering Walden pond, the stones and rotted shore-strewn wood brought back his reading of Kalidasa. "This is the 'sulphur showers' we hear of. Even in Calidas' [sic] drama of Sacontala, we read of 'rills dyed yellow with the golden dust of the lotus.' "[15] And at night-time he remembered that the "Hindoos compare the moon to a saintly being who has reached the last stage of bodily existence."[16] Thoreau was a practical man, but as he viewed the gold rush of the forty-niners to California, he could only think that they matched "the infatuation of the Hindoos who have cast themselves under the car of Juggernaut."[17] He was untouched by the fever for gold. The simple life looked fair to him, "like a Persian city or hanging gardens in the distance, so washed in light, so untried, only to be thridded by clean thoughts."[18] These were some of the natural objects Thoreau wove into simile and metaphor. As with Emerson, there was an aptness and smooth merging of the Hindu's sentences with his own. This is a characteristic of all he wrote:

Live free, child of the mist,—and with respect to knowledge we are all children of the mist. The man who takes the liberty to live is superior to all the laws, by virtue of his relation to the lawmaker. "That is active duty," says the Vishnu Purana, "which is not for our bondage; that is knowledge which is for liberation: all other duty is good only unto weariness; all other knowledge is the cleverness of the artist."[19]

When his scorn was aroused he dipped his pen in vitriol. He used the Hindus to bolster his own thought; and he used them to flay chicanery. "That excitement about Kossuth, consider how characteristic, how superficial it was!—only another kind of politics or dancing." Then he pursued his invective relentlessly, drawing on Indian mythology. "No man stood on truth. They were merely banded together, as usual one leaning on another, and all together on nothing; as the Hindoos made the world rest on an elephant, the elephant on a tortoise, and the tortoise on a serpent, and had nothing to put under the serpent. For all fruit of that stir we have the Kossuth hat."[20]

We may conclude our glance at the effect of the Orientals on Thoreau's prose style with a passage that is as characteristic of the man's mind and life as was the conclusion of "Immortality" in Emerson. Readers of *Walden* may have skipped it, if any one ever skips pages in such a book. I have long thought of it as an allegory of Thoreau's own life, of his love for the Beautiful, the True, and the Good, and of his search for Perfection. I find in it a veiled suggestion of the reason he went to Walden, of his indifference to criticism and the social standards of his time. Thoreau has given the little story an inevitableness of phrase and meaning that dispels all need of explanation. It should not be marred by detracting from its completeness:

There was an artist in the city of Kouroo who was disposed to strive after perfection. One day it came into his mind to make a staff. Having considered that in an imperfect work time is an ingredient, but into a perfect work time does not enter, he said to himself, It shall be perfect in all respects, though I should do nothing else in my life. He proceeded instantly to the forest for wood, being resolved that it should not be made of unsuitable material; and as he searched for and rejected stick after stick, his friends gradually deserted him, for they grew old in their works and died, but he grew not older by a moment. His singleness of purpose and resolution, and his elevated piety, endowed him, without his knowledge, with perennial youth. As he made no compromise with Time, Time kept out of his way, and only sighed at a distance because he could not overcome him. Before he had found a stick in all respects suitable the city of Kouroo was a hoary ruin, and he sat on one of its mounds to peel the stick. Before he had given it the proper shape the dynasty of the Candahars was at an end, and with the point of the stick he wrote the name of the last of that race in the sand, and then resumed his work. By the time he had smoothed and polished the staff Kalpa was no longer the pole-star; and ere he had put on the ferule and the head adorned with precious stones, Brahma had awoke and slumbered many times. But why do I stay to mention these things? When the finishing stroke was put to his work, it suddenly expanded before the eyes of the astonished artist into the fairest of all the creations of Brahma. He had made a new system in making a staff, a world with full and fair proportions; in which, though the old cities and dynasties had passed away, fairer and more glorious ones had taken their places. And now he saw by the heap of shavings still fresh at his feet, that, for him and his work, the former lapse of time had been an illusion, and that no more time had elapsed than is required for a single scintillation of the brain of Brahma to fall on and inflame the tinder of a mortal brain. The material was pure, and his art was pure; how could the result be other than wonderful?[21]

Here is Thoreau; here his philosophy, and here a description of his life. In paraphrase it might be said: the Oriental material from which he drew contained many gems of thought; within the man was poetry; how could his style be other than poetic and beautiful?

There was nothing essentially Confucian in Thoreau's temperament. He was interested in the state, gratified that "even the Chinese philosopher was wise enough to regard the individual as the basis of the empire."[22] But he wrote on, and was a practical exponent of, civil disobedience, whereas Emerson, Confucius, and Mencius all agreed on conformity. No Confucian would ever have gone to Walden. Emerson found in Confucius justification for his remaining in the normal ways of men. Thoreau scorned fine manners, etiquette, ceremonialism; Emerson liked them. It is impossible to find in Thoreau the same parallels that were found between Emerson and Confucius.

Still, Thoreau read the Confucian books, probably just as much as Emerson, but he used them in his own way. His individuality and the eccentricity which baffled the practical Concord villagers was probably never illustrated to better advantage than in the selections from the Chinese books which he chose to quote. How his friends must have wondered at his intent in the following:

What news! how much more important to know what that is which was never old! "Kieou-he-yu (great dignitary of the state of Wei) sent a man to Khoung-tseu to know his news. Khoung-tseu caused the messenger to be seated near him, and questioned him in these terms: What is your master doing? The messenger answered with respect: My master desires to diminish the number of his faults, but he cannot come to the end of them. The messenger being gone, the philosopher remarked: What a worthy messenger! What a worthy messenger!"[23]

Thoreau seems never to have divorced his interest in

nature from his reading of any scripture. His Confucian reading, considered alone, emphatically suggests this. He never tried to read mystical divinity into the Chinese; he quoted them in connection with flora and fauna. "The other day," he wrote, "I picked up the lower jaw of a hog, with white and sound teeth and tusks, which suggested that there was an animal health and vigor distinct from the spiritual." And in connection with this animal vigor he quoted Mencius: " 'That in which men differ from brute beasts,' says Mencius, 'is a thing very inconsiderable; the common herd lose it very soon; superior men preserve it carefully!' "[24] He found a Chinese natural history note was interesting enough to record in connection with his observations on fish. "The Chinese are bribed to carry their ova from province to province in jars or in hollow reeds, or the water-birds to transport them to the mountain tarns and interior lakes."[25] Thoreau's interest even extended to the characters which were engraved on the bathing tub of King Tching-thang. These he quoted: "Renew thyself completely each day; do it again, and again, and forever again." His own comment upon this inscription is reminiscent of his morning renewals in Walden Pond. "I can understand that. Morning brings back the heroic ages."[26] It is in instances such as these that Thoreau used the Chinese. It is fruitless to attempt finding in him a resemblance to the ethics of Confucius.

A final passage from Thoreau's unpublished papers[27] will throw more light on his attitude toward Confucian thought than anything from his pen which has yet appeared in print. The passage is quoted in entirety:

I lately read an anecdote of Confucius and his disciples . . .

Tseu-lou, Thseng-sie, Yan-yeou, Kong-si-hoa, were seated by the side of the Philosopher. The Philosopher said: Make no account of my age more than if I were only a day older than you. Living apart and isolated, then you say: We are not known. If any one knew you, then what would you do?

Tseu-lou replied with a brisk but respectful air: Suppose a kingdom of a thousand war-chariots, hard pressed between other great kingdoms, add even, by enormous armies, and that withal it suffers from want and famine; let Yeou (Tseu-lou) be appointed to its administration, in less than three years I could accomplish that the people of this kingdom should recover a manly courage, and know their condition. The Philosopher smiled at these words.

And you, Khieou, what are your thoughts?

The disciple replied respectfully: Suppose a province of sixty or seventy *li* in extent, or even fifty or sixty *li*, and that Khieou were appointed to its administration, in less than three years I could accomplish that the people should have sufficient. As to the rites and to music, I could entrust the teaching of them to a superior man.

And you, Tchi, what are your thoughts?

The disciple replied respectfully: I will not say that I can do these things; I desire to study. When the ceremonies of the temple of ancestors are performed, and great public assemblies take place, clothed in my robe of azure and other vestments proper for such a place and such ceremonies, I could wish to take part in the quality of a humble functionary.

And you, Tian, what are your thoughts?

The disciple did nothing but draw some rare sounds from his guitar; but these sounds prolonging themselves, he laid it aside, and rising, replied respectfully: My opinion differs entirely from that of my fellow disciples.—The philosopher said: What prevents you from expressing it? Here each one can speak his thought.—The disciple said: Spring being no more, my robe of spring laid aside, but covered with the bonnet of manhood, accompanied by five or six men, and six or seven young people, I should love to go and bathe in the waters of the Y——, to go and take the fresh air in those woody places where they offer sacrifices to heaven to obtain rain, to modulate some airs, and then return to my abode.

The Philosopher applauding these words by a sigh of satisfaction, said: I am of Tian's mind.

The three disciples departed, but Thseng-sie remained yet some time. Thseng-sie said: What ought one to think of the words of these three disciples? The Philosopher said: Each one of them has expressed his opinion; that is all.

The narrator proceeds to tell why the Philosopher smiled; but that is obvious enough. For the most part, when I listen to the conversation of the Reformers, I too am of Tian's mind.

The import of Thoreau's words, also, like the Philosopher's smile, is obvious enough. All other comments on Confucianism which might be culled from his work and placed along side this unpublished passage would be dimmed into insignificance.[28] Thoreau the poet-naturalist of Concord, Thoreau the Yogi, and Thoreau the pseudo-Confucian, in all three rôles there is a man of unvarying consistency. In contrast with the many-sided Emerson, whose words take on now a Platonic and then a Swedenborgian, now a Brahman and then a Confucian complexion, Thoreau is a monotone, but his is the great virtue of consistency. It should be remembered that it was from Saadi he took the motto for a manuscript title-page of *Walden:* "The clouds, wind, moon, sun, and sky, act in coöperation, that thou mayest get thy daily bread, and not eat it with indifference; all revolve for thy sake, and are obedient to command; it must be an equitable condition, that thou shalt be obedient also."[29] The common denominator of all that Thoreau took from the Hindus, Chinese and Persians was a mystical love for Nature. This reading, to be sure, was but a small portion of his wide literary interests which included travel books, natural histories, the seventeenth century poets, and the Latin and Greek classics, but it was the most important of his reading in religious and philosophical literature.

III

To think of Thoreau's years at Walden as a spiritual retreat akin to a Yogi's complete abstraction from all worldly objects is to depart abruptly from the usual interpretation of this episode of his life. Yet Thoreau himself offers the warrant in the words which form the motto of this chapter: " . . . even I am a yogi." Of course no critic can accept these words at their face value and remain unchallenged. The chief objection confronting him would probably state itself in such a question as—"What's in a name? Had Thoreau declared his desire to be a Hottentot, there would have been just as much possibility of his changing the color of his skin, as to change the essentially Yankee temper of his mind into that of an Oriental ascetic." Such an objection seems unanswerable. But the fact remains that Thoreau *did* think of himself as a Yogi, and more than once he affirmed it. Perhaps his words are to be qualified; assuredly they cannot be ignored.

The first step in understanding Walden is to see Thoreau's religious philosophy in its main emphasis. If it is true that the Reality is Brahma—or the Over-Soul—and the phenomenal world is a lie, then the logical end of life for one who believes this is to seek devotedly that Reality.

Not the actualities of the world, but its potentialities would be his interest. His sole spiritual vocation would consist in the discovery of God, not in what serves his temporal ends. Salvation would not be a question of accepting a creed, but of acquiring insight. As Keyserling has suggested, before the period when the average man would enter upon what Wordsworth called the philosophic years, he would strive for greater depth and involution instead of expansion and enrichment. He would long to get beyond the realm of appearance and be released from the fetters of sense. Morality and goodness would not be confused with social values alone, for these are not the whole of values. Thoughts of God would transcend the values established by men. Were one who believed thus to be wrecked on a desert island like Robinson Crusoe—without even a Friday—he would still have supreme values to cherish and a definite end for his life. It would be to know Reality. Thoreau would not have fled from Crusoe's experience. It is quite conceivable that it might have even appealed to him. At one time he remarked that if he were to be confined to a garret-corner all his days, like a spider, so long as he had his thoughts the world would be just as large to him.

Emerson loved the ways of men more than Thoreau. He was more urbane and there was a dash of worldliness and human culture in his idealism. This was the chief difference between the men. And yet it seems a paradox. Thoreau, surveyor and botanist, practical handyman for the chores of his friend's household; Emerson, student, dreamer, happiest among his books and the dreams of mystics and poets. It would seem that Emerson, instead of

Thoreau, should have retired from the world to clear the channels leading to the Over-Soul of all obstructions. But his urbanity forbade. Thoreau, on the other hand, never thought of the simplicity of his manner of living as a virtue in itself. It was for him a path leading towards spiritual self-knowledge and realization. He insisted, as his life amply proved, on living by his beliefs and carrying them to their logical conclusion. In this fact is his greatest affinity with the true philosopher.

The words "even I am a yogi" are to be found in a letter which Thoreau wrote to H. G. O. Blake in 1849. The complete passage adds to their meaning:

"Free in this world as the birds in the air, disengaged from every kind of chains, those who practice the *yoga* gather in Brahma the certain fruit of their works."

Depend upon it that, rude and careless as I am, I would fain practice the *yoga* faithfully.

"The yogi, absorbed in contemplation, contributes in his degree to creation; he breathes a divine perfume, he hears wonderful things. Divine forms traverse him without tearing him, and, united to the nature which is proper to him, he goes, he acts as animating original matter."

To some extent, and at rare intervals, even I am a yogi.[30]

But this, significantly, was not the only instance in which he wrote in this manner. On September 1, 1841, he found that "One may discover the root of a Hindoo religion in his own private history, when, in the silent intervals of the day or the night, he does sometimes inflict on himself like austerities with a stern satisfaction."[31]

What was the specific nature of these austerities he does not confide, but an examination of his life at Walden will disclose much. The main point is that the austerities were Hindu-like and they gave satisfaction, a sense such as Alcott craved, of transcending the daily routine and that of the townsmen, a presentiment of immortality and its successful permeation of life.[32] In common with most Transcendentalists and Hindu philosophers, Thoreau drew no line of demarcation between the present and the eternal. A nexus with God, is, of course, the aim of all mystics.

Moncure Conway, too, who knew both Thoreau and the Hindus, realized what was going on. The language in which he wrote of his friend must have been studied; furthermore it carries the weight of an informed observer who wrote at first hand. "Like the pious Yogi," according to Conway, "so long motionless whilst gazing on the sun that knotty plants encircled his neck and the cast snake-skin his loins, and the birds built their nests on his shoulders, this poet and naturalist, by equal consecration, became a part of the field and forest."[33] Conway was writing specifically of Thoreau at Walden. Such words force us to examine closely what went on there.

IV

If a true estimate of Thoreau's ascetic practice is ever to be obtained, it will most probably be found in *Walden*. Of all confessions, the most unusual that ever came from his pen was the following allegory, which suggests a mystical brooding even before he went to the hermitage:

I long ago lost a hound, a bay horse, and a turtle-dove, and am still on their trail. Many are the travellers I have spoken concerning them, describing their tracks and what calls they answered to. I have met one or two who had heard the hound, and the tramp of the horse, and even seen the dove disappear behind a cloud, and they seemed as anxious to recover them as if they had lost them themselves.[34]

Now to interpret these words in the sense of a falling out of love, or loss of friendship, hardly renders them consistent with many other illuminating, though not so poetic, passages that will be found in his writings. A lover of birds, flowers, and the day-break, one who exulted keenly in life and the wild joys of living intimately with nature, very aptly chose natural symbols to express the pensive longing of the mystic. Thoreau considered his main profession to be always on the alert to find God in Nature, to know his lurking-places, and to attend the oratorios and operas of the outdoors. Of his purpose in going to the Walden hermitage he writes: "My purpose in going to Walden Pond was not to live cheaply nor to live dearly there, but to transact some *private business* with the fewest obstacles."[35] These are hardly the words of a love-lorn or economically embarrassed man.

Model Concordians may have thought of Thoreau's life at the shanty in terms of a lazy hobo dozing in the sun. Perhaps he gave them reason. He also gives critics reason for seeing the Yogi in him, when he pictures the manner in which he spent his time:

Sometimes, in a summer morning, having taken my accustomed bath, I sat in my sunny doorway from sunrise till noon, rapt in revery, amidst the pines and hickories and sumachs, in undisturbed solitude and stillness, while the birds sang around or flitted noiseless through the house, until by the sun falling in my west window, or the noise of some traveller's wagon on the distant highway, I was reminded of the lapse of time. I grew in those seasons like corn in the night, and they were far better than the work of the hands would have been. They were not time subtracted from my life, but so much over and above my usual allowance. I realized what the Orientals mean by contemplation and the forsaking of works.[36]

To draw nice distinctions here between Oriental contemplation in general and the technical processes of the Yoga is to quibble.

Even in the matter of diet Thoreau likened his own to that of the Hindu:

My practice is "nowhere," my opinion is here. Nevertheless I am far from regarding myself as one of those privileged ones to whom the Ved refers when it says, that "he who has true faith in the Omnipresent Supreme Being may eat all that exists," that is, is not bound to inquire what is his food, or who prepares it; and even in their case it is to be observed, as a Hindoo commentator has remarked, that the Vedant limits this privilege to "the time of distress."[37]

No other quotation is needed to clarify Thoreau's position. One who could not even throw a stone into a chestnut tree to dislodge the nuts, because in using the stone he felt as though he were throwing it at a sentient being, was a man with a very intimate sense of his affinity with nature. The reaching of this stage of sensitivity, if we may accept Thoreau's confession at its face value, was not the result of a casual fondness for the outdoors.

It will be remembered that James Russell Lowell blue-pencilled a sentence about an innocuous pine tree in the essay "Chesuncook" which appeared in the *Atlantic Monthly* of July, 1858. The sentence was this: "It is as immortal as I am and perhaps will go to a higher heaven, there to tower above me still."[38] The full implication is

perhaps that man, his body and soul, does not cease existence in this world but mounts to higher and more perfect
articulation in nature. Thoreau's sense of kinship with
trees, his brotherhood with every living object, his identification of personal life with universal life, permeate all his
work. It surely cannot be proved that he was so Hindu as to
desire the total eclipse of his own ego by absorption into
Brahma, yet he wrote lines suggestive of this very thing:

> Fain would I stretch me by the highway-side
> To thaw and trickle with the melting snow;
> That mingled, soul and body, with the tide,
> I too may through the pores of nature flow.[39]

On March 2, 1842, after the death of his brother John,
these were his thoughts: "I do not wish to see John ever
again,—I mean him who is dead,—but that other . . . of
whom he was the imperfect representative."[40] Assuredly
here is something of an *impersonal* attitude toward death
and immortality. It is difficult to see why general Occidental reaction to an impersonal end in Nirvana should be
so violent. Hindus have protested that it is not a state of
utter blankness.[41] The freed soul does not see another, but
sees himself absorbed in the All. George Eliot suggested
something akin to Hindu non-existence in *The Legend of
Jubal*:

> Quitting mortality, a quenched sun-wave,
> The All-creating Presence for his grave.

Finally, Thoreau stated the definite results he obtained
from the Walden experiment. He undoubtedly felt that the
complex and enslaving system of economics which his
neighbors and most of the world thought inevitable and

even excellent was death to the spirit. Yet it is a partiality to construe the following passage as an expression of happy escape from economic and social ills, or the words of a misanthrope who found among men not happiness but ennui. It is only in the light of idealistic philosophy that they can be fully understood.

I learned this, at least, by my experiment: that if one advances confidently in the direction of his dreams, and endeavors to live the life which he has imagined, he will meet with a success unexpected in common hours. He will put some things behind, will pass an invisible boundary; new, universal, and more liberal laws will begin to establish themselves around and within him; or the old laws be expanded, and interpreted in his favor in a more liberal sense, and he will live with the license of a higher order of beings. In proportion as he simplifies his life, the laws of the universe will appear less complex, and solitude will not be solitude, nor poverty poverty, nor weakness weakness.[42]

There is a Hindu flavor in these words. An Indian Yogi may not speak of advancing confidently in the direction of his dreams and with determination living the life he has imagined. Still, there can be no denial that the conclusions to which Thoreau came at Walden are the same as the teaching of Emerson's "Brahma." Poverty, solitude and weakness are things other than themselves in the same sense as in Emerson's poem the doubter is the doubt and the slayer is the slain. This is essential Vedantic teaching. When Walden gave Thoreau these results, it is niggardly to deny him the name of Yogi. But he was a New England Yogi, conditioned by his nativity and his moral and religious heritage. Like the Hindu he courted solitude for the purpose of spiritual discipline, but he worked for men with a most Christian spirit. If his renunciations did not bring him to sack cloth and a seat in ashes, they nevertheless included everything that did not concern his spiritual life. And though he makes ideas positive creative forms, which is not the habit of the Hindu Yogi, yet there seems little doubt that, had he been born among the forest seers who wrote the *Upanishads,* he would have felt neither consternation nor any want.

V

Of course the word *Yogi* suggests certain very definite things that Thoreau never intended. The first of them will be found in Conway's description:[43] ascetic self-torture, the bed of nails, sun-gazing, limbs withered from long disuse. Nor was it probable that Thoreau consciously sought out any of the specific Yogi disciplines such as the Jnana, Raja, Hatha, Mantra, and Karma.[44] He had no interest in systems.

There is another way in which Thoreau was inherently incapable of being a Hindu holy-man. It is best illustrated by a passage from a modern observer:

Of charity in its scriptural meaning I once had a talk with an orthodox old Hindu Sadhu. A friend, just arrived from England, was discussing with him through an interpreter what the Hindu called the "big-little" things. In response to the Hindu's invitation to take my friend on a pilgrimage, he was shown the Englishman's engagement book. The Holy man said that he who kept an engagement book could never attain to holiness. "But," said the Englishman, "my engagements are some of them in the service of my fellowmen. That is surely the way of holiness." "Yes," said the Hindu, "the very bottom-most step

of the ladder." "What! then which is the highest?" "Medita-
tion—perfecting your individual self, losing it, in contemplation." "But while I am making my soul, sitting here meditating,
my brother may be run over by a car in the street. Is not the
higher work to go and rescue him?" "Oh! no," said the Hindu.
"That is for men who are beginning the way of holiness. Works
are for those who need to buy." Then he stopped, puzzled by
his own philosophy. "Or is the rescue of your brother God's
work and not man's?" he said, and left it there.[45]

In the Occident, great thinkers have held that there is a
pathway to God and the goal of human attainment through
the performance of the duties of the good neighbor and
the honest citizen. The kindly Jesus gave the parable of
the Good Samaritan. No thorough-going Vedantic Hindu
would ever have done so. A critic has sensed in Thoreau's
reputed coldness one affinity at least with the Hindus on
this score. He writes: "Thoreau is probably most interesting for his attitude on practical questions concerning
the personal relations. Thoreau's native hatred of philanthropy must have been naturally reinforced by contact with
what Orientalists to-day hold up to the humanitarian West
as the true 'spirit of charity', the Oriental doctrine of cold
benevolence and separation in friendship."[46] No one will
encounter difficulty in finding passages in Thoreau that
would seem to support this view. All Hindus would agree
with him when he writes, "It appears to be a law that you
cannot have a deep sympathy with both man and nature.
Those qualities which bring you near to the one estrange
you from the other."[47] Again, remembering that Nature
to Thoreau was the outward face of God, we may note:
"My acquaintances sometimes imply that I am too cold;

but each thing is warm enough of its kind. . . . You who complain that I am cold find Nature cold. To me she is warm."[48]

In a world where the law of Karma is as permanent and exacting as that of gravitation, all men stand on the level they deserve, according to the Hindu. Every level is necessary, and in so far as it is necessary, it is good. The blossom does not deny the leaf, and the leaf does not deny the stalk, nor the stalk the root. Occidental charity means a desire to do good; Oriental charity signifies wanting every one to come into his own at his own level. Thoreau realized the abuses of both: on the one hand, the tactlessness of folk who insist on improving their fellows; on the other, blindness to medicable woe. He writes coldly of philanthropy: "Philanthropy is almost the only virtue which is sufficiently appreciated by mankind. Nay, it is greatly overrated; and it is our selfishness which overrates it. . . . The kind uncles and aunts of the race are more esteemed than its true spiritual fathers and mothers."[49] But shortly after delivering himself of this seemingly heartless preachment, Thoreau might have been seen bathing the wounds of a fugitive slave, his face beatified with tenderness.

Another practical application of Vedantic thought which Thoreau never could have intended when he applied the name of Yogi to himself is suggested by two sentences from the Hindu scriptures. "When Brahmans know that Self and have risen above the desire for sons, wealth, and worlds, they wander about as mendicants." The same thought is more imperatively stated elsewhere: "Despise home, wealth and country: embrace spiritually beasts and trees."[50] Now Thoreau might have—and did—assent to spiritual embrace of beasts and trees, for his ideal did not primarily express itself in a rich social life; but he never would have condoned the relinquishing of household duties and the dropping of the reins of state as commendable action at any stage in life.[51] Yet it is to this that the *Upanishads* lead. They teach that for him who has attained the philosophical view the ethical is transcended. The way of works is a low way, one to be abandoned, possible consequence notwithstanding. The negation of the phenomenal world tends to negation of reponsibility.

A common story among Anglo-Indians is that of a Hindu who had risen to high honors and a position of great dignity in a native state. Heavy responsibilities were on his shoulders. Through the years he had served the people faithfully and honorably. He had secured the confidence and trust of all with whom he dealt. His subordinates were loyal to him. His superiors counted it a glad day when he rose to power. He had risen through disinterested and great-hearted service. He was a man for whom the future meant unlimited opportunity and the greatest distinction. But he was past the prime of life and the years which had brought him honor had flown by with only too few opportunities for a contemplation of the great eternal verities. An inquietude took hold on him and vexed him. At last as he was on the threshold of greater honors, he arose with the dawn, doffed his responsibilities to the people as lightly as the robes of state, and with a mendicant's begging bowl, barefooted, took the long road through the hills in search of Nirvana. All political chaos which might have resulted from his sudden withdrawal was forgotten in his absorption in the new spiritual business. Were this a solitary instance, it might not be conclusive. The difficulty is that such conduct is fundamentally approved by the Brahman's philosophy of life. All goods are subservient to the spiritual; he who seeks this highest spiritual good is to be exonerated, even though the empire at whose helm he had stood were to crumple into chaos after his withdrawal.

The argument, as it affects India, is of course a telling one. But it is not to be limited in its application. It is probably the explanation of Emerson's sentence, "The view taken of Transcendentalism in State Street is that it threatens to invalidate contracts."[52] The practical man will ever be dubious of the mystic's fitness for responsibility, and even of his normality. As has so often been said, they do not talk the same language. And when mysticism is coupled with a religious sanction for the doffing of duties to one's fellow men, it cannot be argued that the State will benefit. It is only necessary to speak of Thoreau's activity in the Abolition cause to show how incapable he was of being this type of Yogi.

At this juncture it is quite appropriate to consider Thoreau's essays on "Civil Disobedience" and "Life Without Principle." "The most outspoken doctrines of resistance ever penned on this continent," Professor Canby called them. "They are too utterly un-European, too much of the exact antithesis of either socialism or communism, which are the parasites of our industrialism; and that is why, perhaps, they have found their first broad application in the East."[53] Mahatma Gandhi's adoption of Thoreau's principles is in itself the most definite proof that can be found of the latter's Oriental temper.[54] Greater proof is the fact that those principles have become the slogan for millions of Hindus. What is there more unique in the clash of the Eastern and Western cultures than this ready assimilation of a Yankee's thought by the modern Aryans of India? Thoreau's principles were assuredly not for antebellum Americans. They were wasted on a motor-minded people bent on making the most of a new continent. Even the Abolitionists, whose cause Thoreau was abetting with veritable dynamite, failed to realize their potentialities. Nor will they ever be adopted in the West. The fact that Gandhi has used them to shake the British Empire and silence the cotton mills of Manchester, will make little difference. There must be something of Thoreau himself in every lover of Thoreau—at least in every one who would apply his principles to the conduct of life. By this token, consider the intellectual affinity of Gandhi and the recluse of Walden.

A last definite sense in which Thoreau probably never accepted the Yoga is in the Hindu insistence that the man who has reached a stage of true enlightenment is freed from the consequences of his works. The *Chandogya Upanishad* expresses the thought in a most notable passage: "As water does not cling to the lotus leaf, so no evil deed clings to one who knows it."[55] The *Kaushitaki Upanishad* is even more definite: "And he who knows me thus, by no deed of his is his life harmed, not by the murder of his mother, not by the murder of his father, not by theft, not by the killing of a Brahman. If he is going to commit a sin, the bloom does not depart from his face."[56] Few Occidentals could come to such a conclusion. Yet it is perfectly consistent and logical for a Vedantist to think in this manner. Sin belongs to the phenomenal world of

Maya alone. It is unreal. It cannot possibly cling to him who has become one with the Real.

Here the question of Thoreau's belief in the doctrine of Transmigration may aptly be raised, for one of the yearnings of the Hindu Yogi is release from the cycle of rebirth. To reach the stage where sin adheres not, as water does not cling to the lotus leaf, is also to be freed from one's Karma, which determines all rebirth. Emerson, it has been shown, played with the doctrine, but never gave convincing proof of the extent to which he could adjust it to his private uses. Thoreau does little more. There are instances in which it would seem that he found it congenial. For instance he writes of a friend: "Hawthorne, too, I remember as one with whom I sauntered, in old heroic times, along the banks of the Scamander, amid the ruins of chariots and heroes";[57] but this may mean anything from whimsical fun-making to Platonic reminscence, though the latter is extremely unlikely. More definitely does he write in another instance; "Methinks the hawk that soars so loftily and circles so steadily and apparently without effort has earned this power by faithfully creeping on the ground as a reptile in a former state of existence."[58] That is fairly consistent Hinduism: Karma brought its just reward. Not so the following, which he wrote after looking into a spring pool with its teeming insect life: "Yes, I feel positive beyond a doubt, I must pass through *all* these conditions, one day and another; I must go the whole round of life, and come full circle."[59] If by these words Thoreau meant to suggest that after he reached the Brahman, he would begin the long cycle of rebirths beginning with the rain-drop, which is described in the fantastic mythology of the Hindus, he meant more than the most partisan would be willing to read into his words. There would have been no warrant for one of blameless life to retrograde into the insect life.

The truth is that Thoreau never articulated a complete eschatology. When he tells us that like last year's vegetation our human life but dies down to its root and puts forth its green blade into eternity, he constructs a very interesting sentence, but not a full system. Like Emerson, he was influenced by Hindu doctrines of the life after death, and driven to consider them seriously, for the premises of his philosophy closely resembled the Oriental. Death meant to him a release of the vital force, a return to Nature. But here his theism entered and confused the inevitable Hindu logic. He did not dread death. He suffered long from ill health. Once he wished that his soul had been bestowed rather "on some antelope of the plains than upon this sickly and sluggish body."[60] To crave the bounding vitality of the antelope was not unnatural for Thoreau, but the Hindu would not have done so, for the trammels of life with its unreal lures is what he wishes to escape.

VI

Then what positive principles of the Yoga did Thoreau accept? If he never could have been the man certain portions of the Hindu scriptures admonished men to be, on what basis did he find his kinship? The probable key is the *Laws of Menu*. Note what Thoreau wrote of the book on September 2, 1841:

The sublime sentences of Menu carry us back to a time

when purification and sacrifice and self-devotion had a place in the faith of men, and were not as now a superstition. They contain a subtle and refined philosophy also, such as in these times is not accompanied with so lofty and pure a devotion.[61]

These sentences do not express a random impression. They were the result of a frequent reading of Manu through the summer of 1841.[62] The book had not remained an object of curiosity. It had become a very personal discovery.

The "Laws of Menu" are a *manual of private devotion,* so private and domestic and yet so public and universal a word as is not spoken in the parlor or pulpit in these days. . . . It goes with us into the yard and into the chamber, and is yet later spoken than the advice of our mother and sisters.[63]

The title of Manu's work may be misleading to the layman, who very naturally might wonder why Thoreau should have written as he did. The words, *Institutes of Hindu Law; or the Ordinances of Menu, according to the Gloss of Culluca,* suggest a legal treatise, dry as dust, instead of a devotional manual. The truth is that the book may roughly be described as a composite of *Genesis* and *Leviticus,* the *Bhagavadgita* and the *Upanishads.* There are chapters devoted to ceremonial law, it is true. On the other hand, the title of the first chapter is "On the Creation"; of the last, "On Transmigration and Final Beatitude." The first chapter is an apt summary of the Vedantist's concept of the universe; the last chapter expresses his philosophy of the end and purpose of life. A volume that thus attempted to consider both the meaning of the cosmos and the practical affairs of men, necessarily sanctioned both the life of action and the life of contemplation. It reminds one of the admonitions of Krishna to Arjuna in the *Bhagavadgita,* which indicated the manner in which the Hindu compromised the rigorous logic of the Yoga with the more humane Sankhya. There was nothing in either the words of Manu or Krishna to drive Thoreau to a way of life he could not have accepted.

Passages which Thoreau most probably read will be the best basis of understanding what he meant when he spoke of Manu as a manual of private devotion. The following are verses which appeared in the fourth chapter, "On Economicks; and Private Morals":

240. Single is each man born; single he dies; single he receives the reward of his good, and single the punishment of his evil, deeds.

241. When he leaves his corse, like a log or a lump of clay, on the ground, his kindred retire with averted faces; but his Virtue accompanies his soul.

242. Continually, therefore, by degrees let him collect virtue, for the sake of securing an inseparable companion; since with Virue for his guide, he will traverse a gloom, how hard to be traversed!

.   .   .   .

246. He, who perseveres in good actions, in subduing his passions, in bestowing largesses, in gentleness of manners, who bears hardships patiently, who associates not with the malignant, who gives pain to no sentient being, obtains final beatitude.[64]

The last verse of this quotation probably comes closest to suggesting what Thoreau might have had in mind when he called himself a Yogi. But there were verses in the twelfth chapter, "On Transmigration and Final Beatitude," that are also exceedingly suggestive:

10. He, whose firm understanding obtains a command over his words, a command over his thoughts, and a command over his whole body, may justly be called a tridandi, or triple commander; not a mere anchoret, who bears three visible staves.

11. The man, who exerts this triple self-command with respect to all animated creatures, wholly subduing both lust and wrath, shall by those means attain beatitude.[65]

Assuredly there is little in these words to which Thoreau could not have given assent.

The recently published story, entitled *The Transmigration of the Seven Brahmans*,[66] which Thoreau translated from the French of Langlois' *Harivansa,* must also be considered evidence that Thoreau's interest in the Yoga was far more than a passing fancy. The story, in brief, is that of seven brothers who undertook the ascetic disciplines after the death of their father. They were assigned, for one thing, to the task of caring for their teacher's sacred cow and her calf. On one occasion, impelled by hunger, they conceived the mad purpose of slaying the cow. Two of the brothers, Cavi and Swasrima, endeavored to prevent the execution of the plan, but were powerless against the other five. The saving fact in the sacrilegious slaughter was that the cow eventually was offered as a sacrifice in honor of the ancestors. Later, when the brothers met their teacher, they said, "Your cow has been slain by a tiger, but here is her calf." The Brahman never suspected evil, and accepted the falsehood.

When Time came to take the seven brothers from this world, for having been cruel and guilty of impiety towards their preceptor, they were reincarnated as sons in the family of a lowly hunter dwelling in the country of Dasarna. There they all attached themselves with great zeal to the task of redeeming the past. After the death of their parents, "they fixed themselves in the forest, where soon after they themselves also surrendered their souls." In the form of stags with high arching horns they then by turns inspired and suffered the fears of the forest. Later, as geese, they were transported to a beautiful country of lakes where they were "occupied only with divine things." Thus the seven brothers paid the penalty of a tragic fall from their original estate as Brahmans, serving in penance the various incarnations through which they were obliged to pass.

A dramatic incident occurred after they had been incarnated as wild ducks. "In their new condition of inhabitants of the air, they continued their holy practices; in their language they spoke only of sacred things, and the yoga was the only object of their meditations." It chanced, however, that "a prince of the family of the Nipas, brilliant with beauty, illustrious in power, stately, and surrounded by all his house, entered into the forest where these birds lived." One of the brothers, named Soutantra in this incarnation, suddenly dazzled by riches, formed this desire: "Might I become like this king, if I have acquired any merit by my austerities and my penitence! I am unhappy to have fasted and mortified myself without any fruit." Then two of his companions expressed the wish to follow him and share his destiny. Till then, all three had been animated by only religious thoughts. But the four remaining brothers were faithful to their vows, and one of them spoke: "Since consulting only your passion, you reject our pious exercises, in order to form earthly desires, hear my words. Be cursed by us: you shall be king at

Campilya, and these two friends shall follow you there."
Much remains of the story that cannot be narrated here.
All seven brothers continue to experience other incarnations and vicissitudes. The end of the three who permitted
cupidity to enter their minds was that they rose to the
highest positions of the land, one becoming the king and
the others his ministers. But they lost all desire for the
culture of their souls, until they were reminded of their
past by circumstances brought about by the four faithful
brothers who had so grown in devotion and piety by the
practice of the Yoga that they at last "obtained perfection
and the mysterious union with God."

Were Thoreau's interest in the Yoga and the legends
to be found in its literature limited to his translation of
this story alone, it might well be argued that the single
instance is far from conclusive evidence. But it is not the
sole incident of its kind. It has already been pointed out
that Thoreau translated and edited portions of the Buddhist scriptures under the title of "The Preaching of
Buddha" in the *Dial* of January, 1844. He used Burnouf's *Introduction à l'histoire du Buddhisme indien* as
the source of the words of Buddha and his followers upon
the subject of Nirvana. The discussion occupied ten
pages of the magazine. The following was one of the passages selected by Thoreau:

Then this man speaks thus to the Sages: What means must
I employ, or what good work must I do to acquire an equal
wisdom? . . . Then these Sages say thus to the man: If thou
desirest wisdom, contemplate the law, seated in the desert, or
in the forest, or in the caverns of the mountains, and free thyself from the corruption of evil. Then, endowed with purified

qualities, thou shalt obtain supernatural knowledge. Then this man, following this counsel, entering into the religious life, living in the desert, his thought fixed upon a single object, was freed from that of the world, and acquired these five kinds of supernatural knowledge; and having acquired them, he reflected thus; The conduct which I pursued before, put me in possession of no law, and of no quality. Now, on the contrary, I go wherever my thought goes; before I had only little wisdom, little judgment, I was blind.[67]

What, one might ask, making the question more than rhetorical, impelled Thoreau thus to present Oriental asceticism to an American audience, if he did not seriously believe there was essential spiritual health in this asceticism?

As has already been intimated, the *Bhagavadgita* also expressed the ideal of the true Yogi with words of strange and haunting beauty. There are the famous verses, fifty to fifty-five, of the eighteenth chapter, which describe the good man as hateless toward all beings, friendly, pitiful, void of the thoughts of "I" and "mine." He is subdued of spirit, steadfast in his purpose of understanding Brahma, undismayed before the world, void of joy, impatience, and fear, indifferent to honor and dishonor, joy and pain, silent, content with whatever befalls, homeless, firm of judgment, and devoted to his object. Nor was there anything in this kind of Hindu asceticism Thoreau would not have approved.

If it be insisted that the Yoga discipline was very technical, that Buddha and the *Bhagavadgita* recommended that the ascetic abide alone in a secret place, without craving and without possessions, it can be said that the Walden hermitage and its occupant fulfilled this injunction. If it be insisted, furthermore, that the Yogi was expected to affect a certain pose, holding body, head and neck in unmoving equipoise, gaze fixed on the end of the nose, without looking about as directed in the sixth chapter and thirteenth verse of the *Gita*, it can even be suggested that Thoreau in general fulfilled these instructions, although he might not have done so consciously. The Hindu Yogi wrapt in his contemplations is not a far cry from the picture Thoreau gives of himself, sitting in his sunny doorway lost in reverie, oblivious of time from sunrise till noon, oblivious even of the songs of birds. He may not have contemplated the navel; assuredly he never indulged in the grosser practices of the Yoga. But the bhakti of the *Bhagavadgita* was sufficiently indefinite to include him.

Much depends upon the ascetic's object. Some may strive for occult powers, some for control of the necromancer's spells, some for simple recognition without any prejudices. One who is concerned with the highest ideals will hardly develop into a magician on the way. It is absurd even to think of Thoreau as a Yogi in this light. The universal fact is that the Yoga practices heighten the tendencies which its disciple affirms. All that the world's saints claim for the strengthening power of prayer will be easily understood in the psychological effects of even a few minutes of conscious abstractions every morning, which seem to lift one above a narrow individuality into the spirit of a larger universe. Man flows at once to God, Thoreau thought, when the channels of purity are open.

Thoreau is akin to the Yogi, too, in his extreme love of solitude. "I thrive best on solitude," he writes in his

Journal. "If I have had a companion only one day in a week
. . . I find that the value of the week to me has been seriously affected."[68] In solitude and silence he found his soul
unharassed. It seems that they were the only conditions
under which he could hear Truth's speaking-trumpet, and
recognize Reality: "As the truest society approaches always nearer to solitude, so the most excellent speech falls
into Silence. . . . Silence . . . is when we hear inwardly,
sound when we hear outwardly. . . . Who has not hearkened
to her infinite din? She is Truth's speaking-trumpet . . .
through her *all revelations have been made.*"[69] Wisdom is
defined by the *Bhagavadgita* in terms which the average
man will find hard to hear: a constant and invariable
worship paid to God alone, worshipping in a private place
together with a dislike for the society of men. "The Yogee
constantly exerciseth the spirit in private," runs Charles
Wilkins' translation, which Thoreau read. "He is recluse,
of a subdued mind and spirit. . . . He planteth his own feet
firmly on the spot that is undefiled. . . . There he, whose
business is the restraining of the passions, should sit."[70]
This passage strikes very close indeed to the note of
Thoreau's temper. The surest interpretation of the fact
that he called himself a Yogi is to remember that above
all he craved solitude and the inner realization of God.
Most mystics repeat the Yogi's gesture in the largest sense.

VII

It might appear that a study of the Walden years in
terms of the Yoga is to ignore what has been asserted by
other writers on the experiment. For instance, Henry
Seidel Canby writes: "There is no understanding Thoreau

until you forget for a moment the frayed corduroys, the unsociable habits, the eccentricity of one who loved to wade neck deep in the swamps to surprise nature in her secrets, and realize that here was a man who, far from advocating some Oriental mysticism or emotional escape, was engaged upon the central problem of modern life— how to live a good life in an increasingly mechanical world."[71] There is the issue. How much credence can be given to Thoreau's own use of the Oriental in describing his experiences?

In the first place it is useless to deny that Thoreau was a New Englander, interested in the life of Concord folk. And oncoming industrial problems did provoke him. He wrote a good deal about the problem of the good life under untoward circumstances. "I cannot believe that our factory system is the best mode by which men may get clothing," was his opinion in *Walden*. "The condition of the operatives is becoming every day more like that of the English; and it cannot be wondered at, since, as far as I have heard or observed, the principal object is, not that mankind may be well and honestly clad, but, unquestionably that the corporations may be enriched."[72] When he gave his attention to the effects of industrialism on individual men, he found that toil had rendered their fingers too clumsy and trembling to pluck the finer fruits of life. Instead, they were occupied with its factitious cares and superfluously coarse labor, having no leisure for true integrity, or time to sustain what Thoreau called the manliest relations to men, without depreciating their labor in the market. There was time for the machine alone. The finest qualities of human nature died, for they, "like the

bloom on fruits, can be preserved only by the most delicate handling."[3] Yet men do not treat each other tenderly.

Undoubtedly the problems produced by such concentrated industrial centers as the town of Lowell affected
Thoreau. He was too much interested in human worth
to be impervious. Professor Canby is right in asserting
that he advocated no Oriental mysticism for his countrymen. The Yoga would not have solved the problems of
the masses. He realized it, and commenced his appeal for
a humaner social outlook with words which indicate how
he felt about some of the grosser practices of Yogis:

I would fain say something, not so much concerning the
Chinese and Sandwich Islanders as you who read these pages,
who are said to live in New England; something about your
condition, especially your outward condition or circumstances
in this world, in this town, what it is, whether it is necessary
that it be as bad as it is, whether it cannot be improved as
well as not. I have travelled a good deal in Concord; and
everywhere, in shops, and offices, and fields, the inhabitants
have appeared to me to be doing penance in a thousand remarkable ways. What I have heard of Bramins sitting exposed
to four fires and looking in the face of the sun; or hanging
suspended, with their heads downward, over flames; or looking
at the heavens over their shoulders "until it becomes impossible for them to resume their natural position, while from the
twist of the neck nothing but liquids can pass into the stomach"; or dwelling, chained for life, at the foot of a tree; or
measuring with their bodies, like caterpillars, the breadth of
vast empires; or standing on one leg on the tops of pillars,—
even these forms of conscious penance are hardly more incredi-
ble and astonishing than the scenes which I daily witness. . . . I
see young men, my townsmen, whose misfortune it is to have

inherited farms, houses, barns, cattle, and farming tools; for these are more easily acquired than got rid of. . . . Why should they begin digging their graves as soon as they are born? They have got to live a man's life, pushing all these things before them, and get on as well as they can.[74]

An innate kindliness dictated these words.

The *Bhagavadgita,* it will be remembered, was the meeting of the Sankhya and Yoga philosophies. The Sankhya—the way of works—permitted a man to remain in the world and do his duty. The Sankhya was the only possible road for the mass of men. Of course Thoreau knew it; he would never have advocated the insanity of all men building Walden shanties. But the Yoga was the higher road, the *Bhagavadgita* said. The devotee was to enter upon it by himself when he felt called. It was *private business* that Thoreau attended to at Walden; not a social problem.[75]

Furthermore, Walden is hardly the result of personal failure in business or the practical life. After inventing the process by which the most perfect pencil lead known in the country was produced, and standing on the threshold of what could easily have become a most lucrative business, Thoreau says: "I have tried trade; but I found that it would take ten years to get under way in that, and that then I should probably be on my way to the devil. I was actually afraid that I might by that time be doing what is called a good business."[76] The spending of the best years of life in earning money in order to enjoy a questionable leisure during the least valuable portion of it reminded him of the Englishman who went to India to make a fortune first, in order that he might return to his native home and live the life of the poet.[77] He could see no advantage in cutting his *spiritual* bread far thinner than his forefathers did their wheaten.[78]

And when he considers what, in the words of the catechism, is the chief end of man, and "what are the true necessaries and means of life," it seemed to him that men had deliberately chosen the common mode of living because they preferred it or honestly thought that they had no other choice.[79] His own choice was made inevitable by the temper which impelled him to write, "Rather than love, than money, than fame, give me truth."[80] The truest interpretation of Walden is probably to see it neither as an escape from the nerve-rasping shriek of factory whistles, nor the turning by a lover of nature-lore to the most congenial atmospheres. Rather, it is found in this sentence: "To live like a philosopher is to live, not foolishly, like other men, but wisely and according to universal laws."[81] The Yoga also advocated this kind of a good life. To state our conclusion thus may seem, in general, to state a platitude. But Thoreau's application of the principle to life was anything but conventional and platitudinous.

VIII

Whatever may have been the opinions of the critics who have written about Thoreau, one thing seems almost certain: few have been totally indifferent. From the critics of the mid-nineteenth century to those of the present day, Thoreau has received both eulogy and obloquy. And in Thoreau's case it is true, as in probably no other, that the criticism he received was predetermined by the temperament and prejudices of the critics. Very little of it is unbiased. A few examples will serve to illustrate.

It would have required little astuteness to have anticipated the strictures of the jovial and social Robert Louis
Stevenson. Nor is one surprised by the contrast when
Emerson, the idealist, closes the eulogy of his friend with
these words: "His soul was made for the noblest society;
he had in a short life exhausted the capabilities of this
world; wherever there is knowledge, wherever there is
virtue, wherever there is beauty, he will find a home."[82]
Again, Whitman's democratic sympathies, in direct contrast with Emerson's, precluded his castigation of the anti-
social Thoreau: "His great fault was disdain for men,—
for Tom, Dick and Harry; inability to appreciate the
average life, even the exceptional life. It seemed to me a
want of imagination. He could not put his life into any
other life, or realize why one man was so, and another
man was not so; was impatient with other people. It was a
surprise to me to meet in Thoreau such a case of super-
ciliousness."[83]

The essays on Thoreau, which, for example, have been
collected in the anonymous booklet entitled *Pertaining to
Thoreau*,[84] indicate well enough the deep divisions between
critics. Consider such sentences from the essay by C. F.
Briggs as: "But one cannot live on a house unless he
rents it to somebody else, even though he be a philosopher
and a believer in Vishnu";[85] or "Perhaps some practical
people will think that a philosopher like Mr. Thoreau
might have done the world a better service by purchasing
a piece of land, and showing how much it might be made
to produce, instead of squatting on another man's premises, and proving how little will suffice to keep body and
soul together."[86]

If a lack of sympathy with Thoreau's temperament, on the part of critics, has brought an inevitable negative tone into their writings about him, it is no less true that the ignorance of critics has distorted their perspective on the subject. Probably the outstanding instance of this last fact is the famous essay by James Russell Lowell. It is interesting to consider the essay purely from the subject of Orientalism and notice the absurd assertions to which Lowell is led by his opposition to the chief premises of Hindu mysticism:

What, for instance, have Concord and Merrimack to do with Boodh, themselves possessors of an elder and to them wholly sufficient religion, namely, the willing subjects of watery laws, to seek their ocean? We have digressions on Boodh [in the *Week*] . . . and we know not what. We come upon them like snags, jolting us headforemost out of our places as we are rowing placidly up stream or drifting down. Mr. Thoreau becomes so absorbed in these discussions, that he seems, as it were, to *catch a crab,* and disappears uncomfortably from his seat at the bow-oar.[87]

Or consider again Lowell's total scorn for, not Hindu idealism alone, but also the religious philosophy of the people as a whole, when he continues to examine it in connection with Thoreau's predilection for its scriptures. " 'Give me a sentence', prays Mr. Thoreau bravely, 'which no intelligence can understand!'—and we think that the kind gods have nodded. There are some of his utterances which have foiled us, and we belong to that class of beings which he thus reproachfully stigmatizes as intelligences." And Lowell continues: "We think it must be this taste that makes him so fond of the Hindoo philosophy, which would seem admirably suited to men, if men were only oysters."[88] No supposedly informed critic should have been so flippant.

If our primary concern were with the shortcomings or extravagances of Thoreau's critics, it would be possible greatly to extend the discussion of this phase of our subject. Since, however, it is the significance of Thoreau's asceticism and Orientalism that engages us, we hew to that line.

Besides Henry Seidel Canby, Professors Paul Elmer More and Mark Van Doren have most thoroughly examined the significance of the Walden experiment. Professor Van Doren does not share Canby's interest in the industrial interpretation. Rather, he sees it as the result of the German Romanticism filtering into the New England of Thoreau's time, but he writes only to suggest. "The expansion seed," he thinks, "certainly took wing in the beginning from transcendental Germany. But transcendentalism is one thing, and romanticism is another. It has never been determined just how much the movement which grew out of German transcendentalism and which is called German romanticism had to do with American transcendental expansion."[89] This is true enough. The eclectic thought of the American Transcendentalists has never been completely studied. Professor More, in turn, writes of Thoreau's observations on childhood, sleep, and the sacrament of silence as evidence of the thoroughness with which "the transcendental philosophy of New England had absorbed the language and ideas of German romanticism, if not its inmost spirit."[90]

The future may show that Professors More and Van

Doren have probed closer to the heart of the problem than is possible from an Oriental angle. Still, it seems improbable that Thoreau, with his utter disdain of current panaceas for society's ills, would have been influenced by mere romantic sentiment. He was too much of a Realist. He says as early as 1838: "Men are constantly dinging in my ears their fair theories and plausible solutions of the universe, but ever there is no help, and I return again to my shoreless, islandless ocean, and fathom unceasingly for a bottom that will hold an anchor, that it may not drag."[91] Is it taking too great liberty to think of this figure of a shoreless, islandless ocean as not greatly unlike the Brahma of the Hindu, even though other Western writers might offer other similarities? At least it must be admitted that Brahma embraces the object of most mystical seekers. No, Thoreau will not eventually be honored for his contributions to American social and industrial theory. His place is with the mystics.

After examining Thoreau's life, Professor Van Doren finds him little more than a disappointed man. He writes that Thoreau "scarcely suspected that his intensity was distilling the essence out of a vacuum, and not out of life," that "his spiritual existence was more than easy; it was hopelessly, fatally easy,"[92] since he had assured himself that his own will was the will of the Universe, that thought and feeling were one, as also soul and body, that necessity was sweet, and good and evil phantoms easy to dissolve— doctrines long familiar in Emerson. Yet with this start Van Doren thinks Thoreau "never succeeded in stepping entirely out of his little private darkness." Furthermore, he writes, "Thoreau deluded himself, because he was introspective in a certain mistaken, fruitless way,"[93] and the reason for the sterility of his introspection was that "it was a brooding reverie of self-contemplation rather than an effort to measure and correct and check himself by reference to things beyond himself."[94] This point becomes clearer when Van Doren explains: "It is clear enough that he was incapable of distinguishing between fruitless and fruitful expansion—the expansion which merely distends the self at the present stage of its ignorance, and the expansion which really enlarges the self by thrusting it out into play with surrounding selves."[95] It will be easier to determine the justice of such criticism when the contribution of German Romanticism to American Transcendentalism has been examined, as Professor More suggested. From the Oriental point of view it is clear that such criticism is a criticism of the premises from which Thoreau started and not of the man or his life.

Professor Van Doren also came to the conclusion that "Thoreau never gets to the bottom of the law of his being because he fails to keep the other men in mind, because he loses his bearings, because he does not recognize his individual being as in anyway distinguishable from universal being."[96] The answer is a question: Why should a mystic recognize his individuality as distinguishable from the universal being? Emerson did not. No Vedantist would. Thoreau's anchor may never have sunk itself so deep into the bottom of the islandless, shoreless ocean he plumbed that it would not drag. A modern Occidental psychologist may never consider even a Hindu Yogi as successful in the attempt, for there is no gauge by which the mystic's experiences can be measured. Everything depends upon the standards of measurement. With this realization we might let the issue rest.

But, finally, the crux of all Occidental criticism of the Yoga is suggested. "The problem of *self*, like the problem of love, is his sore affliction. 'There is no remedy for love but to love more', said he. So with being; there is no remedy for being but to be indefinitely more—of *nothing*."[97] Of course the last thing an American wants to be is nothing; but the absorption of himself into Brahma is the only thing a pure Vedantist desires. Professor Van Doren has reached the heart of Thoreau's problem. Looking at him through Occidental eyes, weighing his success in Occidental scales, he is right in concluding him a failure, for what a Yogi achieves will never be stated in terms of phenomenal experience. On the other hand, it would be interesting to know what Hindus themselves would say of Thoreau's success as stated in his own words: "I learned this . . . he will meet with success unexpected in common hours . . . he will live with the license of a higher order of beings . . . solitude will not be solitude, nor poverty poverty, nor weakness weakness."[98] This truly implies that the veil of Maya has been pierced.

Thoreau's Transcendentalist contemporary, John Weiss, seems to have anticipated as early as 1865 the conclusion to which our evidence would seem to have led us. "In later years," wrote Weiss, "his chin and mouth grew firmer as his resolute and audacious opinions developed, the curves of the lips lost their flabbiness, the eyes twinkled with the latent humor of his criticisms of society." Thus Weiss continues: "Still the countenance was unruffled: it seemed to lie deep, like a mountain tarn, with cool, still nature all around. There was not a line upon it expressive of ambition or discontent: the affectional emotions had not fretted at it. He went about, like a priest of Buddha who expects to arrive soon at the summit of a life of contemplation, where the divine absorbs the human."[99] We need not amplify the suggestiveness of such incisive sentences as these, for John Weiss was an informed and discriminating observer.

A little mound of stones today marks the site where Thoreau disciplined himself. It rises in the minds of Americans as sharply as an obelisk from a plain, because Thoreau's life was so different from theirs. In India no mounds are ever raised to commemorate the thousands who seek the forest. Whatever else Thoreau's motive may have been, Walden can at least be definitely viewed as the logical consequence of his idealism and the Reality he worshipped. It was an ascetic gesture arising from his own peculiar, Orient-tinged naturalism.

PART FOUR

ALCOTT THE PROPAGANDIST

Very desirable it were since the gates of the East are now opening wide and giving the free commerce of mind with mind, to
collect and compare the Bibles of the races for general circulation
and careful reading.

—Alcott, *Tablets,* p. 135.

I dine and pass the afternoon with the Adams and read 'Bhagavad Gita' to a large audience in the evening, with lively discussions, etc.

—Alcott, *Manuscript Journals.*

The ideal world I might have treated as a cloud-land, had I
not known Alcott, who is a native of that country and makes
it as solid as Massachusetts for me.

—Emerson, *Works,* I, xxxiv.

ALCOTT THE PROPAGANDIST

I

The personality of Amos Bronson Alcott, as did that of
Emerson and Thoreau, determined the nature of his work.
Emerson, as we have seen, was the sage. An iconoclast in
things of the spirit, he nevertheless built, in the place of
the dogmas he had scrapped, a new philosophy, a synthesis
of all the congenial ideas he found in the thought-life of
his time, with much from the Orientals. Thoreau we have
studied in his own peculiar temper. It is easy enough to
charge him in one sense with being an imitator of his elder
friend. He was not in the large sense the pioneer; Emerson
was that. Emerson, it was, who like Tennyson's Ulysses
sailed beyond the utmost bound, not of human but of
Occidental thought. He breathed the yeasty air of intellectual territories which none of his countrymen had explored before him. His essays are the log books of these
journeys. But always he returned home to domestic con-
ventionality and propriety. One may describe Emerson as
he will—level-headed or urbane. The truth is that he never
carried all his theories to their logical conclusion. He is
regarded as the most important exponent of American
Transcendental thought. There are many reasons for this,
the chief being his eloquence and his extensive writing.
Yet Thoreau surpassed his friend in many ways. Emerson's intellectual honesty was superb and his heart stout,
but his was a different rôle. Without the thoughts with

which Emerson returned from his explorations, Thoreau might never have gone to Walden. And Alcott's place in the Transcendental sun was that of educator and dreamer —naturally enough a dreamer. His practical contribution to the cause of the East in America was that of a teacher. His talents were used where they were the most effective. Brilliant as a teacher and conversationalist, in these rôles he sowed the Oriental seed. He also proposed a series of books which no single human being before or since his time has ever written. The plan never was realized, and Alcott, of the three Concord friends, is a man whose influence and work have never been appraised, because so little of his personality ever found its way into the printed page. For this reason his individual color and contribution must be determined from quite a different angle. The bathos[1] which in a purely literary sense is the result of the transition to his pages from those of Emerson and Thoreau, is completely displaced by the fact that in his time Alcott probably had no equal as a popularizer of Orientalism. Though his work was different from that of his friends, it was essentially no less important.

II

The unpublished *Journals* of Bronson Alcott, as they rest securely on their shelves in Concord today, consist of fifty heavy leather-backed volumes. The closely written pages have been preserved from the fate of most scattered loose leaves by the foresight of Louisa Alcott, who ordered the binding of all her father's manuscripts before her death. But slightly explored by Mrs. Morrow[2] and Sanborn, who based his *Life* largely on notes for a biography which Alcott himself had prepared,[3] these diary pages remain unpublished. That they are of value no one who has dipped into them can doubt. There is not the fluency of Emerson's and Thoreau's diaries, but Alcott's nevertheless reflect the high intellectual and spiritual life which he lived, and his personality. Within their covers are embalmed his thoughts after the failure of Fruitlands; the fortitude with which he faced the future after the dismal failures of his Philadelphia and Boston schools; the clear expression of the theories which marked him as an enlightened educator, but unfortunately a prophet whose time was not ripe for his message; the plans he had for regenerating humanity; and, of most value here, a record of his activities and schemes for educating men in the Oriental religions. In the earlier years of his life Alcott wrote at greater length. After the forties, his duties and responsibilities grew, the conversations increased in number, and the labor entailed in preparing them robbed him of time he might have used in elaborating his thought. One must read in between the lines of the entries for these years, if their complete significance is to be grasped.

What is known of the chronology of Alcott's Oriental interests is extremely slight. His earliest reading of consequence was done in the libraries of Philadelphia, while he was a school master there. It was during this period of his life, around the year 1831, that he seems from evidence outside of his *Journals*[4] to have first read about the Orientals. The unpublished journal manuscript pages themselves contain few tell-tale sentences to disclose the fact that Orientalism of any sort was getting a hold. Alcott became expansive when he wrote on the educational

theories which later brought him both fame and oppro-
brium. On other matters he was most laconic. As late as
January 25, 1849, after he had met Emerson and Thoreau
and had become a lover of the Orientals, this sentence,
with its unique spelling, "I read the Bagvat Geeta," was
all that appeared to indicate how a Sunday had been spent.
Emerson and Thoreau would not have failed to expand
that simple sentence into an interesting passage of self-
revelation. But not Alcott. He had less ink. He was not
a born scribbler.

There can be little doubt that Alcott's active Oriental
interests commenced when he, like Thoreau before him,
first met Emerson. There was nothing in the man to make
him immune. Had there been any reason for resistance,
it would nevertheless have been difficult to remain aloof
from such enthusiasm as had taken hold of Emerson and
Thoreau; and rather ungracious, in view of the kindness
they showed him during luckless days. There was a
brotherly bond between the three men. Belonging to the
confraternity of mystics, mutually sharing each other's
sentiments of what was wrong with their world ecclesi-
astically, politically and socially, they lived as neighbors
for many years. During this time Alcott reflected the influence of his friends. But instead of immersing himself in
nature, as did Thoreau, or brooding on and writing about
the Over-Soul, as did Emerson, he made his chief interest
the universal scriptures of men.

III

One of the most interesting pages of all in Alcott's
Journals was drawn up at a time when he was diagram-
ing his tablets, a name which he frequently applied to

the pages of his diary, and subsequently gave to one of his published books.[5] There is the following which appeared under the date of August, 1849:

Tablet   Tuesday 21.

MANKIND LIBRARY

The Sacred Scriptures, with Mythological and Biographical elucidation, first collected and edited: being the Lives, works and times of

Moses	Plato
Confucius	Christ
Zoroaster	Mahomet
Pythagoras	Behmen
Socrates	Swedenborg

Mythology

I. Hebrew and Egyptian	III. Greek and Roman
II. Oriental and Indian	IV. Christian and Cosmic

There can be little doubt as to what it was—the title page of a volume, or series, to be published under the caption of *Mankind Library*. And Alcott was to be the author and editor! Here was one of the man's great plans.[6] No dishonor falls upon him for having failed in the realization. It was a task which no man has ever accomplished, almost commensurate with the editing of *The Sacred Books of the East,* which required the cooperation of the world's best Oriental scholars and thirty-one years of assiduous labor to complete.[7] It is unnecessary to discuss at further length the significance of this dream in Alcott's life work. Nothing could demonstrate more clearly how anxious he was to propagate the Newness. The stark facts are themselves the most eloquent exposition of their own significance.

IV

But the dream persisted and Alcott read constantly in the Oriental scriptures. He had been doing this for several years. On Tuesday, June 17, 1849, the following was entered upon the pages of the diary: "I read the 'Bhagavad Gita'; also write to Louisa and Abby who are passing some weeks at Samuel May's."[8] Reading over other entries we find that two months later he was doing the same thing, re-reading a book which he could have perused at one sitting. On Wednesday, June 27, he writes: "I dine and pass the afternoon with the Adams[9] and read 'Bhagavad Gita' to a large audience in the evening, with lively discussions etc." One is gratified that Alcott's neighbors were capable of entering into "lively discussions, etc." with him on the subject of Hindu mysticism. It may be taken as evidence that the leaven was at work in Concord.

During the month of March, 1849, even before he had drawn upon the proposed title-page for the *Mankind Library,* he planned for a series of public conversations on the teachings of the Oriental sages. One of the most interesting pages of Alcott's diary is that on which he had prepared an advance notice of the meetings, leaving the place and date blank, but probably otherwise ready to turn over to the printer. This notice was confided to the diary on Saturday, March 17:

SUNDAY READINGS AND CONVERSATIONS

Mr. A. Bronson Alcott will give the first of several Readings from the Sacred Books of Mankind, with interpretations and original teachings interspersed at ——— Street, on Sunday morning, next, March ———, commencing at 10 o'clock.

All persons disposed to give hospitable entertainment to the words of illuminated Mind of all times, are respectfully invited to attend the Readings, and express their sentiments on the text, interpretations and teachings. Admission free.

The clergymen of Concord and Boston may have frowned on such competition on the Sabbath day, and their parishioners remained loyal to the established services. Alcott's hope that he could get a following was too venturous, and two years passed before anything came of the plan.

But meanwhile he was reading and collecting material for the course. He consulted James Freeman Clarke, the author of the *Ten Great Religions,* and on March 24 recorded as follows the suggestions he had received:

Oriental Readings. List of Authors to be sought at the Athenaeum. (Given me by J. F. Clarke).
Collier's Four Books of Confucius,
History of China, (by the Jesuit)
The Kings of Confucius,
The Vedas,
The Saama Vedas,
Vishnu Parana,
Saadi,
Firdusi,
The Zendavesta,
The Koran.

This was in 1849, as already intimated. Whether he made an immediate attempt to follow Clarke's suggestions is not indicated in his diary. But that he probably continued to search widely and persistently for books is suggested by the entry of February 11, 1851:

I brought from the Athenaeum, this afternoon, for my Readings, "Marshman's Confucius," containing the Life of Confucius and translation of the "Lun Gnee" or Dialogues, being the third of the Four Classical Books of the Chinese. Also from Burnham's "The Phoenix a collection of Ancient Fragments," "The Morals of Confucius," "The Oracles of Zoroaster" etc. Emerson sent me, a day or two since, the "Hermes Trismegistus," the only copy, I suppose, there is to be had in the country, and which I brought out from England.[10] "Saadi's Gulistan," I can obtain from the Cambridge Library; and of the other Books, from which I propose to give Selections, Socrates, Plato, Behmen, I possess copies; also Dante, by Dr. Carlyle, Buckley's Aeschylus; and Wellington's Swedenborg. Of Goethe I must purchase a copy. Bohn has just published an edition of Faust, Iphigeneia, Torquato Tasso and Egmont.

The fact that Alcott read critically cannot be proved by more substantial evidence than the following passage which was written two days later: "Cory's translations are so superior to Stanley's or Thomas Taylor's of the Oracles of Zoroaster, that I shall transcribe some of them to these pages from my journal of 1849."[11] The transcription followed, five pages of them. They show what Alcott thought the best, and give some conception of what he planned to read to his audiences. "Look not on Nature for her name is Fatal," was one; "Who knows himself knows all things in himself," was another; and still a third was this unique statement of a favorite idealistic doctrine: "Evil, according to the oracle, is more frail than non-entity." The following, which was among the transcribed texts, seems but another way of stating Emerson's favorite doctrine of Compensation: "Our voluntary sorrows germinate in us as the growth of the particular life we lead." More in Alcott's personal manner were these sentences: "The

Furies are the constrainers of men," and "There is a certain Intelligible which it becomes you to understand with the flower of the mind."[12]

Alcott continues under the same date:

"The History of Ancient Philosophy" (Ritter's) is not to be had from our Athenaeum; nor have I been able to find there anything of Saadi's. Harvard College Library, and Longfellow,[13] supplied me with the works of these Orientalists, but I have found less in Ritter for my purposes, than either Stanley or Cudworth had for me.

With all this reading and assiduous preparation for the proposed course, Alcott never lacked for time to share his findings with his friends. Since what is presented here has never been published before, I continue in his own words. It is still February, 1851.

Saturday 15.

Afternoon, came Goodwin[14] to see me, and discussed profoundly on the soul of Music. Mr. G. is recently from Cincinnati; and now organist at St. Paul's in this city. He is familiar with the highest, or Transcendental Music, and himself a composer and critic. Like all minds of this fine cast, he is a receiver of Emerson, and a reader of the biblical literatures of the world. I shall send him tickets to the Select Readings and Conversations on the Poets and Philosophers.

Eight days later H. G. O. Blake, Thoreau's intimate friend and literary executor, called, and we find the following record: "Blake came, and I read some passages from my Diary, the sketch of Thoreau, whom he esteems highly; and the passages from Zoroaster. A man of delicate tastes and much sharpness of intellect is this Mr. Blake; a reader of choice things; and a come-outer in spirit."

At last satisfactory arrangements were made and the

day for the first of the conversations arrived. On Monday, February 24, 1851, Alcott pasted one of the admission cards into the *Journal*. The order of the subjects is interesting evidence of the use he planned to make of some of his reading which we have followed.

ADMIT

to

MR. ALCOTT'S CONVERSATIONS

on the

POETS and PHILOSOPHERS

———

I. Hermes Trismegistus	V. Aeschylus
II. Zoroaster	VI. Pythagoras
III. Confucius	VII. Socrates
IV. Saadi	VIII. Plato

IX. JESUS CHRIST

X. Dante	XIII. Milton
XI. Behmen	XIV. Swedenborg
XII. Shakespeare	XV. Goethe

———

The readings will be held on Monday Evenings, No. 7, Montgomery Place, and will commence Feb. 24, at 7½ o'clock. *Boston, February,* 1851.

Late on the same evening, after the first meeting had passed into history, he wrote:

Evening. Few persons to hear and discuss Hermes, in consequence of the rain. But we had a very good time of it. Mrs. Dall, Miss Parsons, Norton, etc. having something to say about our Egyptian of whom I gave them a taste, with an introduction on the Oracles, Sacred and Profane; their subjects and law. Hermes is the least popular of the names on my card, and of him we know less than of any one of these persons. He is even more fabulous than Zoroaster or Confucius and as mythological as Pythagoras. I did not expect to make much of him but to find a text or two for conversation.[15]

So ended the first of the conversations on that rainy night. If they were continued, I found no evidence of the fact as I browsed through the *Journal*. A few more meetings might have been held, but Alcott did not comment on their success or failure.

But what was Alcott's purpose in holding these conversations? I do not know that scholars have ever told or known. Assuredly any funds that might have accrued from them were negligible. A self-appointed educator and propagator of the things of illuminated Mind, to use his own phrase, Alcott found in these readings and conversations a double outlet. Since he was not a man of the cloth, the occasions afforded him an opportunity to preach his own philosophy to adult audiences, and to gratify the one passion of his life which had never left him, the love of the game of playing school. But let Alcott confess his own purpose in offering the course of 1851. He is writing in his diary on Wednesday, February 12, 1851, a week and a half before the rainy night on which the Egyptian Hermes was used as a spring-board:

A few texts, very few, will serve, and more than serve, for the Readings. Of all Mind, Zoroaster whether he were one or several, a real or mythological Personage, is the more occult and astral, of my cycle, doubled, and opening into a third in Goethe—the void-mind, mythology and history alike twisted into the web of his Genius, and himself but the spokesman of the

Fate that ruled him. Hermes Trismegistus is no less oracular in
the text of his "Divine Pymander" and suggestive of the intellectuals. Behmen and Swedenborg follow, precede perhaps, in
comprehensiveness and depth of insight into natural things, as
Pythagoras includes the wisdom of Society and of Education;
and Christ of Divinity. Plato was the Scholar and Occultist;
Socrates, great master of Practical morals. Saadi is a Persian
Come-outer; Dante and Milton are theological poets; as Aeschylus is a mythic bard, and Shakespeare the pure poet, of humanity. *With such vast and universal cyphers as these minds
afford of existence, I shall not want suggestions of the depth
and height of Being, nor occasion for declaring some private
experiences as they rise.*

With this commitment on the position in human history
of the men with whom he planned to deal, and the confession of what he hoped to do, we may conclude this phase
of Alcott's labors as a propagandist in behalf of the Orientals and turn to another, a work in which the boulders he
started rolling eventually became an avalanche.

V

The marriage of Fannie Maria Adelaide Channing, the
daughter of William Henry Channing, to the famous
author of *The Light of Asia*, brought the American Transcendentalists into close contact with one of the most
eminent popularizers of Buddhism in the Old World.[16] In
a very short time interesting results appeared. Alcott's
Journal is the evidence. The story is best presented with
passages culled from its pages. On August 19, 1879, he
wrote:

I have a letter from my esteemed friend Rev. William Henry
Channing of London, with a book. He dates from 3 Campdon

House Road, Huntington, August 4, and presents the book to
> A. Bronson Alcott,
> Wm. T. Harris,
> F. B. Sanborn, and
> Their confreres in Concord Summer School of
> Philosophy and Literature

The book is entitled:
The Light of Asia, or The Great Renunciation, Being the Life and Teachings of Gautama, Prince of India and Founder of Buddhism. By Edwin Arnold, London, 1879.

The purpose of Channing's writing to Alcott is disclosed when the latter continues:

Channing gives a brief account of the Author, and desired to have the book presented to the school, before its close. It came a day too late. But Harris and Sanborn may review it after perusal. It is written in flowing blank verse, and has great literary merit at best. I shall find time now to give it a closer reading.

Mr. Arnold is, I understand a brother of Matthew, and son of Dr. Arnold of Rugby School. He married a daughter of Mr. Channing.

Alcott must have obtained the concluding note on Edwin's relationship to Matthew Arnold from his own imagination, certainly not from Channing. There is no evidence of any close relationship between the men. Alcott was probably hazarding a guess because of the correspondence in the names.[17] The conclusion of Channing's letter he quotes as follows:

My friend, Edwin Arnold, gave me this volume amongst others to dispose of: and the best use of the gift, as fulfilling the poet's wish seemed to me to be,—the putting it at the disposal of your company. Will our friend, Mr. Harris, introduce it with such notice as he deems most befitting to the readers of his Journal?[18] Will Mr. Sanborn and other friends do likewise in their own appropriate way. Poem and Poet should be widely known, and be heartily welcomed by the nation that providentially serves as mediator between Europe and Asia, to unite the East and West, the Ancient and the Modern Ages, in unity.

And now with hearty friendly regards for yourself, my dear "Ever Young Artist" and with all the company of generous and great compeers around you, believe me,

Yours ever respectfully and hopefully,

WILLIAM HENRY CHANNING.

Channing does not state the fact, but it seems likely that he wrote to Alcott for two reasons. First, he was the dean of the Concord Summer School of Philosophy and Literature, and secondly, Channing probably knew that it would have been difficult to find a more active agitator in all America than Alcott. The suggestion that Sanborn and Harris write notices of the book and that "other friends do likewise in their own appropriate way" was ingenious. Alcott took the hint and went to work. Six days later he notes in his diary that "Sanborn gives . . . notice of Edwin Arnold's 'Light of Asia' in yesterday's *Republican,* with some account of the author taken from Channing's letter to me."[19]

The book arrived in Concord on August 19. The note regarding Sanborn's review which has just been quoted was dated August 25. Alcott was only beginning his work. He made trips forthwith to Boston and arranged for the immediate publication of the American edition. Early in September his *Journal* bears the following entry:

Friday 5. To Boston and find Arnold's *Light of Asia* is already in Press and to be published forthwith. An appendix is to be added of Channing's account of the author, Ripley's and Sanborn's notices, and that of the London Athanaeum. Thus the book will come before our American public chiefly on its own merits. (Holmes also writes a review.)

The parenthetical comment about Holmes does not indicate whether it was at the direct solicitation of Alcott or Channing that the review was written. It might have been either, but most probably Alcott, since he was on the immediate field and Channing was in Europe. What Holmes wrote of Edwin Arnold's book will be discussed presently.

A passage under the date of September 27 from the *Journal* shows that it was from Alcott's personal copy of *The Light of Asia,* the very copy received from Channing, that the Boston printers set type for the American edition. Alcott had moved quickly. Almost immediately he negotiated for the printing, and since he probably possessed one of the very first copies to reach America, and quick action was desirable in presenting to the public so valuable a work as Edwin Arnold's, he gladly relinquished the treasure. But he was not the loser, for he writes:

Mr. Niles[20] gives me the English copy of Arnold's *Light of Asia* in exchange for the copy sent me by Mr. Channing which the printers defaced in printing the American edition, now nearly ready for publication. Dr. Holmes' characteristic review, George Ripley's, and Channing's letter to me, are published as a supplement.

The book will be read with surprise by most, and raise curious questions in the minds of Christians generally.

Alcott had done his work effectively. The nature of the comment he elicted in behalf of the book from his friends will be seen when we take note of the American reviews. The book was safely in press. The business details had all been satisfactorily attended to. Alcott gave himself to enjoyment of the volume, carrying it with him when he called on all his friends. On October 14 he is "At Emerson's. I take my copy of Arnold's *Light of Asia* for his perusal." And he continues the work of sending the good news afield:

Sunday 19th. Also wrote to Mills[21] of Syracuse sending him Sanborn's notice of "Arnold's Light of Asia." Charles Mills has been almost the only American scholar who has cultivated Oriental studies, and written books on Buddhist literature. This poem of Arnold's must interest him, perhaps add to his knowledge of that old learning.

Alcott's excitement and feverish activity gradually subsided. When in January, 1880, *The Light of Asia* was published in Boston, he did not even comment upon the fact in his *Journal,* nor have I found record of his ever having corresponded with Edwin Arnold. The last entry which deals in any way with the book appears in connection with a letter from Channing:

Tuesday 20. My esteemed friend Wm. Henry Channing writes from London dating January 1st. He informs me of his intention of visiting America next April . . . He expects to pass the summer with us, and will doubtless attend our School at the Orchard House. We shall expect good words from him then and there.[22] He forwards thanks for our interest in the reprinting of "Light of Asia."

And thus Alcott's activity in behalf of the book seems to have ended. Nothing could show better the results of the work which he started and the interest of the American public in Orientalism than the words of Edwin Arnold's biographer in the *Dictionary of National Biography:* "The poem aroused the animosity of many pulpits, but there were *sixty editions in England and eighty in America,* and translations were numerous."[23]

VI

The phenomenal success of Edwin Arnold's poem in America was of course due to its own intrinsic merit and appeal. But there can be no doubt that it was also partly due to the warm reception the book received even from the few New England writers whom Alcott mentioned as contributing to an appendix in the American edition.[24] Alcott's account seems to have indicated what was contemplated rather than what actually appeared in the appendix. Nevertheless Ripley, Channing, Sanborn and Holmes did write enthusiastic accounts. It is not outside of the interests of this study to take brief note of the verdict of Alcott's friends.

Ripley's *New York Tribune* review and the excerpt from Channing's letter to Alcott were the only notices printed in the supplement to the 1880 Boston edition of *The Light of Asia* which I have examined. The review from the pen of Oliver Wendell Holmes was the feature article in *The International Review* for October, 1879, and never, to my knowledge, appeared as a supplement in any of the books.[25] The probable reason, and a good one, was the length at which Holmes wrote. As printed in *The International Review,* the article filled twenty-six full pages. It was based on the 1879 edition of the book which appeared in London. One may well imagine the anticipation with which the American audience awaited the volume, after a man of Holmes's literary repute had prepared the way by such pronouncement as:

For it is a work of great beauty. It tells a story of intense interest, which never flags for a moment; its descriptions are drawn by the hand of a master with the eye of a poet and the familiarity of an expert with the objects described; its tone is so lofty that there is nothing with which to compare it but the New Testament; it is full of variety, now picturesque, now pathetic; now rising into the noblest realms of thought and aspirations; it finds language penetrating, fluent, elevated, impassioned, musical always, to clothe its varied thoughts and sentiments.

The concluding sentence of Holmes's essay was:

To lay down this poem and take up a book of popular rhymes is like stepping from the carpet of a Persian palace upon the small tradesman's Kidderminster, or exchanging the shawl of an Indian empress for the printed calico which graces the matinees of the basement.

Writing with greater detail than Ripley, Holmes practically discusses at length each of the eight books which comprised Arnold's poem. The story is told and many of the descriptive scenes repeated. The quotations which were chosen to bait American poet-tasters were fortunate. We may choose one to serve a double purpose as a sample of Holmes's tastes in the poem and an instance of the early experience of the young Buddha which led to his own renunciation:

All things spoke peace and plenty, and the Prince
Saw and rejoiced. But, looking deep, he saw

The thorns which grow upon this stem of life;
How the swart peasant sweated for his wage,
Toiling for leave to live; and how he urged
The great-eyed oxen through the flaming hours,
Goading their velvet flanks; then marked he, too,
How lizzard fed on ant, and snake on him,
And kite on both; and how fish-hawk robbed
The fish tiger of that which he had seized;
The shrike chasing the bulbul, which did chase
The jewelled butterflies; till everywhere
Each slew a slayer and in turn was slain,—
Life living upon death. So the fair show
Veiled one vast, savage, grim conspiracy
Of mutual murder, from the worm to man,
Who himself kills his fellow . . .
The Prince Siddartha sighed. "Is this," he said,
"That happy earth they brought me forth to see?"

But the most interesting thing in Holmes's entire review is the manner in which he prepared his readers, hostile most probably to Buddhism, for what was to follow. One can read in the sentences a deliberate and tactful attempt to break down aversion:

If one were told that many centuries ago a celestial ray shone into the body of a sleeping woman, as it seemed to her in her dream; that thereupon the advent of a wondrous child was predicted by the soothsayers; that angels appeared at this child's birth; that merchants came from afar, bearing gifts to him; that an ancient saint recognized the babe as divine and fell at his feet and worshipped him; that in his eighth year the child confounded his teachers with the amount of his knowledge, still showing them due reverence; that he grew up full of compassionate tenderness to all that lived and suffered; that to help his fellow-creatures he sacrificed every worldly prospect and enjoyment; that he went through the ordeal of a terrible temptation, in which all the powers of evil were let loose upon him, and came out a conqueror over them all; that he preached holiness and practised charity; that he gathered disciples and sent out apostles, who spread his doctrine over many lands and peoples; that this "Helper of the Worlds" could claim a more than earthly lineage and a life that dated from long before Abraham was,—of whom would he think this wonderful tale was told? Would he not say at once that this must be another version of the story of One who came upon our earth in a Syrian village, during the reign of Augustus Caesar, and died by violence during the reign of Tiberius? What would he say if he were told that the narrative was between five and six centuries older than that of the Founder of Christianity? Such is the story of this Poem. Such is the date assigned to the personage of whom it is told. The religion he taught is reckoned by many authorities as the most widely prevalent of all beliefs.

George Ripley's review in the *New York Tribune* was interpretive rather than critical, quoting long passages from the original attempts to retell the story of the Buddha, his princely birth, the palace in which the father confined him in order to shield him from knowledge of the world's evil and pain. With the retelling of the story, Ripley paraphrased Arnold's introduction, which deals with the world-wide scope of the Buddhist faith and its influence as the spiritual stay of "not less than four hundred and seventy millions of our race." A sense of Ripley's verdict on the poem may be gathered from the following passage:

From the dim and shadowy legends of the princely founder of the great religion of the East, scanty and uncertain as they prove to be under the hand of critical research, Mr. Arnold has constructed a poem, which for affluence of imagination. splendor of diction, and virile descriptive power, will not be easily matched among the most remarkable productions in the literature of the day.

The conclusion of Ripley's review was even more laudatory. Readers of the *New York Tribune* could not have failed to be affected by such praise as, "Mr. Arnold's imaginative gifts are combined with a singularly acute historical sense, and a rare perception of the music of rhythmical harmonies and the curious significance of a felicitous phrase. . . . [The poem] is illustrated with all the charms of a fascinating narrative and the enchantments of melodious verse." Such sentences undoubtedly were instrumental in promoting the sale of the book.

But there probably were more reasons for the success of *The Light of Asia* than reviews such as those written by Sanborn, Holmes, and Ripley. In America few English authors have fared better than Edwin Arnold. William Henry Channing would have been interested in the book under all ordinary circumstances. As Arnold's father-in-law he had personal reasons for using all the influence at his command. There is scant reason for believing that his activity in behalf of the book ceased after he had secured Alcott's services in seeing the American edition through the press. Nor was his judgment at fault when he asked Alcott to negotiate with influential men for reviews. Channing knew that Alcott would do his work well, and he did. Also, the poem itself must have counted for a great deal. America was ready to receive it. The reason is best stated in a sentence from the review which W. C. Brownell wrote for *The Nation:* "It [*The Light of Asia*] not only has charm for all students and men of letters, and it is not only the gospel of 'countless millions', as Mr. Arnold says, but to certain Occidental transcendentalists has long offered a comfort and assuagement."[26]

To the end of his life Alcott continued to work as educator and promulgator of mystic lore, but gradually his labor became less personal and centered around his administrative duties as dean of the Concord Summer School of Philosophy. He was not regarded as a great writer by his contemporaries. But they knew him to be a great talker. Lowell, with marked insight, described him in the *Fable for Critics:*

> And indeed, I believe, no man ever talked better,—
> Each sentence hangs perfectly poised to a letter;
> He seems piling words, but there's royal dust hid
> In the heart of each sky-piercing pyramid.
> While he talks he is great, but goes out like a taper,
> If you shut him up closely with pen, ink, and paper;
> Yet his fingers itch for 'em from morning till night,
> And he thinks he does wrong if he don't always write;
> In this, as in all things, a lamb among men,
> He goes to sure death when he goes to his pen.

Posterity will find no reason to change this estimate. It will also add the fact that Alcott's name can never be separated from Fruitlands and the Temple School, important attempts in the social history of America to promote the good life. While it is unfair to think of these ventures as failures, Alcott nevertheless appears as something of a Don Quixote in them, an idealist in conflict with a crass world, and "lamb among men." It is pleasant to think of him as having backed a luckier horse when he took the rôle of propagandist for the new Orientalism. American interest in the Orientals, if it was to take quick hold, needed a man who would work as a house to house colporteur, with his personal enthusiasm and brilliant talk in drawing-rooms doing what the pen of Emerson and Thoreau could not do in the study and hermitage. Alcott was that man. His was a humbler, but essential and successful part.

PART FIVE

CONCLUSION

There is no remedy for musty self-conceited English life made up of fictions, hating ideas,—like Orientalism. That astonishes and disconcerts English decorum. For once there is thunder he never heard, light he never saw, and power which trifles with time and space.

—Emerson, *Journals,* VIII, 36.

CONCLUSION

I

There are several generalizations with which our study may conclude. After all the deference Emerson, Thoreau and Alcott bestowed on the Orientals, there is poetic justice in recording the manner in which some Orientals have responded. Hindus in particular have noticed and appreciated the affinity between themselves and the Transcendentalists.

Shortly after Emerson's death Protap Chunder Mozoomdar, a leader of the Brahmo Somaj,[1] contributed the essay "Emerson as Seen from India" to the memorial symposium edited by Franklin Benjamin Sanborn under the title of *The Genius and Character of Emerson*. One of the most memorable sentences in Mozoomdar's essay was this: "Brahmanism is an acquirement, a state of being rather than a creed. In whomsoever the eternal Brahma breathed his unquenchable fire, he was the Brahman. And in that sense Emerson was the best of Brahmans."[2] The latitude of this sentence does no violence to Hinduism, as the informed will realize; and its indefiniteness will suggest much of Emerson himself. He pretended to settle nothing. He was an endless seeker and experimenter who clung to no definite tradition. He seemed to unsettle everything. But one constant trait was his. It is suggested by other words from Mozoomdar's essay. "Amidst this ceaseless, sleepless din and clash of Western materialism, this heat of restless energy, the character of Emerson shines upon India serene as the evening star. He seems to some of us to have been a geographical mistake. He ought to have been born in India. Perhaps Hindoos were closer kinsmen to him than his own nation, because every typical Hindoo is a child of Nature."[3]

More temperate and scholarly, perhaps, were the words of another Hindu, Herambachandra Maitra, who also wrote on the Indian view of Emerson, but in the *Harvard Theological Review*. Coupling Emerson with Wordsworth, he concludes: "Hence the power with which Wordsworth and Emerson appeal to the Oriental mind. They translate into the language of modern culture what was uttered by the sages of ancient India in the loftiest strains. They breathe a new life into our old faith, and they assure its stability and progress by incorporating with it previous truths revealed or brought into prominence by the wider intellectual and ethical outlook of the modern spirit."[4] Though on the surface it may seem illogical for Emerson to have turned Eastward, the fact remains that he did, and Hindus like Mozoomdar and Maitra have found in him a fresh interpretation of their ancient thought. Both Emerson and the Hindus recognized the affinity.

Thoreau's case was not different from that of Emerson. He received much from the East, but he has also reciprocated. It is really no curious anomaly that Thoreau, who once admitted that his thoughts were constantly plotting against the state, should be the man from whom Mahatma Gandhi has taken much of his philosophy of civil disobedience. It was in the July 7, 1920, number of *Young India* that Mahatma Gandhi wrote an editorial from which the following sentences are taken:

Wiseacres may laugh at the folly of allowing writs of attachment and paying for the collection of fines. Multiply such instances and imagine the consequence to the authorities of executing thousands of writs. Writs are possible when they are confined to a few recalcitrants. They are troublesome when they have to be executed against many high-souled persons who have done no wrong and who refuse payment to vindicate a principle. They may not attract much notice when isolated individuals resort to this method of protest. But clean examples have a curious way of multiplying themselves. They bear publicity and the sufferers instead of incurring odium receive congratulations. Men like Thoreau brought about the abolition of slavery by their personal examples. Says Thoreau: "I know this well, that if one thousand, if one hundred, if ten men whom I could name,—if ten *honest* men only—aye, if *one* honest man, in this state of Massachusetts *ceasing to hold slaves* were actually to withdraw from this co-partnership and be locked up in the county gaol therefor, it would be the abolition of slavery in America. For it matters not how small the beginning may seem to be, what is once well done is done forever." Again, he says, "I have contemplated the imprisonment of the offender rather than the seizure of his goods— though both will serve the same purpose, because they who assert the purest right and consequently are most dangerous to a corrupt State, commonly have not spent much time in the accumulating of property."[5]

Furthermore, Occidentals will be surprised at the long period during which Thoreau has been Gandhi's counselor. Henry Salt, one of Thoreau's earliest biographers, communicated with the Mahatma for the purpose of ascertaining this very point. Here is his account and the answer:

As showing how far Thoreau has travelled since he was "the rural humbug" of Concord, these are the words of Mr. Gandhi, the Indian leader, in reply to my inquiry whether Thoreau had influenced him: "My first introduction to Thoreau's writings was, I think, in 1907, or later, when I was in the thick of the passive resistance struggle. A friend sent me the essay on Civil Disobedience. It left a deep impression upon me. I translated a portion for the readers of *Indian Opinion* in South Africa, which I was then editing, and I made copious extracts for the English part of that paper. The essay seemed to be so convincing and truthful that I felt the need of knowing more of Thoreau, and I came across your Life of him, his *Walden,* and other essays, all of which I read with great pleasure and equal profit."[6]

Thoreau has travelled far indeed. That the thoughts of a Massachusetts villager who died in 1862 should leaven labor agitations in South Africa in 1907, gather indeterminable momentum through subsequent years, and again become a potent factor in the Indian politics of more than a decade of the twentieth century, is a prophecy few of his contemporaries would have ventured to utter. That his force is not yet spent is becoming increasingly apparent to modern critics. The regard of Mahatma Gandhi for Thoreau is as flattering and sincere as any the latter ever gave the Hindus.

II

Emersonian thought was a matter of almost pure mysticism. Men may have come to it by recognition, but never by conviction. It was a religious instinct that spoke through the Concordians, and only those who had ears to hear could receive the message. In this fact is the reason for the short life of the Transcendental Movement in New England. It was not essentially a new departure in literature, such as the Romantic Movement which Wordsworth and Coleridge represented, echoes of which were to be heard even in the last decades of the nineteenth century. Nor did Transcendentalism concern itself with developing a system *ad usum populi*. It was, rather, a peculiarly blended religious and philosophical approach to life. And there were very personal entities which vanished when the men who embodied them passed from the scene, particularly since they had been men who shared the metaphysician's usual indifference to the popularization of their thought. Herein is one reason Transcendentalism is no longer with us.

It was, of course, a way of thinking which the common man had difficulty in understanding. In the metaphysical sense the contradiction of monism and dualism may be no more than that of the English and the metric systems, but it is only the metaphysician who will possess the sane balance necessary to adjust theory to life and avoid vagaries. The plain man's *Weltanschauung* is artless and non-speculative, based on common-sense. That of Emerson, Thoreau, and Alcott was the fruit of the mystical temperament and some metaphysical thinking, mixed with an unusual dash of the urbane. Somewhere Santayana points out that it is impossible to be a transcendentalist all the time. In that case there is nothing left to transcend, for all would be exterminated in the civil war, and the results would be similar to the purposeless Nirvana of the Orientals which few Westerners have been able to condone. The mystic of the West, consciously or unconsciously, finds that the art is to be mystical in spots and to aim the heavy guns of his philosophy at those realities or ideas which he finds particularly galling. What he offers, then, is primarily neither a body nor a conglomerate of truths, but a "technique whereby truth may be discovered." It is only in such a light that we can understand Emerson's catholic and seemingly paradoxical words: "I have very good grounds for being a Unitarian and a Trinitarian too. I need not nibble forever at one loaf, but eat it and thank God for it, and earn another."[7] The reason men who pride themselves on their common-sense and allegiance to hereditary dogma are sometimes unable to share sympathy for such a statement is that they do not usually understand the contemplative men, since they are devoted to the active life. Emerson himself summarized the results of the two ways of life with the usual insight. "If speculation tends thus to a terrific unity, in which all things are absorbed, action tends directly backwards to diversity."[8] There can be no doubt as to the way of life he preferred.

We must realize, then, that in the capacious natures of Emerson, Thoreau, and Alcott, there was room for the expansion and alertness of the West as well as the concentration and serenity of the East. The pervading consciousness of the Infinite was a supreme reality to them, but they also recognized the reality of the individual soul. Herein are the essential differences and similarities between their own and the Oriental mind, and, perhaps, that of many of their countrymen.

This very eclectic capacity has suggested, perhaps inevitably, to many readers the coupling of the names of the Concordians—if not in time at least in spirit—with such modern movements as Theosophy, New Thought, Christian Science, and the hordes of swami and Oriental magi

who have invaded America. The suggestion is superficial.
It is difficult to imagine how any friendship could exist
between Emerson and Thoreau and those religious vag-
rants who almost fortnightly cross the door-step of a new
cult (sometimes contemplating the navel in sumptuously
upholstered, incense-filled salons under the guidance of a
tutor who will return home a veritable Croesus), or the
attendants at lectures for the disconsolate and mentally
unemployed. An excellent study of modern Oriental cults
in the United States will be found in Wendell Thomas'
Hinduism Invades America.[9] None of the Concordians
could possibly be made to fit into the pages of this book.
If answer must be given to the question of the consequences of Concord Orientalism, it will be found in the
lectures presented by Harris and Channing before the
Concord School of Philosophy and the books of such fellow Transcendentalists and reputable students of comparative religions as James Freeman Clarke and Samuel
Johnson, who approached the faiths of mankind with the
Transcendentalist's desire to find the common denominator, but who wrote with the sane judgment of seasoned
scholars. Concord Orientalism is inseparable from its three
exponents. The vagaries of modern, Orientally inspired
prophets should not be laid to them.

For there are practical and moral aspects of the Vedanta to which Emerson and his friends never would have
subscribed. One, in particular, deserves mention. Words
from Ramakrishna (1834-1886), a Hindu saint contemporary with the Concord Transcendentalists, will be the
best illustration. Ramakrishna was a Bengali Brahman,
born of a priestly family, strongly religious in instinct,

who, after a long spiritual pilgrimage, found intellectual refuge in the philosophy of Sankara and emotional appeal in the kindliness of Christianity and the devotional spirit of Mohammedanism.[10] He was an excellent representative of the eclectic blending of the best of three religions; he also represented some of the most important forces of reform in modern Hinduism. Yet his ethical outlook, though consistent with his idealism, was of dubious value for the mass of men, for principle led him in actual practice to bow before the most degraded of moral outcasts as manifestations of God. This was the manner in which he defended his conduct: "When I look upon the chaste women of respectable families, I see in them the Mother Divine arrayed in the garb of a chaste lady; and again, when I look upon the public women of the city, sitting in their open verandas, arrayed in the garb of immorality and shamelessness, I see in them also the Mother Divine, sporting in a different way."[11]

By no flight of the imagination could one ever conceive of Emerson or his friends uttering such words. Walt Whitman might have done so, but not the Concordians—with their Puritan heritage. Yet they logically would have been obliged to give assent, if they were sincere and thoroughly consistent in the postulate of the Over-Soul with its suggestive resemblances to the impersonal Over-Soul of Hinduism. Nor would they have been deterred by the objection that such a postulate made God a participant in all the crimes and evil of a sad world. To understand this, we need only to remind ourselves that the Emersonian mind feared no philosophical anarchy, but on the other hand, its adherents never departed in the least from the most Puritan pattern of the moral life.

The mystery of the attributes of God it is not for us to solve. Our province is here not to question the wisdom and method of His governance of the Universe, or the conclusions at which the Concord men arrived. It is enough for us to realize and in finality restate the chief reason why Emerson, Thoreau, and Alcott turned Eastward, a gesture which brought all the consequences we have studied. They could not live with an absentee God, and they were of Sankara's temper, Sankara, that great sage of ancient India, who on his death-bed prayed that he might be forgiven for having frequented temples, since by doing so he had seemed to deny the omnipresence of God. All that the Concordians thought and did was consequent to this fact. We may be assured that when this is the temper of the best minds of the East and West, the twain do meet in the sympathies of the mystical bond, which is universal.

APPENDIX

BOOKS AND MARGINALIA

Dreary are the names and numbers of volumes . . . to me, who only want to know at the shortest the few steps, the two steps, or the one taken. . . . I want not the metaphysics, but only the literature of them.

—Emerson, *Journals,* X, 248.

In his spiritual astronomy or search for stars he was the observer of single stars as they came into the field of his telescope; he was not making a map of the heavens, or even of a particular region; he had nothing to do with the results of other observers.

—Cabot, *A. Memoir,* I, 288-89.

APPENDIX

BOOKS AND MARGINALIA

The following annotated bibliography is an attempt to make a chronological tabulation of the Oriental reading of Emerson, Thoreau, and Alcott, together with many of the comments and quotations which appear in their published writings. Unpublished marginalia are also included. Besides the standard works, diaries and biographies, the chief sources of information were the library records of the Boston Athenæum and of Harvard College, auction catalogues of Americana, the Emerson and Alcott libraries in Concord, where the books themselves, among them many autographed presentation copies, were examined, and the unpublished Alcott diary. The order in which books are listed was determined from chronological evidence in the journals and the Harvard and Athenæum records. Autographed books in the Emerson and Alcott libraries which were not referred to in the journals are listed under the date of publication.

Undoubtedly there are elusive items that would have escaped the best of drag-nets. A typical instance will be found in Emerson's notation in the *Journals* of 1843, VI, 374-75: "I read in Ward's Chinese book, the other day, of bards; many sentences, purporting that bards love wine. Tea and coffee are my wine, and I have finer and lighter wines than these;" the last clause undoubtedly referring to the wines of the poem "Bacchus." Whether "Ward's Chinese book" was a volume lent to Emerson by his friend Samuel Gray Ward, or one written by an extremely obscure sinologist named Ward, it has been impossible to determine. Another instance of unavailable material will be found in the *Catalog of the Stephen H. Wakeman Collection of Books of Nineteenth Century American Writers*, listing the books auctioned by the American Art Association in New York on April 24-29, 1924. An item in this catalog reads as follows:

985. Thoreau (Henry D.) Manuscript Note Book, containing Transcripts and Extracts of Poems by early English Poets, Translations or Portions of two French Works with his notes on the same. . . . Closely written, in ink, on about 225 Pages and consisting of approximately twenty eight thousand and two hundred words. . . . Translations from the French: Portion of "Confucius et Mencius . . . Traduit du Chinois. Par M. G. Pauthier." Written on 23 pages. Thoreau has translated many paragraphs, and interspersed are notes by Thoreau on the same; Portion of "Harivansa ou Histoire de la Famille de Hari . . . par M. A. Langlois." Written on 11 pages, interspersed with notes. Transcripts of Translations of Indian Works: Portion of Sacontala, or the Fatal Ring. An Indian Drama. Translated by Sir W. Jones. Written on 4 pp.; Portion of "The Sankhya Karika. . . . Translated by Horace H. Wilson." Written on 18 pages. This transcription opens with a full-page account by Thoreau, and four pages at the end of the Transcript relate to the work; Portion of "Vishnu Purana. A System of Hindu Mythology. . . . Translated by H. H. Wilson." Written on 30 pages; Portion of "Translation of Several Principal Books, Passages and Texts of the Veds. By Rajah Rammohun." Written on 11 pages.

This manuscript notebook is now in private hands and

unavailable for scholarly use. It is listed here to indicate the kinds of material which must be made accessible to scholars before any record of the books and marginalia of the Concord men can be completed. It is obvious, therefore, that although the bibliography which follows is extensive, it will be added to as new documents are discovered or made available for scholarly purposes.

Nevertheless, this bibliography, with all the handicaps of being the initial attempt of its kind, will suggestively answer some questions, the chief of which are the extent and sources of the Orientalism of the Concordians, and the nature of their reading. From the beginning there has been doubt of the accuracy of Emerson's information in particular. In an essay which appeared in the *Massachusetts Quarterly Review* for March, 1850, and which was presumably written by Theodore Parker, will be found these words:

Emerson's works do not betray an exact scholarship, which has a certain totality, as well as method about it. . . . Of late years, his work contains allusions to the ancient oriental literature, from which he has borrowed some hard names and some valuable thoughts, but is occasionally led astray by its influence, for it is plain that he does not understand that curious philosophy he quotes from. Hence his oriental allies are brought up to take a stand which no man dreamed of in their time, and made to defend ideas not known to men till long after these antediluvian sages were at rest in their graves.

On the other hand, there are the provocative sentences in the journals of the Concord men which constantly intrude. Of these, there is no better sample than that in Thoreau's *Journal*, IV, 290: "If Sadi were to come back to claim a *personal* identity with the historical Sadi, he would find there were too many of us; he could not get a skin that would contain us all. . . . By sympathy with Sadi I have embowelled him." It is in evaluation of such criticism as Theodore Parker's and such quotations as Thoreau's, that the bibliography which follows will be of use. Readers who are interested in determining the extent the Concord men "embowelled" the Orientals will find the following facts of value.

ACCOUNTS OF TRAVELERS AND GENERAL STATEMENTS OF ORIENTAL THOUGHT AND CUSTOM

1820 EDWARD GIBBON, The History of the Decline and Fall of the Roman Empire, London, 1781-82, 3 vols.
This was the principal edition listed in the *Catalogue of the Library of Harvard University*, Cambridge, Metcalf, 1830. Emerson's *Journals*, I, 84, lists Gibbon among the books quoted from or referred to in 1820. The reason for the presence of Gibbon's volume in this bibliography is the exposition of Zoroastrian religion and scripture which it contains.

1830 JOSEPH MARIE DECÉRANDO, Histoire compareé des systèmes de philosophie, Paris, Alexis Eymery, 1804, 4 vols., 2097 pp.
Emerson drew volumes I and II from the Boston Athenæum on January 1, 1830. On February 1, of the same year, he drew volume IV. The record shows that Emerson again drew Degérando's work on April 6, 1831, but there is no special designation of the volume. This was one of the earliest sources of Emerson's knowledge of Oriental thought; at this time he was only twenty-seven years of age. It is singular that out of the wide range of Degérando's work he should have been most interested in the discussion of Indian, Chinese and Persian literature. The *Journals*, II, 333, contains a most illuminating passage which is a digest of what Degérando had written of Oriental cosmogenies, theogenies and idealism, together with the works of various translators whom Emerson later read.

1840 JACOB BRYANT, A New System, or, An Analysis of Ancient Mythology: Wherein an Attempt is Made to Divest Tradition of Fable; and to Reduce the Truth to its Original Purity, London, Payne, 1774, 2 vols., 1079 pp.

Drawn by Emerson from the Boston Athenæum on November 18, 1840. This book is an ambitious attempt to present a history of the Babylonians, Chaldeans, Egyptians, Canaanites, and similar nations. Many of the chapters are an attempt to examine etymologically the sources of the names of deities, and to compare conceptions regarding them. Legendary heroes and cities are treated in same manner. It is a very learned book. Its appeal for Emerson probably is in the fact that it deals broadly with the relations of all the ancients and quotes Strabo on India and Porphyry on Zoroaster.

1851 HEINRICH RITTER, The History of Ancient Philosophy, Oxford, D. A. Talboys, 1838, 4 vols., 2464 pp.

This book is mentioned in Alcott's diary under date of February 13, 1851. The following are the titles of some of the chapters: "Philosophy of the East in General, and of Some Oriental Nations in Particular"; "Indian Philosophy, the Pre-Historical"; "Oriental Philosophy and Its Influence on Grecian Philosophy." The book contains excellent expositions of Hindu philosophies such as the Sankhya, Yoga, and Nyaya, also discussion of the spread of Oriental ideas into Greek thought, primarily through the Neo-Pythagoreans. A monumental work, typical of the best German scholarship.

1851 THOMAS STANLEY, The History of Philosophy: Containing the Lives, Opinions, Actions and Discourses of the Philosophers of Every Sect, London, W. Battersby, 1701, 722 pp.

This book also was mentioned in Alcott's diary under date of February 13, 1851. It professes to give the lives and opinions of nearly two score Greek philosophers, concluding with a section entitled "The History of the Chaldaick Philosophy," which is an exposition of the writings of the Greeks who came in contact with Zoroastrian thought during the period of the Persian Wars.

1852 IDA PFEIFFER, A Lady's Voyage Round the World: a Selected Translation from the German by Mrs. Percy Sinnett, New York, Harper, 1852, 302 pp.

Thoreau's manuscript fact-book, which is in the Harvard College Library, indicates that he read this work. Among the quotations which he culled from it was the following, to which he gave the title "A Chinese Lady's Foot": "The fore part of the foot was so tightly bound with strong, broad ligatures that all the growth is forced into height instead of length and breadth, and formed a thick lump at the ankle; the under part measured scarcely four inches long and an inch and a half wide." (p. 63). Over twelve chapters are devoted to a discussion of the life and customs of China, India and Persia. See also *Writings*, II, 25.

1855 LYDIA MARIA CHILD, The Progress of Religious Ideas through Successive Ages, New York, C. S. Francis, 1855, 3 vols., 1376 pp.

On November 11, 1855, Emerson wrote from Concord to Lydia Maria Child, after receiving her book: "It is a very slow acknowledgment of your gift to say that it has only come to me on Friday night, and I have only taken a survey and a few soundings here and there. But, as neither now, nor tomorrow, nor for three days, to come, during which I am to be a traveller, can I take any right possession of it, I will not wait longer to say that the Books are here, with all their wealth that their 'Contents' and my dippings into the Indian portion assure me, and that I am deeply beholden to you for a present which, I see plainly, was not made in a month or a year, but which cost many summers to ripen." (Stanley T. Williams, "Unpublished Letters of Emerson," *Journal of English and Germanic Philology*, XXVI, 482-483). Emerson's reference to the "Indian portion" probably meant the chapters of Volume I entitled "Hindostan," "China," "Thibet and Tartary," "Chaldea," and "Persia." Mrs. Child stated in the preface that the purpose of the book was to show that "theology is not religion" and to "give a concise and comprehensive account of religions, in the liberal spirit." Her work was a good beginning in the New England of "baptized hatreds." It is not authoritative but probably served its purpose well. The bibliography lists many of the Oriental volumes Emerson read. It is not beyond possibility that he suggested some of the titles.

1858 THOMAS WITLAM ATKINSON, Oriental and Western Siberia: a Narrative of Seven Years' Explorations and Adventures in Siberia, Mongolia, the Kirghis Steppes, Chinese Tartary, and Part of Central Asia, London, Hurst and Blackett, 1858, 611 pp.

The author states in his preface: "When the journey narrated in the following pages was undertaken, it was not with the intention of publishing either a book of Travels, or any other work. My sole object was, to sketch the scenery of Siberia—scarcely at all known to Europeans." The book is profusely illustrated with these sketches. Thoreau wrote in his *Journal*, VII, 480, on October 3, 1855: "Atkinson, in his Siberian and steppe travels, speaks of the

'Salsola plant' turned a bright crimson. On the Kirghis Steppes, he says, 'in the distance I could see salt lakes: I knew them to be salt by the crimson margins which encircled them.'" I am as yet unable to explain the discrepancy in dates. Atkinson's book appeared after Thoreau's *Journal* entry. Thoreau might have seen newspaper accounts.

1858 S. F. DUNLAP, Vestiges of the Spirit-History of Man, New York, Appleton, 1858, 407 pp.

A volume in the Emerson library, with the following inscription: "Mr. Ralph Waldo Emerson with the author's respect." This was one of the few books written by members of the American Oriental Society which came to be read in Concord. It was an early attempt at a comparative study of religions. The chapter entitled "Brahmanism and Buddhism" was probably the most important for Emerson. There was also an excellent introduction to the bibliography of Oriental translations then extant.

1861 MAX MÜLLER, "Comparative Mythology," Oxford Essays, Contributed by Members of the University, 1856, London, J. W. Parker, 1856, pp. 1-87.

Recorded in Emerson, *Journals*, IX, 350, as read in the year 1861. This essay is more upon the subject of comparative philology than mythology, a fact which probably explains why Emerson's editors listed an essay on the "Science of Language" in conjunction with it. The latter title is not a part of Max Müller's contribution to the symposium. There are numerous excerpts from Greek and Sanskrit literature, which make the essay readable for the layman; but it is primarily a study in linguistics.

1863 LUCY ATKINSON, Recollections of Tartar Steppes and Their Inhabitants, London, John Murray, 1863, 351 pp.

Drawn by Emerson from the Boston Athenæum on August 24, 1863. A volume by the wife of Thomas Witlam Atkinson, whom Thoreau read. It is primarily a book of reminiscences of travel in Siberia, containing general observations on native life and customs.

1867 JULES MICHELET, Bible de l'humanité, Paris, Chamerot, 1864, 503 pp.

A volume listed in Emerson, *Journals*, X, 224, as referred to in 1867. It probably was not of great influence since it is only a popularized discussion of a few Oriental books and ideas. It commences with an account of the Ramayana. The Hindu, Persian and Arabian scriptures are also compared. When Emerson was abroad in 1848, he heard Michelet lecture. He wrote in his *Journals*, VII, 464: "I went to hear Michelet lecture on philosophy, but the sublime creed of the Indian Buddhists was not meant for a Frenchman to analyze and crack his joke and make his grimace upon." Professor R. L. Rusk's forthcoming Emerson letters will indicate that Emerson knew of Michelet as early as 1842. F. H. Hedge and Emerson corresponded about the work of Michelet and certain extracts which Hedge had sent his friend.

1868 HARRIET MARTINEAU, Eastern Life, Present and Past, London, Edward Moxon, 1848, 3 vols., 1011 pp.

A volume listed in Emerson, *Journals*, X, 271, as referred to in 1868, although it is quite probable Emerson knew of this book long before. It deals primarily with travel in Egypt and the Near East. Professor Rusk informs me that in 1848 when Emerson visited Harriet Martineau, he found her "loaded to the lips with her Eastern travel," for which she was then seeking a publisher.

1869 MAX MÜLLER, Chips from a German Workshop, New York, Scribner, 1869, 2 vols., 809 pp.

Drawn by Emerson from the Boston Athenæum on April 4, 1869. This volume is primarily a collection of essays on the science of religion and comparative mythology. It also contains critical reviews of the translations of eminent Orientalists. The following are the titles of some of the essays: "The Veda and Zend-Avesta," "Genesis and the Zend-Avesta," "The Meaning of Nirvana," "The Works of Confucius" and "Semitic Monotheism."

1870 —— An Introduction to the Science of Religion, Four Lectures at the Royal Institution, London, 1870. Sixteen copies privately printed, 61 pp.

A small volume in the Emerson library with the following inscription: "Ralph Waldo Emerson from an old admirer, M. M." This was a privately printed edition which the author sent to personal friends. The enlarged edition appeared in 1873.

1873 —— Introduction to the Science of Religion, Four Lectures Delivered at the Royal Institution, with Two Essays on False Analogies, and the Philosophy of Mythology, London, Longmans Green, 1873, 412 pp.

A volume in the Emerson library, particularly noteworthy because of its dedication, which reads: "Dedicated to Ralph Waldo Emerson in Memory of his Visit to Oxford, in May, MDCCCLXXIII, and in Acknowledgement of Constant Refreshment of Head and

Heart Derived from His Writings During the Last Twenty-five Years." In recognition of this dedication, Emerson wrote in his *Journals*, X, 420: "Professor Max Müller has dedicated his new book to me, and sent me a copy. I have read it, and though I am too dull a scholar to judge of the correctness of his courageous deductions from resembling names, or to relish this as I did his earlier books, I respect and thank his erudition and its results."

1879 NEWMAN SMYTH, Old Faiths in New Light, New York, Charles Scribner, 1879, 391 pp.

A volume in the Alcott House in Concord, which attempts to evaluate religion in the light of the discoveries of modern science.

1880 EDWARD KING, Echoes from the Orient, London, C. Kegan Paul, 1880, 131 pp.

A volume in the Emerson library. It is not a book of translations. The author states that most of his poems were "prompted by a journey in Turkey . . . that strange border land of the East,—a land literally filled with "Echoes of the Orient." A popular Roumanian legend furnished the foundation for "The Sorrow of Manol."

TRANSLATIONS OF THE SACRED AND SECULAR LITERATURES AND EXPOSITIONS OF THE RELIGIONS OF INDIA

1820 RAMMOHUN ROY, Translation of the Ishopanishad, One of the Chapters of the Yajur Veda: According to the Commentary of the Celebrated Shankar-Acharya; Establishing the Unity and Incomprehensibility of the Supreme Being, Calcutta, Hindoostanee Press, 1816, 36 pp.

This volume was very likely recommended to Emerson by his aunt, Mary Moody Emerson. As the title indicates, it is a portion of the *Yajurveda* itself and Sankara's commentary, a valuable introduction to Hindu metaphysics. The preface and introduction by Rammohun Roy are excellent preparation of the layman for reading the Hindu scriptures. There is no reference to this work in Emerson's *Journals*, but Roy was known to Americans in 1820.

1821 JOHN SHORE TEIGNMOUTH, Memoirs of the Life, Writings, and Correspondence of Sir William Jones, London, John Hatchard, 1806, 531 pp.

Emerson read this work in 1821 according to his *Journals*, I, 82. It is the earliest record found of his reading directly the work of famous Orientalists. The latter part of this book deals with Jones's life in India and presents samples of his own poems. Sir William Jones was one of the most influential Orientalists read in Concord.

1823 "Religion and Character of the Hindoos," *Edinburgh Review*, Vol. XXIX, pp. 377-403 (1818).

Emerson's *Journals*, I, 303-4, indicates that this anonymous-article was read and commented upon in 1823. It was a review of several books on India, particularly William Ward's *Account of the Writings, Religion and Manners of the Hindoos*, which Emerson later drew from the Harvard College Library. See page 70 for a statement of Emerson's use of this article.

1830 ANQUETIL DUPERRON, Oupnek'hat (id est, Secretum Tegendum): Opus Ipsa in India Rarissimum, Continens Antiquam et Arcanam, Seu Theologicam et Philosophicam, Doctrinam, é Quatuor Sacris Indorum Libris, Rak Beid, Djedjr Beid, Sam Beid, Athrban Beid, Excerptam, Paris, Levrault, 1801, 2 vols., 1652 pp.

This work is cited in Emerson, *Journals*, II, 334. The word "Oupnek'hat" is a perversion of the word "Upanishad." The other titles listed as "Rak Beid, Djedjr Beid, Sam Beid, Athrban Beid," will be recognized as the Rig, Yajur, Sama, and Atharva *Vedas* respectively. This book is of especial interest and importance because it also contained translations of the *Brihadaranyaka* and *Chandogya Upanishads*.

1836 WILLIAM JONES, Institutes of Hindu Law; or The Ordinances of Menu, according to the Gloss of Culluca, comprising the Indian System of Duties Religious and Civil, London, Rivingtons and Cochran, 1825, 475 pp.

A volume in the Emerson library. The *Journals*, IV, 173, indicate the book was read as early as 1836. It is not to be confused with books on technical law. In many ways a close comparison may be drawn between this and such books as *Genesis* and *Leviticus*. The first chapter, entitled "On the Creation," is a statement of the Vedantic concept of creation of the phenomenal world by emanation from the Brahma. The chapters which deal with the conduct of life emphasize the sacerdotal and the dominant motives behind Hindu religious ethics. The last chapter is entitled "On Transmigration and Final Beatitude." The chief importance of this volume lies in the fact that it is not the exposition of any one school of philosophy, nor concerned with the technicalities of a system. Thoreau's sentences: "Everywhere the speech of Menu demands the widest apprehension and proceeds from the loftiest plateau of the soul. It is spoken unbendingly to its own level, and does not imply any contemporaneous speaker" (*Journal*, I, 268), may suggest something of its effect and tone. This volume must be mentioned in conjunction with Röer's translations in the *Bibliotheca Indica* as among the most important books read in Concord. See pages 164-69 and 214-17.

1837 HORACE HAYMAN WILSON, The Megha Duta or Cloud Messenger: A Poem in the Sanscrit Language, by Kalidasa, London, Richard Watts, 1814, 151 pp.

A volume in the Emerson library. It represents the first attempt made by Wilson to interest European readers in his Sanskrit studies. The story is that of an exiled prince who bids a cloud carry a message of affection to his wife. Much of the poem is devoted to a description of the beauties of the country over which the cloud passes and allusions to the important scenes of Hindu theology and tradition. Emerson first read Wilson's translation at the Boston Athenæum in the *Asiatic Journal* of 1837. See his *Journals*, IV, 317, for the quotation of the lines commencing,

> There in the fane a beauteous creature stands,
> The first best work of the Creator's hands,

which were later used in *Parnassus*.

1840 SIR WILLIAM JONES, Works, London, G. G. and J. Robinson, 1799, 6 vols. Two supplementary volumes appeared in 1801.

This six-volume collection was drawn by Emerson from the Boston Athenæum on July 23, 1840. Thoreau drew it from the Harvard College Library on January 28, 1850. These volumes, each averaging 600 pages, contain Sir William Jones's translations from Oriental literature, his poems on Oriental themes, and his historical and expository essays. They must be numbered among the most influential Oriental books read in Concord. With this reading of Jones's *Works*, interest in Hindu literature increased.

1841 ALEXANDER CHALMERS, The Works of the English Poets, from Chaucer to Cowper, London, 1810, 21 vols.

Thoreau drew the series from the Harvard College Library on November 28, 1841. Volume XVIII contains a brief biographical sketch of Sir William Jones by Alexander Chalmers, the editor of the series. There are also copious selections from Jones's poems, but these are chiefly those which were written in the Oriental manner or addressed to Oriental deities, not his translations. A very valuable essay "On the Poetry of the Eastern Nations" was also included. This volume was probably the source of the lines from "Narayena" which concluded Emerson's youthful account of God. See page 69. Under the date on which Thoreau drew this series from the Harvard library, his *Journal*, I, 288, records: "The twenty-first volume of Chalmers's English Poets contains Hoole's and Mickle's Translations. In the shape of a note to the Seventh Book of the Lusiad, Mickle has written a long 'Inquiry into the Religious Tenets and Philosophy of the Bramins.'" It should be noted that the complete title of William Julius Mickle's translation was: *The Lusiad: or the Discovery of India: an Epic Poem Translated from the Original Portuguese of Luis de Camoens.* This volume of Chalmers' series also contained two essays entitled "The History of the Discovery of India" and "The History of the Rise and Fall of the Portuguese Empire in the East."

1842 CHARLES WILKINS, The Heetopades of Veeshnoo-Sarma, in a Series of Connected Fables, Interspersed with Moral, Prudential, and Political Maxims, Bath, R. Cruttwell, 1787, 334 pp.

This volume is the chief source of the fables of Bidpay, which Sir William Jones called "the most beautiful, if not the most ancient collection of Apologues in the world." Emerson chose selections from this translation to launch the publication of the ethnical sayings in the *Dial*, III, 82 ff. (July, 1842). The following are examples of the passages used: "He, whose inclination turneth away from an object, may be said to have obtained it." "As frogs to the pool, as birds to a lake full of water, so doth every species of wealth flow to the hands of him who exerteth himself." Thoreau wrote in his *Journal*, I, 345, on March 24, 1842: "It is always singular to meet common sense in very old books, as the Veeshnoo Sarma,—as if they could have dispensed with the experience of later times."

1844 EUGÈNE BURNOUF, Introduction à l'histoire du Buddhisme indien, Paris, Imprimerie Royale, 1844, 647 pp.

A fine work of translation and scholarly exposition. Thoreau edited (probably translating himself) portions for the *Dial*, IV, 391-401 (January, 1844), under the title of "The Preaching of Buddha." Nearly two pages of Thoreau's contribution were devoted to commentary and quotation from Burnouf's exposition of Buddhism. Such sentences as the following indicate how the American Transcendentalists probably came to think of Buddhism and Brahmanism as similar: "The philosophic opinion, by which he [Buddha] justified his mission, was shared by all classes, Brahmins, warriors, farmers, merchants, all believed equally in the fatality of transmigration, in the retribution of rewards and pains, in the necessity of escaping in a decisive manner the perpetually changing condition of a merely relative existence. He believed in the truths admitted by the Brahmins."

1845 CHARLES WILKINS, The Bhagvat-Geeta, or Dialogues of Kreeshna and Arjoon, London, Nourse, 1785, 156 pp.

This edition of the *Bhagavadgita* contains very little expository material. D. L. Maulsby in *The Contribution of Emerson to Literature*, 1911, pp. 122-23, presents the following quotation from a letter written by Emerson to Elizabeth Hoar: "The only other event is the arrival in Concord of the *Bhagavad Gita*, the much renowned book of Buddhism [an instance of Emerson's errors in fact], extracts from which I have often admired, but never before held the book in my hands." Professor Rusk's forthcoming edition of Emerson's correspondence will include this letter, which I am informed was written June 17, 1845. On October 19, 1856, Emerson wrote to William Rounseville Alger, the editor of *The Poetry of the East:* "When it was proposed to me once to reprint 'the Bhagvat' in Boston, I shrank back and asked time, thinking it not only some desecration to publish our prayers in the 'Daily Herald', but also that those students who were ripe for it would rather take a little pains, and search for it, than find it on the pavement. It would however be as neglected a book, if Harpers published it, as it is now in the libraries." (Stanley T. Williams, "Unpublished Letters of Emerson," *Journal of English and Germanic Philology*, XXVI, 483-84). Also see Thoreau, *Journal*, IV, 152-53, for a statement on the *Gita*. Professor Rusk also informs me that he is in possession of an Emerson letter of 1873 which indicates that Emerson first got his taste of the *Gita* from a sketch by Cousin.

1845 HORACE HAYMAN WILSON, The Vishnu Purana, A System of Hindu Mythology and Tradition, London, John Murray, 1840, 704 pp.

Emerson's *Journals*, VII, 108, indicates that he read this book in 1845. Thoreau drew it from the Harvard College Library on January 28, 1850, and October 9, 1854. It is a scholarly, carefully annotated and indexed volume. The introduction contributed by Wilson reviewed the activities of Oriental translators and fully discussed the principal features of Hindu thought. See Emerson, *Journals*, VII, 108, for an unusual paraphrase of the Hindu allegory of creation, which he entitled "Vishnu Purana."

1845 HENRY THOMAS COLEBROOKE, Miscellaneous Essays, London, W. H. Allen, 1837, 2 vols., 1005 pp.

Colebrooke's essays, which are in the Emerson library, are expositions of various Hindu schools of philosophy, such as the Yoga, Sankhya, Nyaya and Vaiseshika systems, translations from many of the most important *Upanishads*, accounts of Hindu sects and their practices, and the prefaces to four of Colebrooke's earlier works. In 1845 Emerson quoted from Colebrooke in his *Journals*, VII, 110, as follows: "*Vedanta. The Internal Check.* 'He who eternally restrains this and the other world, and all beings therein; who, standing in the earth, is other than the earth; whom the earth knows not, whose body the earth is, who interiorly restrains the earth, *the same is thy soul,* and the Internal Check immortal." "The internal check is the Supreme Being." The italics are added.

1846 JOHN CALLAWAY, Yakkun Nattannawa: A Cingalese Poem, Descriptive of Demonology . . . and Kolan Nattannawa: A Cingalese Poem, Descriptive of the Characters Assumed by the Natives of Ceylon in a Masquerade, London, Oriental Translation Fund, 1829, 518 pp.

The Harvard College Library records indicate that Emerson drew a volume listed as *Cingalese Poems* on November 18, 1846. This volume, probably here identified, was published under the auspices of the Oriental Translation Fund. Since much of Emerson's Oriental reading was in the books of this series, this translation by Callaway was very probably the volume he read. The title fully suggests the content, which deals with the folk ways of Ceylon more than Buddhistic thought.

1846 EDWARD UPHAM, The History and Doctrine of Buddhism Popularly Illustrated, London, R. Ackerman, 1829, 136 pp.

Drawn by Emerson from the Harvard College Library November 18, 1846. The volume contains numerous illustrations of Buddhist art found in Ceylon, and the fables these illustrations depict. The author deals far more extensively with Buddhist folk-lore than religion.

1847 WILLIAM WARD, A View of the History, Literature, and Mythology of the Hindoos: Including a Minute Description of Their Manners and Customs, and Translations from Their Principal

Works, Serampore, Mission Press, 1818, 2 vols., 1124 pp. Drawn by Emerson from the Harvard College Library on March 30, 1847. The title of this 1124 page work is a good indication of its content, which is exhaustive and scholarly. It was one of the earliest attempts to present a general survey of Hindu civilization. The translations from Hindu literature were excerpts chosen as illustrative samples. For this reason they are not as full as in other books which Emerson read, but the range is wider. Vedic, epic and upanishadic passages are included. There are chapters on the characteristic doctrines of Hinduism and the various sects.

1849 J. H. GARCIN DE TASSY, Histoire de la littérature hindoui et hindoustani, Paris, Oriental Translation Committee, 1839, 2 vols. 1258 pp.
Drawn by Thoreau from the Harvard College Library, September 11, 1849. Volume I has the sub-title "Biographic et Bibliographic"; Volume II, "Extraits et Analyses." A very important work. Volume I would have served as an invaluable guide to Oriental literature. Volume II is an anthology of choice selections from both the epic and philosophic literature of the East.

1849 ALEXANDRE LANGLOIS, Harivansa; ou, Histoire de la famille de Hari, ouvrage formant un appendice du Mahabharata, London, Oriental Translation Fund, 1834, 2 vols., 1147 pp.
Drawn by Thoreau from the Harvard College Library on November 5, 1849. These volumes were the source of his translation *The Transmigration of the Seven Brahmans*, published in 1931. Other quotations from this work will be found in his *Journal*, II, 190-91.

1850 RAMMOHUN ROY, Translation of Several Principal Books, Passages, and Texts of the Veds, and of Some Controversial Works on Brahminical Theology, London, Parbury, Allen, 1832, 282 pp.
Drawn by Thoreau from the Harvard College Library, April 25, 1850. Probably one of the most important Oriental books read in Concord because of the translations contained therein and the expository essays written by Rammohun Roy. The *Translation of the Ishophanishad* published in Calcutta, 1816, and previously listed as a work probably known by Mary Moody Emerson, is included. I quote from the table of contents the additional translations, in order to show the scope of the volume. The archaic form of spelling may indicate the source of some of the spellings by the Concord men. "Translation of an Abridgment of the Vedant, or

Resolution of all the Veds; the most celebrated and revered Work of Brahminical Theology; establishing the Unity of the Supreme Being, and that He alone is the object of Propitiation and Worship"; "Translation of the Uthurvu-Ved"; "Translation of the Cena Upanished, one of the Chapters of the Sama-Veda"; A Translation of the Kut'h-Oopunishud of the Ujoor-Ved"; A Translation into English of a Sungskrit Tract, inculcating the Divine Worship; esteemed by those who believe in the Revelation of the Veds, as most appropriate to the Nature of the Supreme Being." The title of some the expository essays by Rammohun Roy are: "A Defence of Hindoo Theism, in reply to the Attack of an Advocate of Idolatry, at Madras"; "A Second Defence of the Monotheistical System of the Veds; in reply to an Apology for the present State of Hindoo Worship."

1850 JOHN STEVENSON, Translation of the Sanhita of the Sama Veda, London, Oriental Translation Fund, 1842, 283 pp.
Drawn by Thoreau from the Harvard College Library on April 25, 1850. This volume was published for the Oriental Translation Fund. The *Samaveda* consists of a series of verses to be sung at sacrifices. See pages 13-18 for a fuller discussion.

1851 HENRY THOMAS COLEBROOKE, The Sankhya Karika, or Memorial Verses on the Sankhya Philosophy by Iswara Krishna . . . also The Bhashya or Commentary of Gaurapada, translated and illustrated by an original comment by Horace Hayman Wilson, Oxford, Oriental Translation Fund, 1837, 145 pp.
This book presents the scope and leading tenets of the Sankhya philosophy in Karikas, memorial verses or apothegmatical statements, which assert principles rather than discuss arguments. It opens with an examination of the object of philosophy, namely, ascertainment of the means by which the pain of corporeal existence may be finally and absolutely remedied and the soul freed from the body. This is declared alone to be philosophy or the knowledge of the real nature of all that is. The following is a sample (p. 178) of the dogmas asserted: "So, through study of principles, the conclusive, incontrovertible, one only knowledge is attained, that neither I am, nor is aught mine, nor do I exist." Comments to be found in Thoreau's *Journal*, II, 192, indicate that he was reading this book in May, 1851. The Harvard Library charge books listed this volume for Thoreau, January 28, 1851.

1852 W. H. SLEEMAN, Rambles and Recollections of an Indian Official, London, J. Hachard, 1844, 2 vols., 937 pp.

Thoreau's *Journal*, IV, 209, indicates that he read Sleeman on July 9, 1852. He writes: "Sleeman says that no boy in India ever robs a bird's nest. Are they heathenish in that?"

1853 THOMAS ERSKINE PERRY, Cases Illustrative of Oriental Life, and the Application of English Law to India, London, S. Sweet, 1853, 602 pp.

Primarily a volume on legal matters, but also of interest as an exposition of certain phases of Oriental life. Emerson, *Works*, XII, 183-84: "Such is the assimilating force of the Indian climate that Sir Erskine Perry says 'the usage and opinion of the Hindoos so invades men of all castes and colors who deal with them that all take a Hindoo tint. Parsee, Mongol, Afghan, Israelite, Christian, have all passed under this influence and exchanged a good part of their patrimony of ideas for the notions, manner of seeing and habitual tone of Indian society.' He compares it to the geologic phenomenon which the black soil of the Dhakkan offers,—the property, namely of assimilating to itself every foreign substance introduced into its bosom." The date of Emerson's first reading of this work is indefinite.

1854 GEORGE TURNOUR, The Mahawanso in Roman Characters, with the Translation Subjoined; and an Introductory Essay on Pali Buddhistical Literature, Ceylon, Cotta Church Mission Press, 1837, 262 pp.

Drawn by Emerson from the Boston Athenæum on December 1, 1854. Except for the introduction on Pali Buddhistical literature, it is doubtful if this volume was of much use to Emerson. It may best be described as a history of Ceylon in terms of Buddhist birth-stories.

1855 J. R. BALLANTYNE, A Lecture on the Vedanta, Embracing the Text of the Vedanta-Sara, Allahabad, Presbyterian Mission Press, 1851, 84 pp.

A pamphlet in the Emerson Library. It came to him through the Cholmondeley collection.

1855 VISWANATHA PANCHANAN BHATTA, The Bhasha Parichchheda ... Exposition of the Nyaya Philosophy ... with an English Version, Calcutta, Encyclopaedia Press, 1851, 37 pp.

A volume from the Cholmondeley collection which Thoreau bequeathed to Emerson.

1855 EUGÈNE BURNOUF, Le Bhagavata Purana, ou Histoire poétique de Krichna, Paris, Imprimerie Royale, 1840, 599 pp.

A translation in the Cholmondeley collection which Thoreau bequeathed to Emerson. See Emerson, *Journals*, X, 157 and 159 for quotations transcribed in 1866. These passages are unusually full and deal with the Maya. They should be consulted in connection with Emerson's doctrine of Illusions.

1855—— Le Lotus de la bonne loi . . . accompagné d'un commentaire et de vingt et un mémoires relatifs au Buddhisme, Paris, Imprimerie Nationale, 1852, 897 pp.

A volume in the Cholmondeley collection. It forms the sequel to Burnouf's *Introduction à l'histoire du Buddhisme indien,* from which Thoreau edited portions for the *Dial.*

1855 HENRY THOMAS COLEBROOKE, Two Treatises on the Hindu Law of Inheritance, Calcutta, Hindoostanee Press, 1810, 377 pp.

A volume in the Cholmondeley collection dealing with the Hindu laws of succession. There was little of religious or philosophical significance in the book.

1855 SPENCE HARDY, Eastern Monachism: an Account of the Origin, Laws, Discipline, Sacred Writings, Mysterious Rites, Religious Ceremonies, and Present Circumstances, of the Order of Mendicants Founded by Gotama Budha, London, Partridge and Oakey, 1850, 431 pp.

This was one of the volumes which came to Thoreau through the Cholmondeley collection, and at his death passed into Alcott's hands. It is now in the present Alcott library in Concord. The book is predominantly a life of the Buddha and a discussion of the current practices of the ascetic system he founded, rather than an exposition of Buddhist thought. Considerable space is given to a comparison of Buddhist and Western mediaeval monasticism.

A number of very interesting passages have been marked with two kinds of pencils, a red and a black lead pencil of the common variety. It is obviously impossible to determine the identity of the reader who used each pencil, but the passages themselves will suggest an answer that is not altogether untenable. The following was one of the passages marked in red: "The priest is not to eat as a pastime, nor for pleasure; nor to make the body strong, like the public wrestlers; nor to render it beautiful, like the dancers. As a man with a falling house props it up, as a man with a broken waggon puts in a piece of wood; so may the priest eat to preserve his body and prevent untimely death. As hunger is the most powerful of all the appetites, he may eat to ward it off. As a man and woman, when crossing a vast desert with a child, if their food fails them, eat the flesh of their own child in their anxiety to escape from the desert, with similar disgust the priest eats his food, that he may escape from the evils of existence." (Page 96.)

Whoever was sufficiently interested in the above passage to mark it with the red pencil did likewise to the following: "When the food is digested, it does not become gold or gems, but is changed into excrement and urine." (Page 97.) But this was only one of the ten repugnant descriptions of food after it had been eaten, descriptions which could hardly be surpassed if chosen to suppress desire for the Buddhist or turn the stomach of the most redoubtable gourmet. We read that as a shower in the hot season falls upon a village inhabited by low people, and running into the cess on low ground, which abounds with all kinds of filth, forms a decayed compost with a hot sun beating down, of froth and bubbles, so food taken into the body in a little time, mixed with all kinds of impure secretions, becomes similar to the surface of the village cess pool. It is not only the Buddhist monk who would eschew food after reading the eight other descriptions.

Possibly it was Alcott who marked these passages dealing with the subject of diet. No proof can be given to support this surmise except to point out the fact that a red pencil was frequently used in Alcott's manuscript journals during the year the book came into his hands. Another suggestive fact is that Alcott was an ardent vegetarian. Perhaps the Fruitlands ideals were in the mind of the person who used the red pencil in the margin of these sentences: "These are the ten modes by which the defilement arising from food is exhibited; and they are steadily to be meditated on by the priest; that the desire of food may be taken away. By this means, though nirwana should not be obtained, it will secure an inheritance in one of the celestial worlds." (Page 97.) Page 105 was also marked in entirety with a red pencil. It contained commentary on the ascetic diet of monks, both of the Buddhists and mediaeval Christian monasteries. Every passage that was marked with the red pencil in *Eastern Monachism* dealt with the subject of food.

The passages marked with the common lead pencil were characteristically different. They dealt with the values of the ascetic life, but not the asceticism that is concerned with the diet alone. The first marked passage one meets as he turns the pages of the book is this: "Whosoever shall affirm that the conjugal state is to be preferred to a life of virginity or celibacy, and that it is not better and more conducive to happiness to remain in virginity or celibacy, than to be married, let him be accursed." (Page 49). This sounds like good Thoreau. It is not far-fetched to see in the next passage something of the reasoning process which kept the Walden hut so denuded of all unnecessary furnishing: "Francis of Sales did not allow the nuns belonging to the order of the Visitation to have the propriety or even the long use of anything whatever, even their chambers, beds, crosses, beads, and books, were to be changed every year." (Page 64.) Perhaps this is a replica of Mohammed's reputed saying that poverty was his glory. The following was another which received particular attention and a marginal line: "There is in all men a yearning after something that is beyond the limits of the visible world; and although this feeling may too generally be overpowered by the pressure of toil and the strife of passion, there are times when the solemn thought will present itself that a higher destiny is intended for man than that which he now inherits. By some minds, a divinity is communicated to the simplest objects of creation; and a pebble, a flower, a cloud, or a rill, becomes an instrument of music from which are sent forth strains of sweet harmony or lofty measure: this type of mind forms the poet. In other minds there is dissatisfaction with the common affairs of life, a moodiness which scowls at all that is connected with refinement and luxury, and would turn away from the sight of the brightest gem that ever adorned a coronet to contemplate the lack-lustre sockets of a skull: this type forms the recluse. By other minds the attention is directed to voices unheard by the busy multitude; they realize the objective presence of some superior intelligence, to whose influence they implicitly resign themselves, or they lose their own consciousness in the mute contemplation of its more glorious attributes: this type forms the mystic. And there are other minds that seek only to dive into the mysteries of the future, or to gain possession of miraculous energies, either by an increase of their own inherent powers or by allying themselves with the spirits of other spheres: this type forms the soothsayer and the magician. All these types of mind are united in the recluse of India." (Page 356.) The next page was also completely marked. If the surmise that it was Thoreau who checked this paragraph is correct, it is additional proof that there was something Oriental in his own ascetic interests.

The author of *Eastern Monachism* in one instance differentiated between the Sadducee and the Essene. Thoreau seems to have been particularly interested in the description of the Essenes, for he marked it: "The first order of recluses, for the knowledge of whose practices we have to go exclusively to the records of extra-Indian literature, is that of the Essenes. The Pharisees were more nearly allied to the Brahmans of India, whilst the Sadducees partook of the scepticism of the Budhists, and the Essenes of their asceticism. The Essenes gave themselves up to a contemplative mode of life, avoided the ordinary pleasures of existence, and repudiated marriage; they despised riches, and had one common fund; commerce was avoided." (Page 354.) The passages which have been cited are sufficiently similar in temper to Thoreau's interests in general to be presumptive proof that it was he who marked them. Space prohibits the quoting of all the marginally scored passages. These are the pages on which the quotations will be found; in general the complete page was marked, sometimes with two or three lines: 90, 191, 194, 195, 196, 334, 338, 347, 352, 356, 357, and 390. I am inclined to credit all these to Thoreau; also a passage on page 353 which deserves particular mention. It discloses, with quotation from Grote's *History of Greece*, that the century between 650 and 500 B.C., was remarkable for the diffusion of religious brotherhoods and mystic rites, and that this was precisely the age of Buddha. The passage ends thus: "It is said that Lycurgus, in his wanderings, penetrated as far as India; and we can discover many points of resemblance between the precepts promulgated by Gotama and the laws of the Spartans." This was only corroboration of the beliefs of the Concord men.

It was Emerson who carried *Eastern Monachism* to Alcott after Thoreau's death. Because of this fact it is evident that he saw the book. Whether he read it carefully, however, is not known. But there is one sentence that seems to be a veritable model for an Emersonian passage and presumptive proof that Emerson did read the book. Spence Hardy wrote: "Were it possible for a yogi and a rahat from India, a Greek philosopher from one of the schools holding the power of intuition, an ascetic from the wilds of Syria or the mountains of Egypt, a heretic from the school of Alexandria, a monk from one of the monasteries of Europe, a schoolman of the middle ages, and a modern German metaphysician of the school of Schelling to meet together; and were it possible for them to forget their sectarian subtleties and nice distinctions; they would find that there was a vast mass of speculation about the main principles of which they were agreed." (Page 390.) It seems to me there is an unmistakable echo, if not a direct paraphrase of this sentence in Emerson's *Journals*, X, 234: "Can anyone doubt that if the noblest saint among the Buddhists, the noblest Mahommetan, the highest Stoic of Athens, the purest and wisest Christian, Menu in India, Confucius in China, Spinoza in Holland, could somewhere meet and converse together, they would all find themselves of one religion, and all would find themselves denounced by their own, sects and sustained by these believed adversaries of their sects? Jeremy Taylor, George Herbert, Pascal even, Pythagoras,—if these could all converse intimately, two and two, how childish their country traditions would appear!"

This book was probably one of the most influential in disseminating Buddhist lore in Concord. There was far more of the partial partisan in Spence Hardy than in the Concord men. He wrote much in attempted disproof of the Oriental systems, but these pages seem to have been utterly ignored—at least they were never marked.

1855 GRAVES CHAMNEY HAUGHTON, Nanava-Dherma-Sastra; or the Institutes of Menu, London, Cox and Baylis, 1825, 2 vols., 886 pp. This translation was listed by F. B. Sanborn, *The Life of Henry David Thoreau*, 1917, p. 517, as included in the Cholmondeley collection. It is a revision of Sir William Jones's translation, which had gone out of print.

1855 JAIMINI, The Aphorisms of the Mimansa Philosophy . . . with Extracts from the Commentaries, Allahabad, Benares College, 1851, 36 pp.

A small volume in the Emerson library which was originally in the Cholmondeley collection. From the preface: "The great body of Hindu Philosophy is based upon six sets of very concise Aphorisms. Without a commentary the Aphorisms are scarcely intelligible, they being designed not so much to communicate the doctrine of the particular school, as to aid, by the briefest possible suggestions, the memory of him to whom the doctrine shall have already been communicated."

1855 SIR WILLIAM JONES, Sacontala, or The Fatal Ring, London, Edwards, 1790, 109 pp.

A volume listed in the *Catalog of the Stephen H. Wakeman Col-

lection as belonging to Thoreau. It probably came to him in the Cholmondeley collection.

1855 JAMES. MILL, The History of British India . . . with Notes and Continuation by Horace Hayman Wilson, London, James Madden, 1848, 9 vols.

An exhaustive study of Indian civilization, given by Thoreau to the Concord Free Public Library. These volumes most probably came to Thoreau in the Cholmondeley collection, and presumably may be identified as the nine volume work which Thoreau mentioned to Ricketson, when he wrote to his friend of the arrival of the books. See page 47 for a discussion of this correspondence.

1855 HENRY HART MILMAN, Nala and Damayanti, London, Oriental Translation Fund, 1835, 148 pp.

A volume in the Cholmondeley collection which Thoreau bequeathed to Emerson. It comprises an episode in the *Mahabharata,* telling of the love of the characters, despite misfortune and separation. After Emerson read the book, he wrote in his *Journals,* IX, 422 on June 26, 1862: *"Romance.* If we could tell accurately the evanescing effects of an imaginative book on us as we read! Thus Milman's translation of *Nala and Damayanti* is nearer to my business and bosom than is the news in to-day's *Boston Journal.* And I am admonished and comforted, as I read. It all very nearly concerns me. We are elevated by beauty. I walk in marble galleries and talk with kings the while."

1855 E. RÖER, Bibliotheca Indica; a Collection of Oriental Works . . . Translated from the Original Sanscrit, Calcutta, East India Company, 1853, Vol. XV, Nos. 41 and 50, 170 pp.

A volume in the Cholmondeley collection which Thoreau bequeathed to Emerson. It contains translated passages from the following nine *Upanishads:* the *Taittariya, Aitareya, Svetasvatara, Kena, Isa, Katha, Prasna, Mundaka* and *Mandukya.* It was in this volume that Emerson found the model for his poem "Brahma," as well as the conclusion to his essay "Immortality."

1855 J. COCKBURN THOMSON, The Bhagavad-Gita; or a Discourse between Krishna and Arjuna on Divine Matters, Hertford, Stephen Austin, 1855, 274 pp.

A volume in the Cholmondeley collection. This translation contains an introduction of 119 pages, the importance of which may be judged from the following subtitles: "On the Origin of Philosophical Ideas in India," "On the Schools of Indian Philosophy," "The Sankhya System," "The Yoga, of Patanjali," "The Philosophy of the Bhagavad-Gita." There are also full explanatory notes.

1855 HORACE HAYMAN WILSON, Rig Veda Sanhita, a Collection of Ancient Hindu Hymns, London, W. H. Allen, 1850-54, 2 vols., 694 pp.

Volumes which came to Thoreau in the Cholmondeley collection. Emerson drew these books from the Boston Athenæum on May 5, 1855, and again on August 15, 1860. The entry in Emerson, *Journals,* IX, 419, indicates that the Thoreau bequest to him included the "First Ashtaka; Second Ashtaka" of Wilson's translation, which is evidence that the friends probably used only the first two volumes of Wilson's six volume series. Volume III, which appeared in 1857, was published at too late a date to be included in the Cholmondeley list.

1855 ———— Select Specimens of the Theatre of the Hindus, London, Trüber, 1835, 2 vols., 870 pp.

A volume in the Cholmondeley collection which Thoreau bequeathed to Emerson. Six of the classic dramas of India were here presented by Wilson with the avowed purpose of securing "to the Hindu Theatre a place in English literature." The translator did not claim a faithful word for word rendering for his work. A long preface dealt with the different kinds of Hindu dramatic entertainments, conduct of plot, characters, diction and scenic apparatus.

1856 MONIER MONIER-WILLIAMS, Sakoontala or the Lost Ring, Hertford, Stephen Austin, 1856, 288 pp.

An autographed volume in the Emerson library which probably came to him about 1856. This was the famous Hindu drama of which Goethe wrote:

Wouldst thou the young year's blossoms and the fruits of its decline,
And all by which the soul is charmed, enraptured, feasted, fed?
Wouldst thou the earth and heaven itself in one sole name combine?
I name thee, O Sakoontala! and all at once is said.

1857 DAVID URQUHART, The Sraddha, the Keystone of the Brahmanical, Buddhistic, and Arian Religions, as Illustrative of the Dogma and Duty of Adoption among the Princes and People of India, London, David Bryce, 1857, 44 pp.

A pamphlet in the Emerson library. It deals with ancestor worship.

1860 GEORGE HEWIT HODSON, ed., Twelve Years of a Soldier's Life in India: Being Extracts from the Letters of the late Major W. E. R. Hodson. . . . Including a Personal Narrative of the Siege of Delhi and Capture of the King and Princess, Boston, Ticknor and Fields, 1860, 444 pp.

This book deals primarily with soldiering and campaigning in India. Information concerning the country itself, and the life and customs of the natives, is only incidental. See Emerson, *Works*, X, 142-43: "Do not spare to put novels into the hands of young people as an occasional holiday and experiment. . . . If we can touch the imagination, we serve them, they will never forget it. Let him read Tom Brown at Rugby, read Tom Brown at Oxford,—better yet, read Hodson's Life—Hodson who took prisoner the king of Delhi. They teach the same truth,—a trust, against all appearances, against all privations, in your own worth, and not in tricks, plotting, or patronage."

1866 GEORGE SMALL, A Handbook of Sanskrit Literature: with Appendices Descriptive of the Mythology, Castes and Religious Sects of the Hindus, Intended Especially for Candidates for the India Civil Service, and Missionaries to India, London, Williams and Norgate, 1866, 236 pp.

Drawn by Emerson from the Boston Athenæum on September 5, 1866. A brief summary of the table of contents will indicate the nature and value of this book. It is divided into three parts. Part I is entitled "Religious Literature." The chapter headings in this part are as follows: Chapter I, "Introductory and on the Vedas"; Chapter 2, "On the Dharma Sastras, or Sacred Scriptures, Supplementary to the Vedas." Part II is devoted to "Philosophical Literature." The chapters in this section are: Chapter 1, "On the Six Darsanas in General, and the Nyaya and Vaiseshika in Particular"; Chapter 2, "Of the Sankhya and Yoga Schools"; Chapter 3, "On the Vedanta and Mimansa Darsanas." Part III is devoted to "Practical and Miscellaneous Literature." Chapter 1 is "On the Epic Poetry of the Hindus"; Chapter 2, "On the Puranas and Dramatic Works." An appendix attempts to outline briefly the mythological names, castes, and religious sects of the Hindus.

1867 J. TALBOYS WHEELER, The History of India from the Earliest Ages, London, Trübner, 1867, 2 vols., 1418 pp.

Drawn by Emerson from the Boston Athenæum on July 27, 1867. This book contained very important expositions of the literature of the Vedic and Brahmanic periods, and of the epics.

1867 JOHN CLARK MARSHMAN, The History of India, from the

Earliest Period to the Close of Lord Dalhousie's Administration, London, Longmans, Green, Reader and Dyer, 1867, 3 vols., 1504 pp.

Drawn by Emerson from the Boston Athenæum on October 19, 1867. This book is a detailed political and military history of the English administration of Indian affairs down to 1828. Very little attention is given to the religious, literary, social or legendary life of India.

1870 T. ROGERS, Buddhagosha's Parables: Translated from Burmese . . . with an Introduction, containing Buddha's Dhammapada, or "Path of Virtue," translated from Pali by F. Max Müller, London, Trübner, 1870, 378 pp.

A volume in the Alcott House, Concord. Its greatest value lies in Max Müller's long introduction and translation of the most famous text of Buddhism. The parables closely resemble the Jataka tales.

1872 WILLIAM BROCKIE, Indian Philosophy, Introductory Paper, London, Trübner, 1872, 25 pp.

A pamphlet in the Emerson library. The following sentences (p. 3) will indicate its nature: "On the whole, however, Hindu philosophy is fully as logical and profound as any systems of old Greece and Rome. . . . It does not come very far short, perhaps, of the most approved modern systems. . . . Our Lockes, Berkeleys, Kants, Fichtes, Hegels, Mills, Cousins, Hamiltons, and Bains had their fore-runners and counterparts in Kapila, Patanjali, Vyasa, Sankara-Acharya, and others. . . . The systems propounded by these illustrious Brahmans display fully as much metaphysical acuteness as any of those now accepted amongst ourselves." Such writing was acceptable to the American Transcendentalists.

1876 CHARLES D. B. MILLS, The Indian Saint; or, Buddha and Buddhism: a Sketch, Historical and Critical, Northampton, Mass., Journal and Free Press, 1876, 197 pp.

A volume in the Alcott House in Concord. See page 252 for Alcott's comment on Mills. This book is fundamentally an exposition of Buddhism in narrative. The author, who was relatively unacquainted with the translated Oriental literature itself, drew his information principally from the commentaries of Hardy, Müller, Beal and Burnouf. He did little but construct a readable story from the works of Orientalists that were available to him. As a popularization of Buddhistic thought, however, the book is effective. Emerson was also acquainted with Mills and presumably corresponded with him.

1880 E. D. ROOT, Sakya Buddha: a Versified, Annotated Narrative of his Life and Teachings; with an Excursus, containing Citations from the Dhammapada, or Buddhist Canon, New York, Charles P. Somerby, 1880, 171 pp.

A volume in the Emerson library. The following stanza will indicate the general nature and purpose of this book:

> I've conned Milesian fables,
>   Romaunts of olden times;
> With ease which me enables
>   To sketch with flowing rhymes
> The Lord who ne'er was thwarted
>   In deep-laid schemes or plans—
> His laws have been distorted,
>   Reviled by fleering clans.

It is interesting to note that the author called himself "an American Buddhist." The "Excursus," or appendix, contained a representative number of verses from Max Müller's translation of the Dhammapada. In preface the author wrote, "I have epitomized, and brought within the scope of the masses (to whom those volumes are inaccessible) all that is needed to form a correct biographical narrative of the keenest-minded of all religious, Heaven-sent Ariels." The book shows a very limited reading, and in general gives the impression of being the work of a religion-taster.

1883 PROTAP CHUNDER MOZOOMDAR, The Oriental Christ, Boston, Ellis, 1883, 193 pp.

A volume in the Alcott House at Concord. The author is the Hindu who contributed the essay "Emerson as Seen from India" to *The Genius and Character of Emerson*. Mozoomdar here expresses the eclectic idealism which characterized the Brahmo Somaj.

BOOKS RELATING TO SOME MOHAMMEDAN COUNTRIES THEIR PEOPLE, POETRY, RELIGION AND SCRIPTURES

1822 EDWARD WILLIAM LANE, The Thousand and One Nights; or, The Arabian Nights Entertainments, London, John Murray, 1847, 3 vols., 1590 pp.

This was the edition of the *Arabian Nights* in the Boston Athenæum which Alcott drew on September 15, 1851, January 23, 1852, and September 5, 1853. Emerson read the book as early as 1822, but there is no designation of the edition in his *Journals*, I, 204. It probably was Edward Forster's translation, London, 1802, which is listed in the *Catalogue* of the Harvard College Library published in 1830. Thoreau's *Journal*, I, 344, indicates that he read the *Arabian Nights* in March, 1842.

1832 ANQUETIL DUPERRON, "Exposition du système théologique des Perses, tiré des livres Zends, Pehlvis et Parsis," *Histoire de l'Académie des inscriptions avec les mémoires de littérature tirés des registres, de l'Académie royale des inscriptions*, Paris, 1774, Vol. 37, pp. 571-755.

Emerson read this discussion of Zoroastrianism in 1832. On April 17 of that year he transcribed two full pages of quotations to his diary; they will be found in his *Journals*, II, 473-75. This book was probably the most substantial discussion of any Oriental religion which Emerson read before he began writing for publication.

1836 ――――― Zendavesta, Ouvrage de Zoroastre, Paris, Tilliard, 1771, 3 vols., 1942 pp.

Drawn by Emerson from the Boston Athenæum on March 21, 1836. This translation of the main scripture of Zoroastrianism is accompanied with very valuable expository material.

1837 The Phenix; a Collection of Old and Rare Fragments, New York, Gowan, 1835, 298 pp.

This anonymously edited anthology commences with "The Morals of Confucius, a Chinese Philosopher," in which no attempt was made to preserve the divisions of the original. Although this volume holds the most significance because of the Zoroastrian extracts which Emerson used, it is worthy of note as one of the earliest sources of his Confucian readings. The second section, entitled "The Oracles of Zoroaster, the Founder of the Persian Magi," consisted of sayings translated from the Greek by J. P. Cory. This was prefaced with "An Abstract of the Persian Theology of Zoroaster" taken from the history of Edward Gibbon. Only these two sections are of interest here. Alcott wrote in his diary under date of February 13, 1851: "Cory's translations are so superior to Stanley's or Thomas Taylor's of the Oracles of Zoroaster, that I shall transcribe some of them to these pages." See the chapter on Alcott, for these transcriptions and a discussion of the use he made of them. Emerson wrote in his *Journals*, IV, 254, in July,

1837: "Two proverbs I found lately: one, 'He who would bring home the wealth of the Indies, must carry out the wealth of the Indies.' The other may serve as foil to this magnificent sentence, 'Small pot, soon hot.' Then again I found in *The Phenix* the Persian sentence, 'Remember always that the Gods are good,' which for genius equals any other golden saying." In contrast with the transcriptions culled from Alcotts' unpublished diary are the following which Emerson incorporated into his own in 1841, *Journals*, V, 560, the number following each quotation being the number of the page in *The Phenix:*

"Things divine are not attainable by mortals who understand body;
But only as many as are lightly armed arrive at the summit."
    (Page 168.)
"It is not proper to understand the Intelligible with vehemence
But with the extended flame of an extended mind measuring all
    things
Except that Intelligible. But it profits to understand this
For if you incline your mind you will understand it
Not earnestly, but it becomes you to bring with you a pure and
    inquiring eye;
To extend the void mind of your soul to the Intelligible
Because it subsists beyond mind." (Page 167.)
"You will not understand it as when understanding some particular
    thing." (Page 168.)
"There is a certain Intelligible which it becomes you to understand
    with the flower of the mind." (Page 167.)
"Let the immortal depth of your soul lead you." (Page 168.)
"Enlarge not thy destiny" (Page 166.)

1837 ABU-AL-FIDA, Annales Muslemici Arabice et Latine, Hafniae, 1789-94, 5 vols.
This is the volume listed as referred to or quoted from in Emerson, *Journals*, IV, 382. The book is there recorded as Abufelda's *Historia Muslemica*. It is an account of the spread of the Mohammedan Empire under the successors of the Prophet.

1840 WILLIAM OUSELEY, The Oriental Geography of Ebn Haukal, an Arabian Traveller of the Tenth Century, London, Oriental Press, 1800, 363 pp.
Emerson, *Works*, II, 253: "Ibn Haukal, the Arabian geographer, describes a heroic extreme in the hospitality of Sogd, in Bukharia. 'When I was in Sogd I saw a great building, like a palace, the

gates of which were open and fixed back to the wall with large nails. I asked the reason, and was told that the house had not been shut, night or day, for a hundred years. Strangers may present themselves at any hour and in whatever number; the master has amply provided for the reception of the men and their animals, and is never happier than when they tarry for some time. Nothing of the kind have I seen in any other country.' " I place Emerson's reading of Ouseley in the year 1840, since the essay "Heroism" in which he quotes this book first appeared in 1841.

1840 GEORGE SALE, The Koran; Commonly Called the Alcoran of Mohammed; Translated into English Immediately from the Original Arabic, London, Maiden, 1801, 2 vols., 783 pp.

This was the only complete translation of the *Koran* in the Boston Athenæum at the time Emerson and Alcott used its books. It is therefore probably the edition they read, although it does not appear on the records of the library. Other alternatives, which contained excerpts, were: E. W. Lane, *Selections from the Koran*, London, 1843; Barthélemy St. Hilaire, *Mahomet et le Coran*, Paris, 1865; G. Pauthier, *Les Livres sacrés de l'Orient*, Paris, 1843; and S. Green, *Life of Mahomet*, London, 1840. Emerson's *Journals*, V, 501, lists the *Koran* among the books referred to or quoted from in 1840. Though he might have read portions of this scripture earlier, he probably did not come to a complete translation before this time. The following are references to the book in Emerson's published writings. *Works*, IV, 66: "In the doctrine of the organic character and disposition is the origin of caste. 'Such as were fit to govern, into their composition the informing Deity mingled gold; into the military, silver; iron and brass for husbandmen and artificers.' The East confirms itself, in all ages, in this faith. The Koran is explicit on this point of caste. 'Men have their metal, as of gold and silver. Those of you who were the worthy ones in the state of ignorance, will be the worthy ones in the state of faith, as soon as you embrace it.' " Such a passage as this may be taken as supplementary to the discussion of Emerson's doctrine of Compensation. The following passage appears in the essay "Eloquence," *Works*, VII, 64: "The Koran says, 'A mountain may change its place, but a man will not change his disposition'; yet the end of eloquence is—is it not?—to alter in a pair of hours, perhaps in a half hour's discourse, the convictions and habits of years." Finally the following is an excellent illustration of Emerson's eclectic blending of various cultures and doctrines, in this case Platonic, Mohammedan and Hindu. The passage appears in *Works*, IV, 95-96: "All men are commanded by the saint. The Koran makes a distinct class of those who are by nature good, and whose goodness has an influence on others, and pronounces this class to be the aim of creation: the other classes are admitted to the feast of being, only as following in the train of this. And the Persian poet exclaims to a soul of this kind,—'Go boldly forth and feast on being's banquet; Thou art the called,— the rest admitted with thee.' The privilege of this caste is an access to the secrets and structure of nature by some higher method than by experience. In common parlance, what one man is said to learn by experience, a man of extraordinary sagacity is said, without experience, to divine. The Arabians say, that Abul Khain, the mystic, and Abu Ali Seena, the philosopher, conferred together; and, on parting, the philosopher said, 'All that he sees, I know'; and the mystic said, 'All that he knows, I see.' If one should ask the reason for this intuition, the solution would lead us into that property which Plato denoted as Reminiscence, and which is implied by the Bramins in the Tenet of Transmigration. The soul having been often born, or, as the Hindoos say, 'traveling the path of existence through thousands of births', having beheld the things which are here, those which are in heaven and those which are beneath, there is nothing of which she has not gained the knowledge: no wonder that she is able to recollect, in regard to any one thing, what formerly she knew."

1840 SIMON OCKLEY, The Conquest of Syria, Persia and Aegypt, by the Saracens: Containing the Lives of Abubeker, Omar and Othman, the Immediate Successors of Mahomet, London, Knaplock, 1708, 2 vols., 874 pp. Vol. II, published in 1718, entitled History of the Saracens.

Drawn by Emerson from the Boston Athenæum on September 22, 1840, and again on October 25, 1842. See Emerson, *Journals*, V. 465: " 'Paradise,' said Mahomet, 'is under the shadow of swords.' " The editors noted that many other quotations followed, but these were not included in the published *Journals*.

1840 ROBERT MIGNAN, Travels in Chaldea, Including a Journey from Bussarah to Bagdad, Hillah, and Babylon, Performed on Foot in 1827, London, Colburn and Bentley, 1829, 333 pp.

Drawn by Emerson from the Boston Athenæum on November 18,

1840. See also his *Journals*, V, 502. This book is of greater archeological than philosophical or literary interest. The chief emphasis is on the remains of Babylonian civilization and the grandeur of the ancient cities and hanging gardens.

1841 JOSEPH VON HAMMER, Der Diwan von Mohammed Schemseddin Hafis, Stuttgart und Tübingen, 1812, 2 vols., 1070 pp.

See pages 152-54 for a discussion of Emerson's use of this volume.

1842 PAUL ÉMILE BOTTA, "Notice sur un Voyage dans l'Arabie Heureuse," *Archives du Muséum d'Histoire Naturelle*, Paris, 1841, II, 63-88.

A volume of travel and reminiscence from which Thoreau quoted on March 23, 1842. See his *Journal*, I, 343.

1843 MULLA FIRUZ BIN KAUS, The Desatir or Sacred Writings of the Ancient Prophets; in the Original Tongue; Together with the Ancient Persian Version and Commentary, Bombay, Courrier Press, 1818, 208 pp.

See page 13 for a discussion of Emerson's use of this book, and the *Dial*, IV, 59-62 (July, 1843), for the selections he edited as samples of the ethnical scriptures. This volume is listed in the Fruitlands library as imported by Alcott from England. It is now in the Emerson library.

This Persian book was alleged to be a compendium of the saying of fifteen prophets, together with the commentaries of the editors. See Claud Field, *Persian Literature*, 1912, pp. 6 ff. That it proved to be forgery did not seem to concern Emerson. He was perfectly aware of the fact: "Nor do I much care for the question whether the Zend-Avesta or the Desatir are genuine antiques, or modern counterfeits, as I am only concerned with the good sentences; and it is indifferent how old a truth is, whether an hour or five centuries, whether it first shot into the mind of Adam, or your own. If it be truth, it is certainly much older than both of us" (*Journals*, X, 382). It is said that the Desatir was compiled at the time of the Greek occupation of Asia Minor, and that consequently its content is Grecian in its philosophical import as well as Oriental. This is only additional evidence that Emerson was not concerned with the differences between the Greek and Oriental idealism. The volume in Emerson's library has numerous pages on which sentences are heavily underscored. In many instances two or three lines have been placed in the margin in addition to the underscoring; sometimes there were brackets and a neatly drawn hand with the index finger pointing to a choice passage. Since it was Emerson who edited the selections from this book for the *Dial*, there seems little doubt that it was he who marked the pages, possibly with a view to indicating the passages he would reprint. Those which appeared in the *Dial*, were a very small portion indeed of all that were underscored and marginally bracketed. Cabot, it will be remembered, observed that he read "for a touch of suggestion that might help to crystallize the thoughts that were floating within him." It would seem that Cabot is supported by the marginalia of the *Desatir*, for there is in them many an echo of the familiar Emersonian doctrines.

Because there was little of continuity or coherence in the book, the passages Emerson marked may well be arbitrarily grouped around his main doctrines. A natural starting point would be that of God and His nature, the world and the method of creation. Emerson had not read far, only to page 19, when he found this sentence: "The world, like a radiation, is not and cannot be separated from the sun of the substance of the mighty God." In the margin he placed a heavy line. On page 62 he read: "Mezdam is not a substance, and is not unsubstantial; and is more exalted than aught thou canst conceive." These words he underscored. On the same page was the following, with the last pronoun underscored: "He liveth, not by a soul, and life, and body. He liveth of Himself." And turning the page he read, again underscoring: "He is All-Powerful! Whatever He willeth He can do; and is staid in nothing except in creating one like Himself." *eke Nietzsche*

Emerson noted the denial of all finite attributes which the *Desatir* gave to God. Two heavy lines were in the margin opposite this verse: "Thou hast become hidden from the very brightness and extreme brilliance, and excessive light of Thy splendor." (Page 56.) One verse was skipped, but the next was both underscored and bracketed: "Mankind cannot extol or duly praise, in any respect suitably to their excellence, even the meanest of them who stand in the lowest degree." (*Ibid.*) And skipping another verse, we read the sixty-second, bracketed but not underscored: "His worshippers are dejected from their inability to attain the height of His majesty." (*Loc. cit.*)

The prophets of the *Desatir* admonished: "Say unto mankind, Look not upon the Self-Existent with this eye: ask for another eye." (Page 98.) In the margin a large cross. The next marked passage was the theme of the essay ["Circles": "The Perfect Man reacheth God as the line of the circle returneth to the point whence it began." (*Ibid.*) In the margin of this thought was a heavy line, as also that of the next marked passage: "The roads tending to God are more in number than the breathings of created being." (*Loc. cit.*) Opposite the last checked passage on this page was again a heavily pencilled cross: "True Self-knowledge is knowledge of God." Perhaps Emerson felt this was but another way of stating his doctrine of self-reliance.

There is a curious medley of the mundane and the sublime in this book. Of these Emerson significantly failed to notice the former. He followed closely all the searching after the nature of the Prius, ignoring what was irrelevant to his own thoughts. "Let us ask assistance from Mezdam, the self-Existent, the Uncompounded, the Artificer of qualities! The Necessarily-existent is the Creator of the conditionally-existent." (Page 149.) The first of these sentences received a marginal line; the second was underscored. The authors of the *Desatir* used harsh, condemnatory words against the dualist, in a passage that was both underscored and marginally checked: "That man is a perverter of truth who imagineth that likeness, or quantity, or locality, or body, or any accident among accidents, or any property among properties can be predicated of Thee; save from necessity, as a form of speech, or for the purpose of intimation." (Page 57.) The reason for this was given. "The eyes of purity saw Thee by the lustre of Thy substance. Dark and astounded is he who hath seen thee by the efforts of the Intellect. . . . The Perfect seeth unity in multiplicity, and multiplicity in unity." (Pages 55 and 97, double marginal lines and underscoring.) To these verses the commentator added much pertinent information which was both underscored and bracketed. He explained that a man "is dark and confounded who would see God as He is, by the light of the understanding: seeing that the understanding, however sublime, cannot discover Him as He is: And this proceeds not from the weakness or imperfection of the understanding, but from the greatness, the exaltedness and dignity of the essence of the Governor of the world." (Page 55.) The commentator later explained that the "discriminative nature of God is the essence of His substance, and is not external to or separable from Him. For, His self-existence is the essence of His substance; inasmuch as nothing can in any respect be joined or united, or conceived as joined or united to Him. Things therefore receive existence and being in this sort: they have an absolute dependence and cling firmly on the being of God, and there is a light reflected on them from the most Just, the Bestower of Existence; but not so that being is to be understood as a quality essentially inherent in or united with them." (Pages 55 and 56; passage underscored; marginal check opposite last two lines.)

The most blessed of men were those who belonged to a special class. "The chief class see the Really-Existent, and observe the Creation through Him, and mark God in whatever exists: those who are of this class do not believe that to discover unity in multiplicity, and multiplicity in unity is an obstruction to a knowledge of real unity; the name of this blessed class is Semrud Semrud which means United-in-Unity." (Page 97; passage underscored.)

The substance, the nature, and the impossibility of labelling God with attributes, we have noted. The following is the *Desatir's* description of the manner in which God creates: "The Simple Being, without hope of return, of his own beneficence and love of good first of all, created a substance free and unconfined, unmixed, immaterial, not subject to time, without body or aught material, or dependence on body, or matter, or quality, named Behnam, whose title is *The Chief of Angels*." (Pages 2 and 3; double marginal check. Pages 165, 166, and 167 also deal with the creative processes. There were double marginal lines on all pages.)

The laws of Compensation and Retribution were not differentiated in Emerson's mind. If it was he who marked the *Desatir*, as we have assumed, this was probably the reason that double marginal lines were placed opposite the following text as well as the commentator's explanation. The text: "Whosoever is an evil-doer, on him He first inflicted pain under the human form: for sickness, the sufferings of children while in their mothers' womb, and after they are out of it, and suicide, and being hurt by ravenous animals, and death, and being subjected to want from birth till death, are all retributions for past actions: and in like manner as to goodness." The commentator's explanation of this passage: "Observe that he says that every joy, or pleasure or pain that affects us from birth till death, is wholly the fruit of past actions, which is now reaped." (Page 12.)

In the Oriental mind, Karma is the immediate cause of transmigration and the endless cycle of rebirth for the soul. The law is thus expounded in a marked passage of the *Desatir:* "The lion, the tyger, the leopard, the panther and the wolf, with all ravenous animals, whether birds, or quadrupeds, or creeping things, have once possessed authority: and every one whom they kill hath been their aider, or abetter, who did evil by supporting, or assisting, or by the orders of, that exalted class; and having given pain to harmless animals are now punished by their own masters." (Page 13.) Opposite this a single marginal line: "If a man be possessed of excellent knowledge, yet follow a wicked course of action, when this vile body is dissolved he doth not get another elemental body, nor doth his soul get admittance into the upper abode, but his evil dispositions becoming his tormentors, assume the form of burning fire, of freezing snow, of serpents, dragons and the like, and inflict punishment on him." (Pages 15-16.)

The following is suggestive of Emerson's teaching on the relation of man's soul to the Over-Soul: "There is in thy soul a certain knowledge, which, if thou display it to mankind, they will tremble like a branch agitated by a strong wind." (Page 93; double marginal lines.) Note the injunction with regard to prayer: "In prayer, turn to any side: but it is best to turn to the stars and the light." (Page 17; single marginal line.) The commentator's explanation of this injunction was also checked with a single marginal line: "He says, that, to that Being who is without place, you may pray in all directions; and that prayer is good whithersoever you turn in praying to Him: but nevertheless that it is best to pray towards the stars and lights, and that prayers made towards the stars and celestial luminaries are most acceptable." (*Ibid.*)

Most mystics have found an ascetic life of some sort the most congenial. It is the austere life that seems to abet the soul in its search for God. Approval of the austere life is thus indicated in this Persian book on page 23: "A band will appear who are knowers and doers of good, mortifying the senses." Here one marginal line. "And this Band are in a blessed road." This sentence was underscored. "And there is a different Band who know and do good, without practicing austerities, and who investigate the real nature of things by the guidance of reason, and live as *Sirdasp.*" This pretty well describes Emerson himself, a man who preferred to explore Reality from his study instead of a lonesome Walden hut or some pantisocratic Fruitlands. In the margin were two heavy lines. And opposite this note: "The Sirdasp are such as seek good without mortifying their bodies in devotion," was a heavy bracket. One can imagine Emerson saying to himself that here was a writer after his own heart—whoever this Oriental might have been; that here was described a life to which he had naturally and spontaneously come, for he loved the good life, and he constantly sought the highest, but he saw no necessity for the mortification of the flesh.

Finally, it may be noted that the *Desatir* was not only interesting for its speculative thought. If a departure from the common habit of indicating approval with marginal lines, brackets and underscoring means anything, there was one instance in which, added to the usual bracket, was a distinct drawing of a hand, pointing, with the index finger extended. The sentence to which the hand pointed was this: "The spider said, Animals do not transfer the secrets of Mezdam from a living heart to a lifeless body." (Page 138.) Here is a kind of Aesopian context. Animals have usurped the place of men and supernatural beings. Mankind comes out the worse for some of the encounters of wit. The following complete passage was marked, the verses appearing in the order of the original text, with nothing omitted: "129. The wise tortoise next advancing said, What proof is there of the superiority of man? 130. The sage, named Shalish-herta said, Kings and ministers, and generals, and physicians, and astronomers afford proofs of man's superiority. 131. The tortoise said, Animals too possess the classes you have mentioned. 132. Observe the sovereignty of the bee and of the ant in their kind: 133. And attend to the visiership of the fox; 134. And recollect the generalship of the elephant; 135. And learn medicine from the dog, who healeth wounds, by licking them with his tongue; 136. And the cock is an astronomer, who knoweth right well the time of the day and night. 137. On hearing these observations Shalish-herta remained silent. 138. Next the sage peacock sailing in, said; What proof is there of man's superior dignity? 139. The wise visier, Vizlur by name, said, Mankind possess the faculty of judgment and discrimination. 140. The sage peacock answered, If during the darkness of a single night, a hundred sheep have young, each knoweth its own lamb; and in like manner each lamb knoweth (its mother)."

The most significant marked passages have been given. If it was

Emerson, as has been surmised for various reasons earlier presented, who did the marking, the marginalia in the *Desatir* must
lead to one definite conclusion. It is this: a good sentence was one
which echoed his own thought.

1844 THOMAS TAYLOR, Iamblichus on the Mysteries of the Egyptians,
Chaldeans, and Assyrians, Chiswick, Whittingham, 1821, 389 pp.
A volume in the Emerson library. The first paragraph of the introduction states the scope of the work and the probable reason for
its appeal to Emerson: "It appears to me that there are two
descriptions of persons by whom the present work must be considered to be of inestimable worth, the lovers of antiquity and the
lovers of ancient philosophy and religion. To the former of these it
must be invaluable, because it is replete with information derived
from the wise men of the Chaldeans, the prophets of the Egyptians,
the dogmas of the Assyrians, and the ancient pillars of Hermes; and
to the latter, because of the doctrines contained in it, some of which
originated from the Hermaic pillars, were known to Pythagoras and
Plato, and were the sources of their philosophy; and others are
profoundly theological, and unfold the mysteries of ancient religion
with an admirable conciseness of diction, and an inimitable vigor
and elegance of conception." Probably no volume was more influential than this in augmenting Emerson's natural tendency to see
one source as the origin of all systems. Alcott also imported a
volume for the Fruitlands library. The ethnical scriptures which
appeared in the *Dial*, IV, 529-36, (April, 1844), under the heading
"Oracles of Zoroaster and the Theurgists," although from Thomas
Taylor's translation, were not taken from this book. Instead, the
source was the *Monthly Magazine and British Register for 1797*,
III, 509-26. Emerson quoted from this source in his *Journals*, VI,
500. Other references to the Chaldæan Oracles will also be found
in Emerson, *Journals*, V, 560; VI, 499-500; VIII, 534. See pages
244-45 for the Oracles collected by Alcott. Taylor's translations also
appeared in the *Classical Journal*, XVI, 333-44 and XVII, 128-33.

1845 W. F. THOMPSON, The Practical Philosophy of the Muham-
madan People, Exhibited in Its Professed Connection with the
European, so as to Render Either an Introduction to the Other;
Being a Translation of the Akhlak-I-Jalay, the Most Esteemed
Work of Middle Asia, from the Persian of Fakir Jany Muhammad
Asaad, London, Oriental Translation Fund, 1839, 560 pp.
Numerous quotations in Emerson, *Journals*, VII, 107 ff. show that

this book was much read in 1845. This volume was originally compiled during the period of the Byzantine Empire, and consequently reflects the fusion of Greek and Mohammedan thought. There are three main parts, entitled respectively, "The Individual State," "The Domestic State," and "The Political State." The expositions in these sections occasionally resemble a Socratic dialogue, and at other times the form of the proverbs found in the *Desatir*.

1846 JAMES ATKINSON, The Shah Nameh of the Persian Poet Firdausi, London, Oriental Translation Fund, 1832, 639 pp.

Drawn by Emerson from the Harvard College Library on September 2, 1846, and July 26, 1847. This poem has often been called the Persian *Iliad*. Matthew Arnold used one of its episodes as the basis for "Sohrab and Rustum," which poem will serve as a suggestion of the nature of the epic.

1846 ALEXANDER CHODZKO, Specimens of the Popular Poetry of Persia, as found in the Adventures and Improvisations of Kurroglou, the Bandit-Minstrel of Northern Persia; and in the Songs of the People Inhabiting the Shores of the Caspian Sea, London, Oriental Translation Fund, 1842, 602 pp.

Drawn by Emerson from the Harvard College Library on September 2, 1846, and again on July 26, 1847. See his *Journals*, VII, 153, 280, and 291 for quotations. Longfellow's famous poem "The Leap of Roushan Beg" is based on the account of an adventure of the bandit-hero of this book. It is interesting that Emerson also both quoted from and paraphrased this same story in his *Journals*, VII, 280.

1849 JOSEPH VON HAMMER-PURGSTALL, Geschichte der schönen Redekunste Persiens, mit einer Bluthenlese aus Zwehhundert Persischen Dichtern, Wien, Heubner und Wolfe, 1818, 444 pp.

This anthology of Persian poetry is the source of the lines Emerson translated from Saadi in his *Journals*, IX, 538 ff. The German rendering of Saadi's "Kassaid" and "Old Age," will be found on pages 208 and 210 respectively. For other instances of Emerson's use of German models in his so-called "translations" see pages 152-54 of this study.

1850 AUSTEN HENRY LAYARD, Nineveh and Its Remains: with an Account of a Visit to the Chaldaean Christians of Kurdistan, and the Yezidis, or Devil-Worshippers; and in Inquiry into the Manners and Arts of the Ancient Assyrians, New York, Putnam, 1849, 2 vols., 707 pp.

Quoted from by Thoreau, June 9, 1850. See his *Journal,* II, 35; also VI, 9-11. Emerson drew this volume from the Boston Athenæum on September 16, 1869. The title is sufficiently definitive of the content.

1853 CHARLES FELLOWS, Travels and Researches in Asia Minor, London, John Murray, 1852, 520 pp.

Drawn by Emerson from the Boston Athenæum on Nov. 30, 1853. This book is an account of travel in such portions of Asia Minor as had not yet been opened by the Royal Geographical Society. The chief interest lies in the archaeological remains which depict the life of the Greek colonists. There is relatively little discussion of Oriental thought.

1856 J. W. DE FOREST, Oriental Acquaintance: or, Letters from Syria, New York, Dix Edwards, 1856, 290 pp.

A volume in the Emerson library, containing the following inscription: "Mr. Ralph Waldo Emerson from his affectionate cousin C. Upham Shepard." This book is a personal account of the author's encounters with the natives and discomforts while travelling in the Near East. There is no exposition of such subjects as the literature, religion or civilization of the countries travelled.

1856 WILLIAM ROUNSEVILLE ALGER, The Poetry of the East, Boston, Whittemore, Niles and Hall, 1856, 288 pp.

On October 19, 1856, Emerson wrote to Alger after the receipt of this book: "I have delayed thanking you for the gift of your Book, till I could look a little into it: And though I have not yet nearly done with it, I have made some eager search into the heart of it. The enterprize is very welcome to me, this brave sally into Orientalism, and the attempt to popularize some of its richest jewels. . . . Your introductory Chapter is rich and interesting, and every taste will find something to thank you for in your collections." (Stanley T. Williams, "Unpublished Letters of Emerson," *Journal of English and Germanic Philology,* XXVI, 483-84). Alger's book was an anthology of excerpts from translations of Hindu and Persian poetry, selected from the work of European Orientalists. An introduction of 92 pages presents an admirable survey and exposition of the subject. Many of the items which comprise the present bibliography are listed in this introduction, and it is quite likely that the attention of the Concordians was thus attracted. Later editions of Alger's anthology bore the title *Specimens of Oriental Poetry.*

1857 RICHARD FRANCIS BURTON, Personal Narrative of a Pilgrimage to El-Medinah and Mecca, New York, Putnam, 1856, 498 pp.

This volume is primarily of geographic interest. The preface to the American edition states: "Burton's narrative is especially valuable for his full and accurate particulars of the religious observances of the pilgrimage, and the various formulas of salutation and prayer. In this respect there is no other work of the kind equal to it. His descriptions of the holy edifices are scrupulously technical and careful; and he gives us, for the first time, sketches of the sacred cities which impress us with their fidelity to nature." On February 10, 1857, Thoreau commented on and quoted freely from this book. See his *Journal*, IX, 251-52.

1862 JOSEPH EUGÈNE DAUMAS, Les Chevaux du Sahara, et les mœurs du désert, Paris, Michel Levy, 1858, 275 pp.

Emerson read this book in 1862. See his *Journals*, IX, 408, for quotations. See also *Works*, VI, 176. This book deals primarily with the Arab's love of horse-flesh, and the origin, care, and various uses of the Arabian horse.

1864 JOHN MALCOLM, The History of Persia, from the Most Early Period to the Present Time: Containing an Account of the Religion, Government, Usages, and Character of the Inhabitants of that Kingdom, London, John Murray, 1815, 2 vols., 1380 pp.

Drawn by Emerson from the Boston Athenæum on March 26, 1864. This book is by a colonel of the British Army who served as Minister Plenipotentiary to the Court of Persia. He was a man of catholic interests who examined the literature and religion of Persia, as well as its political history. The title gives a good suggestion of the scope. This was probably one of the best existing volumes on the subject that Emerson could have found.

1864 BARTHÉLEMY D'HERBELOT, Bibliotheque orientale, ou Dictionnaire universel, La Haye, Neaulme und Daalen, 1777-1879, 5 vols.

This work is mentioned in Emerson, *Journals*, X, 86, as read in 1864. It is primarily an encyclopedia of Arabian, Persian and Turkish religions, sects, arts, sciences and literature, averaging nearly 700 pages to the volume.

1867 WILLIAM GIFFORD PALGRAVE, Narrative of a Year's Journey through Central and Eastern Arabia, London, Macmillan, 1865, 2 vols., 876 pp.

Drawn by Emerson from the Boston Athenæum on May 13, 1867. This book is an interesting, familiar account of Arabia by an English army officer well acquainted with the country. The descriptions are of the natives and the country in which they live rather than their thought and literature.

1869 EUGÈNE FROMENTIN, Un Été dans Le Sahara, Paris, Michel Levy, 1857, 291 pp.

A book listed in Emerson, *Journals*, X, 306, as read in 1869. It deals with French military campaigns and contacts with the natives of the desert.

1869 DAVID SHEA AND ANTHONY TROYER, The Dabistan, or School of Manners, Paris, Oriental Translation Fund, 1843, 3 vols., 1420 pp.

A book listed in Emerson, *Journals*, X, 305, as read in 1869. The "Preliminary Discourse," written by Anthony Troyer, contains a thirty-five page discussion of the *Desatir* and a long synopsis of the present Persian work which gives particular attention to the "mixture, fusion, and resemblance of Persian and Indian doctrines and institutions." This book is reputed to be a tract on twelve different religions written by a Mohammedan traveller named Mohsan. The first chapter deals with the religion of Huchang, which was long anterior to Zoroastrianism, and continued to be secretly professed. Like the *Desatir*, the *Dabistan* is discounted by modern scholars.

1872 EDWARD FITZGERALD, The Rubaiyat of Omar Khayyam, London, Quaritch, 1872, 36 pp.

An autographed presentation copy in the Emerson library with the following inscription: "R. W. Emerson, with the grateful affection of C. E. N. December, 1873." In his *Life and Letters*, I, 508-09, Norton tells of introducing Emerson to Omar Khayyam while they were travelling together on shipboard: "I lent him Omar Khayyam, and he forgot that he had condemned him six months before . . . he became deeply interested in the little volume, and kept it through the voyage to read and reread it. Found it good as the best Persian poetry; very lofty in its defiance; with rare depths of feeling and imagination."

1875 HENRY BICKNELL, Hafiz of Shiraz: Selections from His Poems, London, Trübner, 1875, 404 pp.

A volume in the Emerson library. The introduction to these translations contained little with which Emerson was not already acquainted when they were published.

1876 THOMAS GOLD APPLETON, A Nile Journal, Boston, Roberts, 1876, 307 pp.

A volume in the Emerson library. The author wrote in dedication: "This is a Journal I kept on the Nile for your entertainment and my own. It is like a thousand other journals, full of trivial details, and without learning or eloquence."

1877 ———— Syrian Sunshine, Boston, Roberts, 1877, 308 pp.

A volume in the Emerson library, very similar to the author's *Nile Journal*. It is a record of six weeks of travel in the Holy Land in the spring of 1875.

1877 JOHN WEISS, Goethe's West-Easterly Divan, Boston, Roberts, 1877, 264 pp.

A volume in the Emerson library. It consists of original poems by Goethe in the Persian manner, not translations. John Weiss's edition contains copious notes.

CHINA AND THE CONFUCIAN TEXTS

1830 ABEL RÉMUSAT, "L'Invariable milieu," *Notices et extraits des manuscrits de la Bibliothèque du Roi*, Paris, 1818, Vol. X, pp. 269-426.

Emerson wrote in his *Journals*, II, 334, on October 27, 1830: "The rule 'Do as you would be done by' is found in the 'Invariable Medium' of the Chinese, but thrown into the 3d paragraph of the 3d chap. So the *Invariable Milieu* begins with these promising definitions. 'The order established by heaven is called *Nature*. What is conformed to nature is called *Law*, the establishment of law (in the mind?) is called *Instruction*.' (This '*Invariable Milieu*' M. Abel Rémusat has translated into French in *Tome II. des Notices des Manuscrits*, 1818.)" The citation of the volume is incorrect. Rémusat's work appeared in the tenth volume of the series. The correspondence between Emerson's *Nature* and the tenor of the quotation he recorded in his *Journals* is indeed significant.

1836 JOSHUA MARSHMAN, The Works of Confucius; Containing the Original Text, with a Translation . . . to which is Prefixed a Dissertation on the Chinese Language and Character, Serampore, Mission Press, 1809, 742 pp.

See Emerson, *Journals*, IV, 10, for quotations taken from this volume in 1836. The Boston Athenæum charge-book shows that Emerson drew it out on February 16, 1836. It is evident therefore the source of the quotations was probably the Athenæum edition. Alcott drew it from the Athenæum on March 28, 1849, and February 11, 1851. Thoreau used it as the source of selections published in the *Dial*, III, 493-94 (April, 1843). There was no preliminary note. The following are illustrations of his choices: "Chee says, if in the morning I hear about the right way, and in the evening die, I can be happy." "To worship at a temple not your own is mere flattery."

1837 "A Sketch of Lord Napier's Negotiations with the Authorities at Canton," *Asiatic Journal and Monthly Register*, XXIII (new series), 267-79 (May-August, 1837).

This essay was an account of the earliest trade negotiations of the British with the Chinese. After a visit to the Boston Athenæum, Emerson wrote in his *Journals*, IV, 318-19, on October 13, 1837. "I read with great content the August number of the *Asiatic Journal*. Herein is always the piquancy of the meeting of civilization and barbarism. Calcutta or Canton are twilights where Night and Day contend. A very good paper is the narrative of Lord Napier's mission to China (who arrived at Macao 15 July, 1834, and died 11 October). . . . There is no farce in fiction better than this historical one of John Bull and the Yellow Man: albeit it ends tragically, as Lord Napier died of vexation apparently. I must get that book again." In *Journals*, IV, 317, Emerson quoted lines from Wilson's translation of Kalidasa's *Megha Duta*, which appeared in the same number of the *Asiatic Journal*.

1842 LUDOVICI MAGNI, Confucius Sinarum Philosophus, Sive Scientia Sinensis, Paris, Danielem Horthemels, 1787, 296 pp.

A Latin translation listed among the books in the Fruitlands library. No mention was found in the published works of Emerson, Thoreau, or Alcott. A catalogue of the books imported from England by Alcott will be found in the *Dial*, III, 545-48 (April, 1843), and the appendix of C. E. Sears's *Fruitlands*. See Thoreau, *Writings*, I, 288-99, for quotations from other translations of Confucian texts.

1843 DAVID COLLIE, The Chinese Classical Work, Commonly Called the Four Books, Malacca, Mission Press, 1828.

This translation was read by Emerson in 1843. See his *Journals*, VI, 483, where the author's name was misspelled "Collier" by the editors. Thoreau used this book as the source of selections in the *Dial*, IV, 205-10 (October, 1843). The following is from his preliminary note: "This translation . . . is the most valuable contribution we have yet seen from the Chinese literature. That part of the work, which is new, is the Memoirs of Mencius in two books, the Shang Mung and the Hea Mung, which is the production of Mung Tsze (or Mencius), who flourished about a hundred years after Confucius. The subjoined extracts are chiefly taken from these books." Some of these extracts follow: "He who employs his whole mind, will know his nature. He who knows his nature, knows heaven." "He who offends heaven, has none to whom he can pray." "Chung Kung asked, What is perfect virtue? Confucius said, What you do not wish others to do to you, do not to them."

1849 JOSEPH A. M. M. DE MAILLA, Histoire générale de la Chine, ou Annales de cet empire, Paris, Imprimerie du Grand-Conseil du Roi, 1777, 2 vols., 939 pp.

This is most probably the history of China "by the Jesuit" suggested to Alcott by James Freeman Clarke. The author's complete name on the title page was "Père Joseph-Anne-Marie de Moyriac de Mailla, Jésuite Francois, Missionaire á Pékin." The book was in the Boston Athenæum. It is a study of Chinese history in the traditional manner, and a record of Jesuit missionary activity. Professor A. W. Hummel informs me that de Mailla's History is a translation of the substance of Chu Hsi's *Mirror of History,* hence it is not a "study" made by himself.

1852 EVARISTE REGIS HUC, Travels in Tartary, Thibet, and China, During the Years 1844-5-6, New York, Appleton 1852, 2 vols., 493 pp.

Thoreau's *Journal,* IV, 15, indicates that he read this work in 1852. In this passage he writes as follows: "The salutations and commonplaces of all nations, which would sound to us formal often, are always adapted to their circumstances, and grow out of their necessities. The Tartar inquires, 'Has the rain been abundant? Are your flocks in prosperity? Have your mares been fruitful?' and the answer is, 'All is at peace in our pastures.' Serene and Biblical, and no man's invention. M. Huc met with a family in China remarkable for hospitality." See also Emerson, *Journals,* VIII, 510, where this book is listed and the author's name misspelled "Hue."

1854 JOHN FRANCIS DAVIS, The Chinese: a General Description of the Empire of China and its Inhabitants, London, Charles Knight, 1836, 2 vols., 900 pp.

This book is listed in Emerson's *Journals,* VIII, 510, as read in 1854. The author was an English diplomat in China for more than twenty years. In preface he states: "It is singular that no general and systematic work on China has yet been produced in this country, notwithstanding that our immediate interest in the subject has been vastly greater than that of any other European nation." The book is for the general reader and covers everything from the Chinese penal code, marriage ceremonies, amusements and modes of travel, to the kidnapping of children and the cultivation of rice.

1856 G. PAUTHIER, Confucius et Mencius les quatre livres de philosophie morale et politique de la Chine, Paris, Charpentier, n. d., 465 pp.

Among Thoreau's comments on Confucius is the following written in a letter dated December 12, 1856, which will be found in his *Writings*, VI, 299: "I do not remember anything which Confucius has said directly respecting man's 'origin, purpose and destiny.' He was more practical than that. He is full of wisdom applied to human relations,—to the private life,—the family,—government, etc. It is remarkable that, according to his own account, the sum and substance of his teaching is, as you know, to do as you would be done by. He also said (I translate from the French), 'Conduct yourself suitably towards the persons of your family, then you will be able to instruct and to direct a nation of men." Thoreau translated from this edition.

1858 ABEL RÉMUSAT, Iu-kiao-li; ou, Les Deux cousines; roman chinois, Paris, Moutardier, 1826, 4 vols., 863 pp.

Thoreau's interest in this Chinese novel is indicated by quotations copied in 1858 into the *Journal*, XI, 65-66: "In the Chinese novel 'Ju-Kiao-Li, or The Two Fair Cousins', I find a motto to a chapter (quoted): 'He who aims at success should be continually on his guard against a thousand accidents. How many preparations are necessary before the sour plum begins to sweeten! . . . But if supreme happiness was to be attained in the space of an hour, of what use would be in life the noblest sentiments?" There are other quotations in this Thoreau context. Thoreau wrote in *Journal*, XI, 81: "The author of the Chinese novel 'Ju-Kiao-Li', some eight hundred years ago, appears to have appreciated the beauty of the willows. Pe, his principal character, moved out of the city late in life, to a stream bordered with willows, about twenty miles distant, in order to spend the rest of his days drinking wine and writing verses there. He describes the eyebrow of his heroine as like a willow leaf floating on the surface of the water." See also Emerson, *Journals*, IX, 550: "It is with difficulty that we wont ourselves in the language of the Eastern poets, in the melodramatic life. . . . As, for example, in the Chinese *Two Fair Cousins.*" An English edition, rendered from Rémusat's French by an anonymous translator, was published in London in 1827. This is essentially a novel of manners and social satire. Rémusat remarked in his preface that "Chinese romances are, therefore, excellent in their way of supplying the information wanting in the accounts of voyagers and the common geographical authorities. . . . What so many continental readers have experienced on the perusal of the English Clarissa, has often been felt by me in running over for the first time certain Chinese romances."

1860 LAURENCE OLIPHANT, *Narrative of the Earl of Elgin's Mission to China and Japan,* New York, Harper, 1860, 650 pp.
Drawn by Emerson from the Boston Athenæum on June 9, 1860. This volume deals primarily with the expansion of Occidental trade in the Far East. It contains much information about Indian, Chinese and Japanese customs, methods of trade, civilization, and relations with the West, but little of religious significance.

1863 JAMES LEGGE, The Chinese Classics: with a Translation, Critical and Exegetical Notes, Prolegomena, and Copious Indexes, London, Trübner, 1861, Vols. I and II, 873 pp.
On October 7, 1863, Emerson copied three pages of quotations from Legge's translation of the Confucian texts. See *Journals,* IX, 533-35. "I am reading a better Pascal," Emerson wrote in recording his impressions. Legge's translations of the Chinese classics extended to eight volumes, the last appearing in 1872. It seems Emerson used only the first two volumes.

THE ORIENTAL LIBRARY OF HENRY WADSWORTH LONGFELLOW

ALGER, W. R., The Poetry of the East, Boston, 1856.
APPLETON, T. G., A Nile Journal, London, 1876.
—— Syrian Sunshine, Boston, 1877.
ATKINSON, JAMES, Lailí and Majnum, A Poem, London, 1836.
BERTACCHI, COSIMO, History of the Capitol of Asia, Boston, 1856.
—— Stories in Bengali, American Mission Press, 1843.
—— Chants populares de l'Inde, Paris, 1854.
—— A Trip to Rangoon, Calcutta, 1853.

BRETON, J. B. J., La Chine en miniature, Paris, 1811.

BROWN, T. R., The Essentials of Sanscrit Grammar, Southwick, 1841.

BURRITT, ELIHU, A Sanskrit Handbook, Hartford, 1876.

CALLAWAY, JOHN, Yakkun Nattannawa and Kolan Nattannawa, Cingalese Poems, London, 1829.

CARLYLE, J. D., Specimens of Arabian Poetry, London, 1810.

CHODZKO, ALEXANDER, Specimens of the Popular Poetry of Persia, London, 1842.

CLERK, MRS. GODFREY, 'Ilam-en-Nas. Historical Tales Translated from the Arabic, London, 1873.

CORNER, JULIA, China, Pictorial, Descriptive and Historical, London, 1853.

—— India Before the Sepoy Mutiny, London, 1891.

CORY, J. P., Ancient Fragments of the Phoenician, Chaldean, Egyptian . . . and Other Writers, London, 1932.

COSTELLO, L. S., The Rose Garden of Persia, London, 1845.

CURTIS, G. W., Nile Notes of a Howadji, New York, 1851.

CURZON, ROBERT, The Monasteries of the Levant, New York, 1849.

D'ISTRIA, MME. DORA, La poésie des Ottomans, Paris, 1877.

FITZGERALD, EDWARD, Rubaiyat of Omar Khayyam, London, 1872.

—— Rubaiyat of Omar Khayyam, Boston, 1878.

GLADWIN, FRANCIS, The Gulistan, Boston, 1865.

GREEY, EDWARD, The Golden Lotus, and Other Legends of Japan, Boston, 1883.

GRIFFITH, T. T. H., Idylls from the Sanscrit, London, 1856.

HOLUB, EMIL, Seven Years in South Africa, Boston, 1881.

JOHNSON, SAMUEL, Oriental Religions and their Relation to Universal Religion, India, Boston, 1872.

JOLOWICZ, HEYMANN, Polyglotte der Orientalischen Poesie, Leipzic, 1856.

JULIEN, STANISLAS, Hoei-lan-ki, ou l'Histoire du cercle de craie, drame, en prose et en vers, London, 1832.

KEENE, H. G., The Mogul Empire, London, 1866.

KNATCHBULL, WYNDHAM, Kalila and Dimna, or The Fable of Bidpai, Oxford, 1819.

LACK, MRS. E., An Anglo-Bengali Primer, Calcutta, 1850.

MAUGHAM, R. C. F., The Alps of Arabia, London, 1875.

MONIER-WILLIAMS, MONIER, Sakoontala, or the Lost Ring, Hertford, 1855.

MUIR, JOHN, India as Represented in the Hymns of the Rig Veda, Edinburgh, 1868.

NARDI, FRANCESCO, Ricordi di un Viaggio in Oriente, Roma, 1866.

NEWMAN, FRANCIS W., The Text of the Iguvine Transcriptions with Interlinear Translation and Notes, London, 1864.

OGILBY, JOHN, Asia, London, 1623.

—— China, London, 1661.

RIDLEY, JAMES, Tales of the Genii, London, 1895.

ST. NICHON, ABBÉ DE, A Religious Journey in the East, London, 1853.

SALE, GEORGE, The Koran, London, 1825.

SCHACK, A. F. VON, Poesie und Kunst der Araber in Spanien und Sicielien, Berlin, 1865.

SCHIER, CHARLES, Fables de Lokman surnommé le Sage, en Arabe, Paris, 1850.

TAYLOR, BAYARD, A Visit to India, China and Japan, New York, 1855.

—— Egypt and Iceland, New York, 1874.

TIFFANY, OSMOND, The Canton Chinese, Boston, 1849.

TUCKEY, J. K., Expedition to the River Zaire, London, 1818.

VINCENT, FRANK, The Land of the White Elephant, New York, 1884.

WARNER, C. D., My Winter on the Nile, Hartford, 1876.

—— Mummies and Moslems, Hartford, 1876.

—— In the Levant, Boston, 1877.

WEBER, ALBRECHT, History of Indian Literature, London, 1878.

WILKINS, CHARLES, The Bhagvat-Geeta, or Dialogues of Kreeshna and Arjoon, London, 1785.

—— The Bhagvat-Geeta, or Dialogues of Kreeshna and Arjoon, New York, 1867.

NOTES

PART ONE: INTRODUCTION

1. Oliver Wendell Holmes, *Ralph Waldo Emerson,* Boston, Houghton Mifflin, 1885, p. 287.

2. *Ibid.*

3. *The Complete Works of Ralph Waldo Emerson, with a Biographical Introduction and Notes,* ed. Edward Waldo Emerson (Centenary Ed.), Boston and New York, Houghton Mifflin, 1903-12, VIII, 193. In all future citations this collection will be referred to as *Works.* The passage appears also in the *Journal* of Aug. 10, 1834 (III, 324).

4. *Journals of Ralph Waldo Emerson with Annotations,* ed. E. W. Emerson and W. E. Forbes, Boston and New York, Houghton Mifflin. 1909-14, X, 220-21. In all future citations this series will be referred to as *Journals.*

5. Amos Bronson Alcott, *Table-Talk,* Boston, Roberts, 1877, p. 35.

6. Amos Bronson Alcott, *Tablets,* Boston, Roberts, 1879, p. 135.

7. *The Writings of Henry David Thoreau,* ed. Bradford Torrey (Walden Ed.) Boston and New York, Houghton Mifflin, 1906, II, 192. This series consists of both Thoreau's published works and the *Journal,* which appeared posthumously. To distinguish between them, in all future citation, the former will be referred to as *Writings* and the latter as the *Journal.*

8. Holmes, *Emerson,* p. 381.

9. Mark Van Doren, *Thoreau, A Critical Study,* Boston and New York, Houghton Mifflin, 1916, p. 95.

10. Thoreau, *Journal,* VIII, 134-35. See Appendix for the editions of the *Rigveda* known in Concord. This passage suggests that Thoreau read German translators. I have, however, found no specific reference to the work of any German scholar. The italics are added.

11. Emerson, *Journals,* X, 248.

12. Emerson, *Works,* VII, 218-19.

13. Moncure Conway, *Emerson at Home and Abroad,* Boston, Osgood, 1882, p. 359.

14. Emerson, *Journals,* IX, 422.

15. Thoreau, *Writings*, II, 110.

16. Emerson, *Journals*, II, 55.

17. *Ibid.*, VII, 256-57.

18. *Ibid.*, IV, 190.

19. *Ibid.*, VII, 510.

20. James Eliot Cabot, *A Memoir of Ralph Waldo Emerson*, Boston and New York, Houghton Mifflin, 1887, I, 290.

21. Thoreau, *Writings*, I, 72.

22. F. B. Sanborn, *The Life of Henry David Thoreau*, Boston and New York, Houghton Mifflin, 1917, p. 260.

23. F. B. Sanborn and W. T. Harris, *A. Bronson Alcott, His Life and Philosophy*, Boston, Roberts, 1893, I, 165.

24. *Ibid.*, I, 332.

25. *The Dial*, III, 82 (July, 1842).

26. *Loc. cit.*

27. *Ibid.*, III, 83.

28. *Ibid.*, III, 85.

29. *Ibid.*, III, 331.

30. *Loc. cit.*

31. *Ibid.*, III, 340.

32. G. W. Cooke, *An Historical and Biographical Introduction to The Dial*, Cleveland, The Rowfant Club, 1902, pp. 196-211. This is the most complete analysis of the *Dial* and its contributors.

33. The exact editions from which selections were made and additional illustrative quotations will be found in Appendix.

34. The texts to which I am most indebted for this survey of Indian literature are those of Arthur A. Macdonnell, *A History of Sanskrit Literature*, London, 1917; and Moriz Winternitz, *A History of Indian Literature*, University of Calcutta, 1927.

The following is a list of the standard translations into English of the sacred scriptures of India. Of the *Rig Veda*, or "The Veda of Psalms": H. H. Wilson and E. B. Cowell, *Rig Veda Sanhita*, London, 1854-88; R. T. H. Griffith, *Hymns of the Rig Veda*, Benares, 1896-97; Max Müller and H. Oldenburg, *Vedic Hymns*, Oxford, 1891-97. Of the *Yajur Veda*, or "The Veda of Formulas": R. T. H. Griffith, *Texts of the White Yajur Veda*, Benares, 1893; A. B. Keith, "The Veda of the Black Yajur School," *Harvard Oriental Series*, 1914. Of the *Samaveda*, or "The Veda of Chants": J. Stevenson, *The Sanhita of the Sama Veda*, London, 1842; R. T. H. Griffith, *Hymns of the Sama Veda*, Benares, 1893. Of the *Atharvaveda*, or "The Veda of Charms": R. T. H. Griffith, *Hymns of the*

Atharva Veda, Benares, 1895-96; W. D. Whitney and C. R. Lanman, "Atharva-Veda Sanhita, with Critical and Exegetical Commentary," *Harvard Oriental Series*, 1905; M. Bloomfield, *Hymns of the Atharva Veda*, Oxford, 1897.

Very few readers of this book will be likely to explore the *Brahmanas*, or "Priestlies," and *Aranyakas*, or "Forest Treatises." The English translations will therefore not be tabulated here. It may be noted, however, that the list of translators includes the names of J. Eggeling, H. Oertel, M. Bloomfield, M. Haug, and A. B. Keith.

Of the *Upanishads*, or "Philosophic Seances," the best modern translation, already referred to, in the preface of this study, is R. E. Hume, *The Thirteen Principal Upanishads*, Oxford, 1921. Other books containing both translation and exposition are: A. E. Gough, *The Philosophy of the Upanishads and Ancient Indian Metaphysics*, London, 1882; S. C. Vasu, *Sacred Books of the Hindus*, Allahabad, 1911; M. Monier-Williams, *Indian Wisdom; or Examples of the Religious, Philosophical and Ethical Doctrines of the Hindus*, London, 1875; J. Muir, *Metrical Translations from Sanskrit Writers, with an Introduction, Many Prose Versions, and Parallel Passages from Classical Authors*, London, 1879; Anonymous, *The Spirit of the Upanishads; or, the Aphorisms of the Wise: A Collection of Texts, Sayings, Proverbs . . . Expressing the Cream of Hindu Philosophic Thought*, Chicago, 1907; L. D. Barnett, *Brahma-Knowledge: An Outline of the Philosophy of the Vedanta as Set Forth by the Upanishads and by Sankara*, London, 1911; R. G. Milburn, *Religious Mysticism of the Upanishads: Selected Texts, Translations and Notes*, Calcutta, 1919.

While the above list of English translations is by no means complete, it will probably serve the purposes of the general reader, since it contains the outstanding mystical or religious documents. Translations of other Hindu scriptures, such as the sutras and puranas, may be found by consulting the files of the *Harvard Oriental Series, Trübner's Oriental Series, Sacred Books of the East, Wealth of India Series, Sacred Books of the Hindus Series*, and the *Bibliotheca Indica Series*. See Note 58 for the *Bhagavadgita*.

35. *Rigveda*, X. 129. Quoted in Sydney Cave, *Redemption Hindu and Christian*, Oxford University Press, 1919, pp. 34-35. The name of the translator is not cited. The title of this book suggests Christian apologetics, but it does not strictly belong in this field. Few books contain more valuable analyses of the beginnings of Brahmanic speculation and Vedanta doctrine. This is one of the most scholarly works in these fields. Another rendering of this *Rigveda* passage, together with a discussion, may be

found in John Muir, *Original Sanskrit Texts*, London, Trübner, 1872, V, 356.

36. Winternitz, *op. cit.*, p. 161.

37. *Ibid.*, p. 187.

38. Max Müller, *Chips from a German Workshop*, New York, Scribner, 1869, I, 113. See also Julius Eggeling, "The Satapatha-Brahmana," *Sacred Books of the East*, ed., F. Max Müller, Oxford, 1882, XII, ix: "In the whole range of literature few works are probably less calculated to excite the interest of any outside the very limited number of specialists, than the ancient theological writings of the Hindus, known by the name of Brahmanas. For wearisome prolixity of exposition, characterized by dogmatic assertion and a flimsy symbolism rather than by serious reasoning, these works are perhaps not equalled anywhere. . . . [But] The Brahmanas, it is well known, form our chief, if not our only, source of information regarding one of the most important periods in the social and mental development of India. They represent the intellectual activity of a sacerdotal caste which, by turning to account the religious instincts of a gifted and naturally devout race, had succeeded in transforming a primitive worship of the powers of nature into a highly artificial system of sacrificial ceremonies, and was ever intent on deepening and extending its hold on the minds of the people, by surrounding its own vocation with the halo of sanctity and divine inspiration." Another interesting comment will be found in J. N. Farquhar, *An Outline of the Religious Literature of India*, Oxford University Press, 1920, p. 27: "One's first reading of a Brahmana is an extraordinary experience. It seems as if the men who composed these interminable gossiping lectures had left realities far behind them, and were living in a dreary realm of shadowy gods and men and topsy-turvy morality and religion, in which nothing belongs to the world we know except the sacrificial meats and drinks and the fees paid to the priestly dreamers. Yet in the midst of this waste of arid ritualism and childish speculation one finds the beginnings of grammar, of astronomy, of etymology, and of the philosophy of the *Atman*."

39. Paul Deussen, *The Philosophy of the Upanishads*, trans. by A. S. Geden, Edinburgh, 1906, p. 39.

40. Winternitz, *op. cit.*, I, 264.

41. On this subject consider Richard Garbe, *The Philosophy of Ancient India*, Chicago, Open Court, 1897, pp. 3-4: "The origin of the Indian belief in metempsychosis is unfortunately still shrouded in obscurity. In the old Vedic time a joyful view of life prevailed in India in which we discover no germs whatever of the conception which subsequently dominated and oppressed the thought of the whole nation; as yet the nation

did not feel life as a burden but as the supreme good, and its eternal continuance after death was longed for as the reward of a pious life. In the place of this innocent joy of life suddenly enters, without noticeable evidences of transition, the conviction that the existence of the individual is a journey full of torments from death to death. It is natural enough, therefore, to suspect foreign influence in this sudden revolution of thought. . . . It is well known that the belief that the human soul passes after death into the trunks of trees and the bodies of animals is extremely widespread among half-savage tribes. On the basis of this fact . . . the Aryans, on their amalgamation with the original indigenous inhabitants of India, received from these the idea of the continuance of life in animals and trees."

42. F. B. Sanborn, "Thoreau and Confucius," *The Nation*, XC (May 12, 1910), 481.

43. Emerson, *Journals*, VII, 511. See Stanley T. Williams, "Unpublished Letters of Emerson," *Journal of English and Germanic Philology*, XXVI (1927), 475-84, for interesting correspondence which identifies this friend as H. G. O. Blake, Thoreau's literary executor.

44. Emerson, *Journals*, VII, 511.

45. Thoreau, *Writings*, II, 328-29. The italics are added.

46. Sidney Cave, *Introduction to Living Religions of the East*, London, Duckworth, 1921, p. 42.

47. Arthur W. Ryder, *The Bhagavad-Gita*, University of Chicago Press, 1929, pp. xvi-xvii.

48. See Hastings, *Encyclopedia of Religion and Ethics*, for excellent expositions of the Sankhya and Yoga philosophies. These systems are the most prominent in Hindu thought; they are discussed in practically all books dealing with the subject. Several sentences from the article contributed by Professor Richard Garbe to Hastings' *Encyclopedia* will offer some understanding of the systems here. Of the Sankhya Professor Garbe writes: "Its origin must be sought in a reaction against the idealistic monism of the *Upanishads*, and its rise may be attributed to the same district of India as produced Buddhism. . . . The Sankhya system is throughout .rationalistic. It recognizes two uncreated substances, existing from all eternity, but differing essentially from one another." Of the Yoga Professor Garbe writes: "The characteristics of the Yoga philosophy, apart from points of less importance, are—(1) the rejection of the atheistic views of the Sankhya, and (2) the treatment of the doctrine of absorption as the most effectual means for the attainment of the knowledge that secures emancipation."

49. *Bhagavadgita*, II. 71; Cave, *Redemption*, p. 103.

50. Charles Wilkins, *The Bhagvat-Geeta*, London, Nourse, 1785, p. 57. This was the source of Emerson's quotation. The general *Gita* reference is V, 4-5. In the dedicatory epistle written in 1784 by Warren Hastings for Wilkins' translation appears these remarkable words: "It is not very long since the inhabitants of India were considered by many, as creatures scarce elevated above the degree of savage life; nor, I fear, is that prejudice yet wholly eradicated, though surely abated. Every instance which brings their real character home to observation will impress us with a more generous sense of feeling for their natural rights, and teach us to estimate them by the measure of our own. But such instances can only be obtained in their writings: and these will survive when the British dominion in India shall have long ceased to exist, and when the sources which it once yielded of wealth and power are lost to remembrance." (Page 13.)

51. Emerson, *Journals*, VII, 68.

52. *Bhagavadgita*, XI. 55; Cave, *Redemption*, p. 108

53. *Ibid.*, II. 31; *loc. cit.*

54. *Ibid.*, V. 2; *ibid.*, p. 109.

55. *Ibid.*, VII. 17; *ibid.*, p. 110.

56. *Ibid.*, IV. 5-8; *loc. cit.*

57. *Bhagavadgita*, IX. 34; Cave, *Living Religions*, p. 46.

58. Emerson, *Journals*, VII, 511. The extensive interest of the West in the *Bhagavadgita* is indicated by the following list of translations into English, arranged in the chronology of their appearance: Charles Wilkins, *The Bhagvat-Geeta*, London, 1785; J. Cockburn Thomson, *The Bhagavad-Gita*, Hertford, 1855; Kashinath Trimbak Telang, *Bhagavad Gita, Translated into English Blank Verse*, Bombay, 1875; William Oxley, *The Philosophy of Spirit, Illustrated by a New Version of the Bhagavat Gita*, Glasgow, 1881; John Davies, *The Bhagavad Gita, or The Sacred Lay*, London, 1882; Edwin Arnold, *The Song Celestial, or Bhagavad-Gita*, London, 1885; Mohini M. Chatterji, *The Bhagavad Gita, or The Lord's Lay*, Boston, 1887; H. Bower, *The Bhagavadgita, Translated into English and Tamil*, Madras, 1889; Kali Prasanna Sarkar, *Srimath Bhagabath Gita, or The Song Celestial*, Comilla, 1894-1901; Annie Besant, "The Bhagavad Gita, or The Lord's Song," *Lotus Leaves*, London, 1895; Pramada Das Mitra, *The Bhagavad Gita, or The Divine Ode*, Benares, 1895; A. Mahadev Sastri, *Vedic Religion, The Bhagavad Gita*, Mysore, 1901; Manmathanath Shastri, *Gita, or The Teachings of Sri-krishna*, Calcutta, 1903; L. D. Barnett, *Bhagavad Gita, or The Lord's Song*, London, 1905 [Temple Classics]; S. Subha Rao, *The Bhagavad Gita, Trans-*

lated into English, Madras, 1906; Charles Johnston, *Bhagavad Gita, The Songs of the Master,* Flushing, 1908; C. C. Caleb, *The Song Divine, or The Bhagavad-Gita: A Metrical Rendering,* London, 1911; William Q. Judge, *The Bhagavad-Gita, The Book of Devotion,* New York, 1913; Swami Paramananda, *Srimad-Bhagavad-Gita, or The Blessed Lord's Song,* Boston, 1913; Swami Swarupananda, *Bhagavad Gita,* Calcutta, 1918; Tookaram Tatya, *The Bhagavadgita, The Song of the Divine One, The Lord,* Bombay, 1920; Arthur W. Ryder, *The Bhagavad-Gita,* Chicago, 1928; W. D. P. Hill, *The Bhagavadgita,* Oxford, 1928; D. G. Mukerji, *The Song of God,* New York, 1931.

59. R. E. Hume, *The World's Living Religions,* New York, Charles Scribner, 1927, p. 117.

60. *Ibid.,* pp. 124-25.

61. *Loc. cit.*

62. H. A. Giles, *Confucianism and Its Rivals,* London, Williams, 1915, pp. 165-67.

63. Hume, *The World's Living Religions,* p. 119.

64. *Sacred Books of the East,* III, 89-90.

65. *Mencius,* VI. 1.2.2; James Legge, *The Chinese Classics,* London, Trübner, 1861, II, 272.

66. Emerson, *Works,* III, 72-73; *Mencius,* II. 1.2.11-14.

67. James Legge, *The Chinese Classics,* II, 65-66.

68. Lim Boon Keng, "The Confucian Way of Thinking of the World and of God," *Asiatic Review,* XV (April, 1919), 175-76.

69. *Ibid.*

70. See W. E. Soothill, *The Three Religions of China,* Oxford University Press, 1923, and James Legge, *The Life and Teachings of Confucius,* London, Trübner, 1887, for excellent discussions of Confucianism and its scriptures. In brief, there are three books from which a clear insight into the character and teaching of Confucius may be obtained. These are the *Analects,* which contain his sayings and dialogues; the *Great Learning,* which shows the aim of education; and the *Doctrine of the Mean,* which presents the teaching of Confucius as to the golden mean of character and conduct. This work and the *Analects* were said to have been committed to writing by disciples. The fourth great book of the Confucian canon, entitled *Mencius,* contains the words of Mencius, the most famous follower of Confucius, not as written by himself, however, but by his disciples.

71. Edward G. Browne, *A Literary History of Persia,* London, Unwin, 1902. See also Margaret Smith, *Studies in Early Mysticism in the Near*

and Middle East, London, Sheldon Press, 1931. Some scholars are of the opinion that there is a relation between Sufism and Hinduism.

72. See also R. A. Nicholson, *The Mystics of Islam,* London, Bell, 1914, p. 3. With reference to the derivation of the name of the sect Nicholson writes: "Until recently its derivation was in dispute. Most Sufis, flying in the face of etymology, have derived it from an Arabic root which conveys the notion of 'purity'; this would make 'Sufi' mean 'one who is pure in heart' or 'one of the elect.' Some European scholars identified it with σοφος in the sense of 'theosophist.'" But Nöldeke, in an article written twenty years ago, showed conclusively that the name was derived from *sūf* (wool), and was originally applied to those Moslem ascetics who, in imitation of Christian hermits, clad themselves in coarse woollen garb as a sign of penitence and renunciation of wordly vanities." Professor Nicholson also traces the connections of Sufism with Hinduism, Buddhism, Neo-Platonism, and mediaeval theology. Other valuable books that will serve as excellent introduction to the subject are Claud Field's *Mystics and Saints of Islam,* and Shaikh Muhammad Tobal's *The Development of Metaphysics in Persia.*

73. For a tabulation of Sufi doctrine, see *Selections from the Rubaiyat and Odes of Hafiz the Great Mystic and Lyric Poet of Persia . . . together with An Account of Sufi Mysticism,* by a Member of the Persia Society of London, London, John M. Watkins, 1920, pp. 16-17.

74. This list of symbols is adapted from the *Selections from the Rubaiyat and Odes of Hafiz,* London, 1920.

75. Nicholson, *The Mystics of Islam,* p. 103.

76. *Ibid.,* p. 104.

77. *Selections from the Rubaiyat and Odes of Hafiz,* p. 11.

78. *Centenary Review of the Asiatic Society of Bengal,* published by the Society, Calcutta, 1885, p. 3.

79. *Ibid.,* p. 2.

80. Winternitz, *A History of Indian Literature,* I, 11: "Jones had already in his youth occupied himself with Oriental poetry, and translated Arabic and Persian poems into English."

81. *Centenary Review A. S. of B.,* p. 2.

82. *Ibid.,* p. 12.

83. *Ibid.,* p. 75. See this same source for other details of Jones's life. He was born in 1746.

84. *Ibid.,* p. 55.

85. *Ibid.,* pp. 55-56.

86. *Ibid.,* p. 75.

87. Colebrooke lived from 1765 to 1837 (*Ibid.*, p. 75).

88. *Ibid.*, pp. 75-76.

89. Sir Charles Wilkins (1750-1833) came to India as a writer in the employ of the East India Company's Civil Service (*Ibid.*, p. 76).

90. *Ibid.*, p. 76.

91. Winternitz, *History of Indian Literature*, I, 11. See notes 50 and 58 for complete bibliographical information and a quotation from Warren Hastings' dedicatory epistle.

92. *Loc. cit.*

93. The *Dial* selections were credited to the "Veeshnoo Sarma."

94. The article in the *Dictionary of National Biography* states that during Wilson's entire stay in India he was secretary of the Asiatic Society of Bengal. He lived from 1786 to 1860.

95. *Centenary Review A. S. of B.*, p. 78

96. *Loc. cit.*

97. *Loc. cit.*

98. Brian Houghton Hodgson lived from 1800 to 1894. A valuable article on Hodgson's work in India will be found in the supplement to the *Dictionary of National Biography*. Note the following passage from this article: "Of Sanscrit manuscripts he collected more than four hundred, which are now divided among the libraries of Calcutta, London, and Paris. The portion sent to Paris supplied Eugène Burnouf with the materials for his two epoch-making works, which first placed the knowledge of Northern Buddhism on a scientific foundation. Burnouf's posthumous 'Le Lotus de la Bonne Loi' (Paris, 1852) is dedicated to Hodgson, 'comme au fondateur de la veritable étude du Bouddhisme par les textes et les monuments.'"

99. *Centenary Review A. S. of B.*, p. 80.

100. *Loc. cit.*

101. *Centenary Volume of the Royal Asiatic Society of Great Britain and Ireland, 1823-1923*, ed. Frederick Eden Pargiter, published by the Society, London, 1923.

102. *Ibid.*, p. xi.

103. *Ibid.*, p. vii.

104. *The Journal of the Bombay Branch of the Royal Asiatic Society*, XXIV (1917), 316 ff.

105. Moriz Winternitz, *A History of Indian Literature*, I, 19.

106. *Loc. cit.*

107. *Encyclopedia Britannica*, XIVth edition.

108. Winternitz, *op. cit.*, I, 20-21.

109. *New International Encyclopedia*, New York, Dodd, Mead, 1928.

110. Most of the Thoreau-Cholmondeley correspondence was edited by F. B. Sanborn. See his "Thoreau and his English Friend Thomas Cholmondeley," *The Atlantic Monthly*, LXXII (December, 1893), 741-56.

111. *Ibid.*, p. 745.

112. *Loc. cit.*

113. *Ibid.*, p. 746.

114. *Daniel Ricketson and His Friends*, ed. Anna and Walton Ricketson, Boston and New York, Houghton Mifflin, 1902, pp. 52-53. The correspondence of Ricketson and Thoreau published in this volume presents a suggestive picture of the manner in which Thoreau's Oriental enthusiasm affected his friends. On March 7, 1858, Ricketson wrote as follows to Thoreau (p. 62): "I no longer wonder that you had Homer, Valmiki, Vyasa, etc. in your Walden shanty. They have already peeped into my windows, and I shall not be surprised to have them seated within as my guests ere long. You need not be astonished if you hear of my swearing in Sanscrit or at least in Pan crit! I have just got a taste of these old fellows, and what a glorious feast awaits me! What a lucky mortal are you to be the possessor of those priceless treasures, sent you from England! I am about starting upon a pilgrimage into the country of these ancient Hindus. . . . Give me your hand, Gabriel, and lead the way." In the same letter (p. 63) Ricketson sent Thoreau his " 'Orphics' by a Modern Hindu." Ricketson was a Quaker. His orphics were after the manner of Alcott's contributions to the *Dial*.

115. Sanborn, *Thoreau*, 1917, p. 306.

116. Emerson, *Works*, IV, 53-54. See Robert Hume, *The World's Living Religions*, New York, Scribner, 1927, pp. 200-1: "The Greek writers were deeply impressed by the religion of their combatants from Asia. Herodotus visited and described Persia. Plato was prevented from fulfilling his desire to go to Persia and study Zoroastrianism by the Graeco-Persian Wars, which ended with Alexander's complete victory."

117. Emerson, *Works*, IV, 48.

118. *Ibid.*, IV, 52.

119. *Ibid.*, IV, 49.

120. *Atlantic Monthly*, LI, 826.

121. Garbe, *The Philosophy of Ancient India*, p. 38.

122. F. W. Bussell, *Religious Thought and Heresy in the Middle Ages*, London, Robert Scott, 1918, p. 171.

123. *Ibid.*, p. 169.

124. Sir William Jones, *Works*, London, Robinson, 1799, I, 360-61.

125. H. T. Colebrooke, *Miscellaneous Essays*, London, Trübner, 1873, I, 436-37 Pythagoras' chief indebtedness is in the doctrine of metempsychosis. Modern Egyptology seems to prove he could not have taken the doctrine from the people of the Nile. Garbe, *op. cit.*, pp. 41-42, writes: "In an . . . exhaustive and comprehensive manner, but without knowledge of his predecessors, Leopold von Schroeder has also treated this subject in an essay, *Pythagoras und die Inder* (Leipsic, 1884)."

126. Garbe, *The Philosophy of Ancient India*, p. 32.

127. Garbe lists the following works as valuable aids in the study of Greek and Oriental parallels, but insufficient in knowledge of Oriental sources (p. 37) : Ed Röth, *Geschichte unserer abendländischen Philosophie*, 1846; C. B. Schlüter, *Aristoteles' Metaphysik eine Tochter der Samkhya-Lehre des Kapila*, 1874.

128. Bussell, *op. cit.*, p. 169.

129. *Loc. cit.*

130. *Ibid.*, p. 173.

131. *Loc. cit.*

132. *Loc. cit.*

133. *Loc. cit.*

134. *Ibid.*, p. 174.

135. *Loc. cit.*

136. *Ibid.*, p. 176.

137. Lassen, *Indische Alterthumskunde*, III, 379 ff.

138. Garbe, *The Philosophy of Ancient India*, p. 46.

139. *Ibid.*, p. 49.

140. *Loc. cit.*

141. *Loc. cit.*

142. *Ibid.*, p. 51.

143. *Loc. cit.*

144. W. S. Urquhart, *The Vedanta and Modern Thought*, London, Oxford University Press, 1928.

145. *Ibid.*, p. 192.

146. *Ibid.*, p. 193.

147. *Ibid.*, p. 194.

148. *Loc. cit.*

149. *Ibid.*, p. 195.

150. *Loc. cit.*

151. *Ibid.*, p. 198.

152. Loc. cit.

153. Two very valuable books, dealing with comparative thought, may well be noted as a conclusion to this section. M. G. Pauthier, *Mémoire sur l'Origine et la Propagation de la Doctrine du Tao,* Paris, Librairie Orientale, 1831, discusses the connections between the pantheism of Lao Tsu and the *Kena* and *Isha Upanishads.* Rudolf Otto, *Mysticism East and West,* New York, Macmillan, 1932, is a comparative analysis of the nature of mysticism and aims "to comprehend such great spiritual phenomena as, for instance, the German Meister Eckhardt, the Indian Sankara, the Greek Plotinus, the mystics of the Buddhist Mahayana School, in all their characteristic individuality." Unfortunately this book was published at too late a date to be used in this study.

PART TWO: EMERSON

1. Cabot, *A Memoir,* I, 103.
2. *Ibid.,* I, 104.
3. *Loc. cit.*
4. *Loc. cit.*
5. *Ibid.,* I, 80-81.
6. *The Christian Register,* probably the outstanding Unitarian journal of the time, printed on Dec. 7, 1821, over eight columns of intelligence regarding the writings and work of Rammohun Roy. All other news was excluded from the four-column front page. It is easy to understand why the editors were aroused by the so-called "Indian Unitarian Controversy." As editorially explained in a later number (June 7, 1822), Rammohun Roy, after having become acquainted with Christianity and convinced of its superiority over the religions of India, selected and published for the use of his countrymen the preceptive parts of the *Gospels,* omitting what he called "abstruse doctrines and miraculous relations." The reasons for the omissions were that the former were subject to dispute and the latter were not more wonderful than the miraculous relations handed down in Indian literature. The book was published in Calcutta in 1829 under the title of *The Precepts of Jesus a Sufficient Guide to Peace and Happiness.* It is reprinted in *The English Works of Raja Ram Mohun Roy,* ed. J. C. Ghose, Calcutta, 1887. But Baptist missionaries in Calcutta attacked the work with great severity, and a journalistic war was waged in the magazines published in India. Roy eventually defended his religious activities and his book in another work to which he gave the

ironic title of *An Appeal to the Christian Public, in Defence of 'The Precepts of Jesus.'* The controversy in many ways duplicated the Unitarian-Trinitarian debates in New England. This was probably natural, for the contestants were, on the one hand, a Hindu widely read in the monistic scriptures, and on the other, a Trinitarian missionary, Joshua Marshman.

In the introduction to *The Precepts of Jesus,* Rammohon Roy had candidly stated the purpose of his work. Pointing out that much of the traditional Christian dogma and ecclesiasticism was unintelligible to the natives of Asia, he insisted that the morals of Christ were alone "intelligible alike to the learned and the unlearned," and effective in elevating men to a high and liberal notion of one God, or in regulating the conduct of life and assuaging disappointment, pain and death. The rub came when Roy questioned the effectiveness and reasonableness of the Trinitarian missionary program in India. *The Christian Register* on May 24, 1822, pointed out that Roy's chief objection to the religion presented by missionaries to his countrymen was "those doctrines which Unitarians deem *corruptions* of Christianity, and no part of Christianity itself— viz., against the doctrines of the *trinity, innate moral depravity, unconditional election, etc.*" The missionaries found a subtle opponent in this Hindu. A telling example of his method of debate is found in his *Appeal to the Christian Public.* What peace of mind, he asked, could be bestowed upon an Asiatic, a total stranger to the Christian world, by communicating to him such a doctrine as that found in the first verse of *St. John:* "In the beginning was the Word, and the Word was with God, and the Word was God." Would not the Asiatic find himself totally at a loss to reconcile this dogma as follows: A is B, and A is also with B? Continuing, he wrote that although "the interpretations given us of such texts by truly learned and candid divines be ever so satisfactory, yet to those that are strangers to these explanations, they cannot be intelligible; nor can it be expected from the order of things, that each can happily find at hand an able interpreter, to whom he can have recourse for an explanation, whenever he may be involved in difficulties or doubts." (*The English Works of Raja Ram Mohun Roy,* II, 92-93.)

So it was natural that American Unitarians should rejoice in the work of a Hindu who eschewed the dogmas of the Church but embraced the moral precepts of Jesus, and the founding of a Unitarian Society in Calcutta. *The Christian Register* of May 17, 1822, expressed the sentiment in Boston with these words: "It must be a source of high gratification to our readers thus to perceive the progress of what we deem the truth, in remote parts of the world, and against all the obstacles presented, either by interest or prejudice. For ourselves we will not dissemble that we received this intelligence with the most lively satisfaction; partly because every new instance of the triumph of Unitarian principles amongst those who have once been Trinitarians, must, necessarily, in some degree shake the confidence of those who remain, in the soundness of their own principles, and induce them not only to cherish feelings of greater tenderness to Unitarians, but to listen with greater candor to their reasons 'for the hope that is in them.' "

An excellent scholarly evaluation of Rammohun Roy and the early Brahmo Somaj will be found in J. N. Farquhar, *Modern Religious Movements in India,* New York, Macmillan, 1919.

7. Cabot, *A Memoir,* I, 80-81.

8. Emerson, *Journals,* I, 5.

9. *Ibid.,* I, 21.

10. *Ibid.,* I, 69.

11. *Ibid.,* V, 82.

12. *Ibid.,* I, 108.

13. *Ibid,* I, 157.

14. "Religion and Character of the Hindus," *The Edinburgh Review,* XXIX (1818), 388.

15. *Loc. cit.*

16. Emerson, *Journals,* I, 327.

17. *Ibid.,* I, 341.

18. *Ibid.,* IV, 318-19.

19. *Ibid.,* II, 63-64.

20. Emerson, *Works,* X, 226-27. Note also *Works,* XI, 489-90, from which I quote: "I find something stingy in the unwilling and disparaging admission of these foreign opinions—opinions from all parts of the world—by our churchmen, as if only to enhance by their dimness the superior light of Christianity."

21. *Ibid.,* I, 126.

22. Emerson, *Journals,* V, 334-35.

23. *Ibid.,* VII, 241-42.

24. *Ibid.,* IX, 15.

25. *Ibid.,* IV, 425.

26. Emerson, *Works,* I, 91.

27. Other passages in which Emerson discloses his attitudes toward the Oriental religions and scriptures will be found in *Journals,* II, 58; IV, 256; V, 81; VI, 168; VII, 106; IX, 116 and *Works,* II, 7, 9, 28; III, 72, 73; IV, 4, 5; VII, 166; VII, 179; X, 544.

28. Emerson, *Journals*, III, 321.

29. *Chandogya Upanishad*, VI. 1 ff; Hume, *Thirteen Principal Upanishads*, p. 240.

30. Emerson, *Journals*, III, 402. The italics are added.

31. *Ibid.*, II, 323.

32. The statement occurs nine times in the *Chandogya Upanishad;* the references are as follows: VI.8.6; VI.9.4; VI.10.3; VI.11.3; VI.12.3; VI.13.3; VI.14.3; VI.15.3; VI.16.3.

33. Emerson, *Journals*, III, 399.

34. Emerson, *Works*, II, 271-72. See Thoreau, *Writings*, I, 70-71: "The wisest man preaches no doctrines; he has no scheme; he sees no rafter, not even a cobweb, against the heavens. It is clear sky." Also Thoreau, *Writings*, IV, 475: "Knowledge does not come to us by details, but in flashes of light from heaven." Alcott offers a passage in *Tablets* (p. 164), closely akin to Emerson's Over-Soul: "The new calculus is ours. An organon alike serviceable to metaphysician and naturalist—whereby things answer to thought, facts are resolved into truths, image into ideas, matter into mind, power into personality, man into God; the One soul in all souls revealed as the Creative Spirit pulsating in all breasts, immanent in all atoms, prompting all wills, and personally embosoming all persons in one unbroken synthesis of Being."

35. Emerson, *Works*, II, 294.

36. *Ibid.*, II, 292. An interesting connection appears between these sentences and the motto on the title page of Anquetil Duperron's *Oupnek' hat*, which reads: "Quisquis Deum intelligit, Deus fit."

37. *Ibid.*, II, 269.

38. *Loc. cit.*

39. *Ibid.*, XII, 20.

40. Emerson, *Journals*, III, 200.

41. *Ibid.*, IV, 403. It may be that Emerson's reticence was largely due to his desire to avoid unsettling the cherished beliefs of others.

42. Cabot, *A Memoir*, II, 499-500.

43. Emerson, *Journals*, IV, 416.

44. Cabot, *op. cit.*, I, 341.

45. Emerson, *Works*, VIII, 223.

46. Emerson, *Journals*, IV, 424.

47. Emerson, *Works*, VIII, 221.

48. S. Radhakrishnan, *Indian Philosophy*, New York, Macmillan, 1922, I, 173. But it should be remembered that in Emerson's mind there is perhaps some confusion of the Vedantic principles of the Brahman and the law of Karma in the interest of idealistic Platonism.

49. Emerson, *Works*, X, 8.

50. For a fuller discussion of these Hindu concepts see Surendranath Dasgupta, *A History of Indian Philosophy*, Cambridge University Press, 1922, I, 44, 45, 61, 65, and 110.

51. William James, *Varieties of Religious Experience*, New York, Longmans, Green, 1928, p. 416. *Cf.* St. Augustine's famous sentence, "We can know what God is not, but not what He is." (Trinity, VIII, 2.) *Cf.* also Rudolf Otto, *The Idea of the Holy*, Oxford University Press, 1928, p. 189: "But this 'negative theology' does not mean that faith and feeling are dissipated and reduced to nothing; on the contrary, it contains within it the loftiest spirit of devotion, and it is out of such 'negative' attributes that Chrysostom fashions the most solemn confessions and prayers. He thereby shows once more that feeling and experience reach far beyond conceiving, and that a conception negative in form may often become the symbol (what we have called an "ideogram") for a content of meaning which, if absolutely unutterable, is none the less in the highest degree positive. And the example of Chrysostom at the same time shows that a 'negative theology' can and indeed must arise . . . from purely and genuinely religious roots, namely, the experience of the numinous."

52. Vasudeva Kirtikar, *Studies in Vedanta*, Bombay, Taraporevala, 1924, p. 29.

53. Quoted by Kirtikar, *ibid.*, p. 29.

54. Edward Emerson, *Emerson in Concord*, Boston, Houghton Mifflin, 1890, p. 249. Emerson's youthful acquaintance with Platonic thought must not be forgotten in this connection.

55. Emerson, *Journals*, IX, 302-3.

56. *Loc. cit.*

57. *Ibid.*, X, 162. The editors of the *Works* note that the passage also appeared in Emerson's notebook called *Orientalist*. If there was thus a double entry, the emphasis on this passage cannot be stressed too much.

58. Emerson, *Works*, VI, 324.

59. *Ibid.*, VI, 313.

60. *Ibid.*, IV, 178.

61. Kirtikar, *Studies in Vedanta*, p. 40.

62. *Ibid.*, p. 39.

63. S. Radhakrishnan, *The Vedanta, According to Sankara and Ramanuja.*, London, Allen and Unwin, 1928, p. 146.

64. *Ibid.*, p. 135.

65. *Ibid.*, p. 149.

66. From Ramdas' *Dasa Bodha*, VI, 5. Quoted by Kirtikar, *op. cit.*, p. 40 *note*.

67. In this connection consider the following passages from Emerson, *Works*, I, 64-65. "The world proceeds from the same spirit as the body of man. It is a remoter and inferior incarnation of God, a projection of God in the unconscious. But it differs from the body in one important respect. It is not, like that, now subjected to the human will. Its serene order is inviolable by us. It is, therefore, to us, the present expositor of the divine mind." Consider also the following sentence in *Emerson in Concord*, p. 61: "The rock seemed good to me. I think we can never afford to part with Matter." For other references to Emerson's view of matter see his *Works*, I, 26, 27, 33, 34; VIII, 5, 8, 9, 10, and XII, 16, 17.

68. *Ibid.*, III, 48.

69. *Loc. cit.* George Williamson, in an interesting article, "Emerson the Oriental," *University of California Chronicle*, XXX, 271-88 (July, 1928), also discusses this, and other points, in Emerson's Orientalism. I am indebted to this article for valuable suggestions.

70. *Ibid.*, IX, 287.

71. *Ibid.*, IX, 348.

72. *Ibid.*, VI, 425. Before presenting passages from Thoreau and Alcott to show their kinship in belief with Emerson, a last passage from the *Journals* should be included, since it is too suggestive to be excluded. In 1855 (*Journals*, VIII, 578) Emerson wrote: "In this gale of warring elements, it was necessary to bind souls to human life, as mariners in a tempest lash themselves to the mast and bulwarks of a ship; so Nature employed certain illusions as her ties and straps. A rattle, a red coral, a doll, an apple, a horse-chestnut for a child keeps him going, climbing and tumbling about, and educates his muscle, blood and bones; skates, a river, a boat, a horse, a gun, the boy; (*esprit-du-corps*) party-spirit, and maids draw the youth; money and power and his children, the man. Slowly and rarely and condescendingly the masking veil falls, and he is allowed to see that all is one stuff cooked and painted under a hundred counterfeit appearances. When the boys come into my yard for leave to gather horse-chestnuts, I enter into Nature's game, and affect to grant the permission reluctantly,—fearing that any moment they will find out they are fooled." For further passages on Maya and Illusion in the *Journals*, see III, 285, 289; V, 179; VII, 505; VIII, 414. In the *Works*, III, 50, 51, 52; VI, 325; VIII, 169; IX, 243. Cabot, *A Memoir*, I, 217, 218 and II, 641 also offer valuable commentary.

Thoreau writes in his *Writings*, II, 106-7: "Children, who play life, discern its true law and relations more clearly than men, who fail to live it worthily, but who think that they are wiser by experience, that is, by failure. I have read in a Hindoo book, that 'there was a king's son, who, being expelled in infancy from his native city, was brought up by a forester, and, growing to maturity in that state, imagined himself to belong to the barbarous race with which he lived. One of his father's ministers having discovered him, revealed to him what he was, and the misconception of his character was removed, and he knew himself to be a prince. So soul,' continues the Hindoo philosopher, 'from the circumstances in which it is placed, mistakes its own character, until the truth is revealed to it by some holy teacher, and then it knows itself to be Brahme.' I perceive that we inhabitants of New England live this mean life that we do because our vision does not penetrate the surface of things. We think that that *is* which *appears* to be." For another passage from Thoreau see his *Journal*, I, 276.

Alcott also speaks specifically, using the Hindu term Maya in *Table-Talk*, pp. 113-14: "Nature urges herself to complete introversion, and the 'breath of Life' is compelled to sustain itself by contest with the clay dwelling in which it finds itself. In satisfying the physical, the spiritual is excited to activity, and gradually gains ascendance and independence. The 'mask of life' and the subjection of the spiritual to material ends is seen to be only Maya,—a mere delusion of the sense. All this servitude and slavery has been only for self-knowledge, of the Universal in the Particular." For other passages from Alcott see *Table-Talk,* p. 130, and *Tablets,* p. 176.

73. Radhakrishnan, *The Vedanta*, p. 205.

74. Kirtikar, *Studies in Vedanta*, p. 37.

75. Emerson, *Works*, IX, 57-58. This passage, with the Hindu metaphor of the world sleeping as an egg of stone in subsequent lines will be discussed in the later section. The Hindu source of the metaphor is added proof to the Vedantic aspect of Emerson's doctrine of emanation.

76. Emerson, *Journals*, V, 533.

77. Kirtikar, *Studies in Vedanta*, p. 37.

78. Radhakrishnan, *Indian Philosophy*, I, 181.

79. *Aitareya Aranyaka*, II. 1.8.1. Quoted by Radhakrishnan, *op. cit.*, I, 181. The most accessible translation for the general student is that by A. B. Keith, Oxford, 1909.

80. Kirtikar, *Studies in Vedanta*, p. 36.

81. *Ibid.*

82. Note the editorial comment in Emerson, *Works*, I, xxvi: "The

early recognition by Emerson of Evolution as the plan of the Universe in his first book, and everywhere in his prose and verse, has often attracted notice, first, I think, of Mr. Moncure D. Conway."

83. Cabot, *A Memoir,* II, 734.

84. Henry David Gray, *Emerson A Statement of New England Transcendentalism as Expressed in the Philosophy of its Chief Exponent,* Stanford University Press, 1917, p. 43. The doctrine has been common in Christian thought since Augustine.

85. Emerson, *Journals,* IV, 247.

86. *Ibid.,* V, 484.

87. *Ibid.,* VI, 419. And yet how contrary to the Oriental is this implied enthusiasm for the individual!

88. Emerson, *Works,* VIII, 10.

89. Alcott offers an interesting parallel thought to Emerson's doctrine in *Tablets,* p. 193: "As the male impregnates the female, so mind charges matter with form and fecundity; the spermatic world being life in transmission and body in embryo."

90. *The Cambridge History of American Literature,* New York, Putnam, 1918, II, 24.

91. See the *Autobiography and Letters of Orville Dewey,* ed. Mary E. Dewey, Boston, Roberts, 1884, p. 158, and the comment by his daughter on contemporary acceptance of Emerson's thought. Though out of sympathy on many points, Dewey defends compensation in a sermon: "But the law does stand fast. Nothing ever did, ever shall, ever can escape it. Take any essence-drop or particle of evil into your heart and life, and you shall pay for it in the loss, if not of gold or of honor, yet of the finest sense and the finest enjoyment of all things divinest, most beautiful and most blessed in your being. I know of no writer among us who has emphasized this fact, this law, more sharply than Waldo Emerson."

92. Emerson, *Journals,* VII, 123.

93. Emerson, *Works,* VI, 12.

94. *Ibid.,* II, 88.

95. Emerson, *Journals,* III, 331.

96. *Cf.* a passage in Emerson, *Works,* VI, 5, in this connection.

97. *Cf. Brihadaranyaka Upanishad,* III. 2.13. "Verily, one becomes good by good action, bad by bad action." Also *Chandogya Upanishad,* III. 14.1: "Man is a creature of will. According as he believes in this world, so will he be when he is departed." Hume, *Thirteen Principal Upanishads,* p. 209.

98. Cabot, *A Memoir,* I, 70-71. It might be suggested that the doctrine

was the result of an attempt to deal with the Christian problem of evil in terms of evolutionary idealism. However, evidence does not conclusively show that Emerson was concerned with the problem of evolution during his early youth.

99. Edward Emerson, *op. cit.*, p. 22.

100. Emerson, *Works*, I, 334-35. Alcott writes in *Table-Talk*, p. 163: "The Orientals defined Fate to be the penalty of deeds committed in a former state of existence." This is Hindu, but he continues, showing his loose understanding of the law of Karma: "And the like penalty is re-affirmed by Jews and Christians, ancestral sins being visited upon the children even to the third and fourth generation,—by imputation upon the race itself." In another passage Alcott strikes a truer Hindu tone (*Table-Talk*, p. 166): "Evil is retributive: every trespass slips fetters on the will, holds the soul in durance till contrition and repentance restore it to liberty. Not even in Pandemonium may sinners run at large, nor in Paradise without their tether. The eternal laws prevail and must be obeyed throughout the universe."

Thoreau offers little to elucidate his understanding or adoption of the Karmic law. Two passages may be noted. In the *Journal*, I, 280, he writes: "I was informed to-day that no Hindoo tyranny presided at the framing of the world,—that I am a free man of the universe, and not sentenced to any caste." See also *Writings*, II, 131: "Every path but your own is the path of fate. Keep on your own track, then."

101. Emerson, *Works*, IV, 95-96. Whether the Hindus deny the Platonic doctrine of recollection is besides the point here. Emerson obviously was not interested in possible differences between the Greek and Hindu views.

102. *Ibid.*, IV, 124.

103. *Ibid.*, IV, 145.

104. Emerson, *Journals*, VII, 93-94.

105. *Ibid.*, VII, 94.

106. *Ibid.*, VII, 120-21.

107. *Ibid.*, VII, 121.

108. Emerson, *Works*, II, 32. *Cf.* also *Journals*, V, 444: "Tantalus is but a name for you and me. *Transmigration* of Souls: that is no fable."

109. Emerson, *Journals*, X, 288.

110. *Ibid.*, VI, 419-20.

111. *Ibid.*, V, 192.

112. *Brihadaranyaka Upanishad*, IV. 4.3; Hume, *Thirteen Principal Upanishads*, p. 140.

113. *Ibid.*, IV. 4.4.

114. *Ibid.*, VI 2.15; *Ibid.*, p. 163.

115. *Ibid.*, VI. 2.16.

116. *Katha Upanishad*, I. 6.

117. Emerson, *Journals*, II, 211.

118. Emerson, *Works*, VIII, 342-43.

119. *Ibid.*, VIII, 329.

120. *Ibid.*, XII, 28.

121. *Ibid.*, X, 512.

122. *Ibid.*, IX, 126.

123. Cabot, *A Memoir*, II, 725.

124. For an exhaustive discussion of Emerson's scientific information see Harry Hayden Clark, "Emerson and Science," *Philological Quarterly*, X (July, 1931), 225-260.

125. Emerson, *Works*, III, 75.

126. *Ibid.*, III, 181-82. This thought is stated in the essay "Experience." It is fully conceded that too much may be made of an isolated passage, but the present interpretaton would logically be a consistent part of Emerson's pseudo-Vedantism.

127. *Ibid.*, I, 73-75.

128. *Ibid.*, I, 124.

129. *Ibid.*, XII, 55.

130. *Ibid.*, IV, 177.

131. John Morley, *Ralph Waldo Emerson, an Essay*, New York, Macmillan, 1884, 50.

132. Edward Emerson, *op. cit.*, p. 245.

133. Cabot, *op. cit.*, II, 506-7.

134. Edward Emerson, *op. cit.*, p. 245.

135. *Loc. cit.*

136. *Letters of Charles Eliot Norton*, ed. Sara Norton and M. de Wolfe Howe, 1913, I, 484-85.

137. Emerson, *Works*, VIII, 138.

138. Norton, *op. cit.*, I, 503-4.

139. *Ibid.*, I, 505. *Cf.* also the following from Garnett, *Emerson*, p. 192: "He insists that all things gravitate towards the good, and that this progression is infinite; which, if we look back only as far as the time when the worm first essayed 'to mount the spires of form,' seems an irrefragable conclusion. From the moral indifference often justly chargeable upon optimists of Oriental type, Emerson is protected by the Marcus Aurelius element in his constitution."

140. An excellent survey of some writers who have dealt with the problem will be found in Gray, *op. cit.*, pp. 77-78. The following summary is based on this survey.

141. Spinoza, it will be recalled, went through a similar evolution, which is in varying degrees probably the experience of all idealists. For a further discussion, see W. T. Harris' chapter "Emerson's Orientalism" in *The Genius and Character of Emerson*.

142. Deussen, *System of the Vedanta*, p. 403. Quoted by John McKenzie, *Hindu Ethics*, Oxford University Press, 1922, pp. 157-58.

143. Emerson, *Works*, I, 73-74. The italics are added.

144. The Confucian texts from which parallel passages are cited in the following notes are those which Emerson and his friends read. They are: Joshua Marshman, *The Works of Confucius*, Serampore, 1809; David Collie, *The Chinese Classical Work, Commonly Called the Four Books*, Malacca, 1828; James Legge, *The Chinese Classics*, London, 1861. See annotated bibliography for further information. I have, for the most part, used Legge's translation in my discussion because it is probably the most available for the general reader who might wish to read further in the Chinese. Supplementary translations from Collie and Marshman have been supplied in the notes. These will be of interest, since it is obvious that the Concordians often paraphrased. Citations from Collie are listed with the Chinese title and page to facilitate reference, since his work does not in all instances follow the standard divisions of chapter and verse in Legge. A Master's thesis entitled *Some Traces of the Influence of the Four Books of the Chinese Classics on the Writings of R. W. Emerson* was written at Columbia University by Mr. Robert E. Bundy in 1926. I am indebted to this essay for some suggestions.

145. An article, too detailed to be discussed here, may interest the reader because of its disclosure of the parallels between the Chinese and ancient Greek conceptions of filial piety. See W. A. P. Martin, "Plato and Confucius: a Curious Coincidence," *Journal of the American Oriental Society*, XIV (October, 1888), xxxi-xxxiv.

146. Gray, *op. cit.*, p. 71.

147. Emerson, *Works*, XI, 472.

148. *Ibid.*, XI, 637.

149. *Ibid.*, VII, 100; *Analects*, VII. 11; Legge, *op. cit.*, I, 62.

150. Emerson, *Journals*, VI, 403.

151. *Ibid.*, VI, 459. Emerson's transcription is a rearrangement and paraphrase of a passage in *Mencius*, I. 4, which will be found in Collie, "Shang Mung," pp. 78-79.

152. *Ibid.*, VII, 126.

153. Emerson, *Works*, II, 156; *Mencius*, IV. 1.15; Legge, *op. cit.*, II, 182.

154. *Ibid.*, II, 159.

155. Emerson, *Journals*, IV, 10.

156. *Analects*, II. 10; Marshman, *op. cit.*, pp. 102-3.

157. Emerson, *Works*, II, 157.

158. *Analects*, IV. 14; Collie, "Shang Lun," p. 14; Legge, *op. cit.*, I, 33.

159. *Analects*, XIV. 32; *Legge, op. cit.*, I, 151; Collie, "Hea Lun," p. 69: "Confucius says, be not vexed that you are not known, but be concerned that you want abilities."

160. *Analects*, I. 8; Marshman, *op. cit.*, pp. 35-36.

161. Emerson, *Works*, II, 211-12.

162. *Analects*, II. 12; Legge, *op. cit.*, I, 14; Collie, "Shang Lun," p. 5: "Confucius says, the superior man is not a mere machine, which is fit for one thing only."

163. Emerson, *Works*, III, 4.

164. *Ibid.*, III, 95. The italics are added.

165. *Mencius*, VI. 1.2.2; Legge, *op. cit.*, II, 271-72; Collie, "Hea Mung," p. 141: "The virtue of man's nature resembles the downward flowing of water. Men are all naturally virtuous, the same as all water naturally flows downwards."

166. Emerson, *Works*, III, 110.

167. Walt Whitman, "Emerson's Books (the Shadows of them)," *Literary World*, XI (May 22, 1880), 177.

168. Emerson, *Works*, III, 137. The italics are added.

169. *Doctrine of the Mean*, XXII; Legge, *op. cit.*, I, 279-80; Collie, "Chung Yung," p. 21, renders the passage thus: "It is only the man possessed of the highest sincerity, that can perfect his own nature—he who can perfect his own nature, can perfect the nature of other men;—he who can perfect the nature of other men, can perfect the nature of things;—he who can perfect the nature of things, can assist heaven and earth in producing and nourishing things. When this is the case, he is united with heaven and earth so as to form a trinity." It is interesting to note that Ku Hung Ming's translation of the *Doctrine of the Mean* was given the title *The Conduct of Life or the Universal Order of Confucius*, London, Murray, 1908 (Wisdom of the East Series).

170. Emerson, *Works*, III, 122.

171. *Doctrine of the Mean*, XX. 18; Legge, *op. cit.*, I, 277. Collie renders the passage and its context thus ("Chung Yung" p. 19): "Sin-

cerity is the Taou or way of heaven. To aim at it, is the way (or duty) of man. The sincere (or perfect) hit the due medium without effort, obtain it without thought, and practise it spontaneously."

172. Emerson, *Works*, III, 123.

173. *Doctrine of the Mean*, XX. 4-5; Legge, *op. cit.*, I, 269.

174. Emerson, *Works*, III, 132.

175. *Mencius*, IV. 2.28; Legge, *op. cit.*, II, 209; Collie, "Hea Mung," p. 115: "Mencius says, that by which the superior man differs from other men, consists in keeping his heart. The superior man, keeps his heart by virtue and propriety. The virtuous (or benevolent) love others, and the polite respect others. Men constantly love those who love them, and he who treats others with respect, is always respected by others."

176. Emerson, *Works*, III, 142.

177. *Ibid.*, III, 220.

178. *Great Learning*, Introduction; Legge, *op. cit.*, I, 223; Collie, "Ta Heo," p. 2. "The ancient (Princes) who felt desirous that the brilliancy of resplendent virtue might shine through the whole Empire, first promoted good order in their own provinces;—wishing to establish order in their own provinces, they first regulated their own families;—in order to effect the regulation of their own families, they first adorned their persons with virtue; in order that they might adorn their persons with virtue, they first rectified their own hearts; wishing to rectify their hearts, they first purified their motives; in order to purify their motives, they first extended their knowledge to the utmost."

179. *Mencius*, IV. 1.4; Legge, *op. cit.*, II, 171; Collie, "Hea Mung," p. 100: "If you do not succeed according to your wishes, turn round upon yourself. If you be correct in your own conduct, all under heaven will follow you."

180. Emerson, *Works*, III, 221.

181. *Ibid.*, III, 204.

182. *Doctrine of the Mean*, XX. 2-4; Legge, *op. cit.*, I, 269; Collie, "Chung Yung," p. 16: "The true principles of man naturally produce good government, just as the earth naturally produces trees. Good government is like the Poo Loo tree (i.e. easy and speedy in its growth). Good government depends on obtaining proper men."

183. Emerson, *Works*, III, 216.

184. *Mencius*, IV. 1.5; Legge, *op. cit.*, II, 171; Collie, "Hea Mung," p. 100: "Mencius said, men are all in the habit of speaking of the Empire and of the Provinces: Now, the foundation of the Empire lies in the provinces, the foundation of the provinces in families, and the foundation of families in individuals."

185. Emerson, *Works*, X, 120. Emerson took this passage from *Analects*, XII. 18-19. See Legge, *op. cit.*, I, 122. Collie renders the latter passage thus in "Hea Lun," p. 55: "Ke Kang asked of Confucius respecting government, saying, how would it answer to put to death the vicious, in order to bring forward the virtuous. Confucius replied, Sir, if you wish to govern well, why put men to death. If you only wish for virtue, the people will be virtuous. The virtue of the superior man (or of superiors) resembles the wind, that of inferiors resembles the grass. When the wind blows on the grass it must yield." Another very pertinent passage will be found in *Analects*, IX. 13; Legge, *op. cit.*, I, 85: "The Master was wishing to go and live among the nine wild tribes of the east. Some one said, 'They are rude. How can you do such a thing?' The Master said, 'If a superior man dwelt among them, what rudeness would there be?' "

186. Francis Gladwin, *The Gulistan or Rose Garden, by Saadi,* preface by Ralph Waldo Emerson, Boston, Ticknor and Fields, 1865.

187. Holmes, *Emerson*, p. 224.

188. Joseph Von Hammer, *Der Diwan von Mohammed Schemsed-din Hafis,* Stuttgart und Tübingen, 1812.

189. Holmes, *op. cit.*, p. 224.

190. Emerson, *Works*, VIII, 237.

191. *Ibid.*, VIII, 240.

192. *Loc. cit.*

193. *Ibid.*, VIII, 241.

194. *Ibid.*, VIII, 242.

195. *Ibid.*, VIII, 242-43.

196. See pages 35-38.

197. Emerson, *Works*, VIII, 249.

198. See W. R. Inge, *Christian Mysticism,* New York, Scribner, 1899, pp. 369-72, for a valuable history of the interpretations given to the *Song of Solomon.*

199. Saadi, *The Gulistan or Rose Garden,* Boston, 1865, p. vii.

200. *Ibid.*, pp. iv-v.

201. *Ibid.*, p. vi.

202. *Ibid.*, p. ix. The italics are added.

203. *Ibid.*, p. x.

204. *Ibid.*, p. xi.

205. Joel Benton, *Emerson as a Poet,* New York, Holbrook, 1883, p. 29.

206. *Ibid.*, pp. 28-29.

207. *Ibid.*, p. 29.

208. Emerson, *Works*, IX, 296.

209. Edward Emerson, *Emerson in Concord*, p. 231.

210. Holmes, *Emerson*, p. 338.

211. Emerson, *Works*, IX, 443.

212. William Sloane Kennedy, "Clews to Emerson's Mystical Verse," *The American Author*, II (June, 1903), 18.

213. Emerson, *Works*, IX, 125-26.

214. W. R. Alger, *The Poetry of the East*, Boston, Whittemore, Niles and Hall, 1856, p. 166.

215. Benton, *op. cit.*, p. 26.

216. Emerson, *Works*, IX, 122.

217. Benton, *op. cit.*, pp. 26-27.

218. This poem first appeared in *The Dial*, I, 37 (Cincinnati, January, 1860).

219. Benton, *op. cit.*, p. 29.

220. Emerson, *Works*, IX, 275-76.

221. *Ibid.*, IX, 496.

222. These lines reappear in the motto to the essay on "Persian Poetry," but with a difference:

> God only knew how Saadi dined;
> Roses he ate, and drank the wind.
> As Jelaleddin old and gray,
> He seemed to bask, to dream and play ...

223. Emerson, *Works*, IX, 325.

224. See pages 147-48.

225. See pages 147-48.

226. Joseph Von Hammer, *Der Diwan von Hafis*, II, 548, stanza 3.

227. *Loc. cit.*

228. Emerson, *Journals*, IV, 57.

229. *Ibid.*, VII, 169.

230. Emerson, *Works*, XII, 326. In the *Journal* of 1847 (VII, 291) Emerson writes: "*Orientalist*. Says Goethe, 'The English translator of the Cloud-Messenger, Meghaduta, is likely worthy of all honor, since the first acquaintance with such a work always makes an epoch in our life."

231. Emerson, *Works*, XII, 297.

232. *Ibid.*, VII, 13.

233. Emerson, *Journals*, IX, 552.

234. *Ibid.*, III, 310.

235. Emerson, *Works*, II, 136-37.

236. *Ibid.*, VIII, 311.

237. *Ibid.*, XII, 174.

238. *Ibid.*, II, 278-79.

239. *Ibid.*, X, 191.

240. *Ibid.*, XII, 159.

241. *Ibid.*, VIII, 121.

242. See page 68.

243. Emerson, *Journals*, VI, 458.

244. *Ibid.*, VII, 52-53.

245. *Ibid.*, V, 550-52.

246. *Ibid.*, IX, 58. The *Katha Upanishad* commences with this story. Next to the *Bhagavadgita*, it may safely be said that the *Katha* was the most influential of the Hindu scriptures in Emerson's work, since it was from Röer's translation of this text that Emerson took also the main model for the poem "Brahma."

247. Emerson, *Works*, VIII, 349-52. Emerson paraphrased and quoted Roër. The following is a list of references to Oriental literature and thought in Emerson's *Journals* and *Works*. They are, of course, exclusive of the references that have already been used. *Journals*, II, 474; III, 260; V, 29, 444, 449, 560; VII, 103, 109, 110, 291, 512; VIII, 79, 547-49; IX, 145, 536, 538, 539, 550; X, 100, 134, 156, 235. For references in Emerson's *Works* see I, 213, 216, 222; II, 79, 243; III, 151; IV, 39, 66, 94, 95, 96, 139, 140, 172, 217, 224, 263; VI, 18, 233, 235, 272, 296; VII, 64, 70; VIII, 98, 280, 283, 343; IX, 100, 107, 294, 506; X, 100, 120, 177, 243, 546; XI, 236, 504; XII, 35, 80, 148, 235.

248. Holmes, *Emerson*, pp. 396 ff. See also *The American Author*, II (June, 1903), 204, for an article entitled "Clews to Emerson's Mystical Verse", in which William Sloane Kennedy describes the bewilderment of New Englanders in the face of the metaphysics of the poem, concluding that "to the Hindoo, or the reader of Hindoo Scriptures, 'Brahma' is only an elementary primer of metaphysics." In my discussion of the poem which follows I am much indebted to Kennedy's article. Holmes's approach to the poem can best be shown by the following words: "Of course no one can hold Emerson responsible for the 'Yoga' doctrine of Brahmanism, which he amused himself with putting into verse. The Oriental side of Emerson's nature delighted itself in these narcotic dreams, born in the land of the poppy and hashish. They lend a peculiar charm to his poems, but it is not worth while to try to construct a philosophy out of them." It must be remembered that Holmes was a doctor of medicine. The mystic was a pathological problem to him.

249. C. A. Bartol, "Letter to the Editors," *Critic*, new ser., IX (March 3, 1888), 104: "The store Emerson at one time set by this poem appears

from his resisting, as Mr. J. T. Fields told me he did, a proposal to omit it from a collection the publishers were making of his works. This he said, must go in, whatever else stayed out. . . . To Dr. F. H. Hedge he said that he composed lines because he happened to have a nice lead-pencil and some good paper. . . . He disparaged his own rhymes and put none of them into 'Parnassus.' Perhaps it was his admiration of the Oriental genius that made him insist on the claim of Brahma. It went, indeed, to the heart of his religion and philosophy, in which the One was all."

250. See Emerson, *Journals*, IX, 56, for the first draft of the poem, there entitled "Song of the Soul (Brahma)." There this line appears as "The vanished gods not less appear." Immediately preceding the poem are the following quotations:

"Until man is able to compass the ether like leather, there will be no end of misery, except through the knowledge of God."—*Upanishad*.

"From whom the sun rises, and in whom it sets again, him all the gods entered; from him none is separated; this is that.

"What is here, the same is there, and what is there, the same is here. He proceeds from death to death who beholds here difference.

"He (Brahma, or the Soul) does not move; is swifter than the mind: not the gods (the senses) did obtain him, he was gone before. Standing, he outstrips all the other gods, how fast soever they run.

"He moves, he does not move. He is far, and also near."

Then appear the four stanzas of the poem, with the single exception of the altered line in the second stanza which has been noted. Following these come three more quotations:

"Know that which does not see by the eye; and by which they see the eyes, as Brahma, and know what is worshipped as this.

"Know that which does not think by the mind, and by which they say the mind is thought, as Brahma, and not what is worshipped as this.

"The soul declared by an inferior man is not easy to be known, but when it is declared by a teacher who beholds no difference, there is no doubt concerning it, the soul being more subtle than what is subtle, is not to be obtained by arguing."

This is the context of the poem as it is originally found in the pages of the *Journal,* yet these quotations do not form the model for Emerson's lines, as will be shown presently.

251. Edward Emerson, *Emerson in Concord,* p. 162.

252. Emerson, *Journals,* II, 343. *Cf.* also, particularly the third stanza, with an entry of 1832 (*Journals* II, 480) : "He counts very unskillfully who leaves God out of his reckoning."

253. Emerson, *Works*, IX, 465.

254. Harris' articles are to be found in *Poet-Lore*, I, 253-59 (1889), and *The Genius and Character of Emerson*, ed. F. B. Sanborn, Boston, 1885, pp. 372-85. The first of the articles is entitled "Emerson's *Brahma* and the *Bhagavad Gita*"; the second, "Emerson's Orientalism."

255. David Lee Maulsby, *The Contribution of Emerson to Literature*, Tufts College Press, 1911, pp. 121-30.

256. *The American Author*, II, 195-230.

257. *The Genius and Character of Emerson*, p. 373.

258. The theme is the basis of Krishna's discourses in the second book. "Brahma" recapitulates almost verbatim *Katha Upanishad* II. 19, which in turn occurs in *Bhagavadgita*, II. 19.

259. E. Röer, "Katha Upanishad," *Bibliotheca Indica* Calcutta, 1853, XV, 105. The translator consistently uses parentheses instead of square brackets for interpolations.

260. *The Genius and Character of Emerson*, p. 377. Harris does not give the Hindu source of this passage.

261. *Bhagavadgita*, VIII. 15-16. W. T. Harris, "Emerson's 'Brahma' and the 'Bhagavad Gita,'" *Poet-Lore*, I (1889), 259. An anonymous correspondent in *The Galaxy*, VI (July, 1868), 147-48, suggests as a source for "Brahma" lines from John Fletcher's "Hymn to Venus":

> O divinest star of heaven,
> Thou, in power above the seven;
> Thou, sweet kindler of desires
> Till they grow to mutual fires;
> Thou, O gentle queen, that art
> Curer of each wounded heart;
> Thou, the fuel and the flame;
> Thou, in heaven, here, the same;
> Thou, the wooer and the wooed;
> Thou, the hunger and the food;
> Thou, the prayer and the prayed;
> Thou, what is or shall be said;
> Thou, still young and golden tressed,
> Make me by thine answer blessed.

In suggesting these lines as a source the reviewer insisted that Emerson was acquainted with Fletcher's poetry. This is an interesting suggestion and supplement to the Oriental interpretation.

262. Emerson, *Journals*, VIII, 36.

263. Emerson, *Works*, IX, 357.

264. *Ibid.*, XII, 10.

265. *Ibid.*, IV, 49-50.

266. *Ibid.*, IV, 50-51.

267. The word *Hamatreya* has confused scholars. There seems to be no such word in the Hindu vocabulary, and the only explanation is that it is a form of the word *Maitreya,* the name of a character in the *Vishnu Purana.*

268. Emerson, *Works,* VI, 324.

269. Emerson, *Journals,* VII, 108.

270. *Ibid.*, VII, 127-30.

271. Emerson, *Works,* IX, 35-36.

272. *Ibid.*, IX, 221. See also W. S. Kennedy, *op. cit.*, II, 221-22, for a discussion of this poem and T. W. Higginson's conjectures as to the source. See also the notes in the Centenary Edition of Emerson's writings.

273. Emerson, *Works,* IX, 115.

274. On the other hand William Sloane Kennedy writes (*Op. cit.*, p. 200) : "I think I have put my finger on the very passage in the Rig Veda which Emerson had in mind,—i.e., the lines which speak of 'the triple-naved everlasting Wheel that nothing can arrest, *on which repose all being*' ('Night of the Gods,' ii, 597)."

275. H. H. Wilson, *Vishnu Purana,* London, Oriental Translation Fund, 1840, Bk. II, chap. VI, pp. 205-6.

276. Emerson, *Works, IX,* 115.

277. Emerson, *Journals,* VII, 127.

278. Emerson, *Journals,* VIII, 549. See A. A. Macdonell, *Vedic Mythology,* Strassburg, Trübner, 1897, pp. 37-39 for various interpretations of Vishnu's three steps. Many scholars are of the opinion that these steps refer to the course of the sun, its rising, culminating, and setting.

279. *Ibid.*, IX, 489.

280. Röer, *op. cit.*, XV, 116; *Katha Upanishad,* VI.1.

281. Emerson, *Works,* IX, 57-58.

282. H. H. Wilson, *Vishnu Purana,* 1840, pp. 18-19.

283. *Parnassus,* ed. R. W. Emerson, Boston, James R. Osgood, 1875, p. 56.

284. *Ibid.*, p. 58.

285. The only other Oriental selection in the anthology is Sir William Jones's "Narayena: Spirit of God" (p. 180) :

> Blue crystal vault and elemental fires
> That in the aerial fluid blaze and breathe!
> Thou tossing sea, whose snaky branches wreath
> This pensile orb with intertwisted gyves;—

Mountains whose lofty radiant spires
Presumptuous rear their summits to the skies;
Smooth meads and lawns that glow with vergant dyes
Of dew-bespangled leaves and blossoms bright!

Then follow the lines which Emerson used in an early *Journal* to conclude his discussion of God.

PART THREE: THOREAU

1. Franklin Benjamin Sanborn, *The Life of Henry David Thoreau*, Boston and New York, Houghton Mifflin, 1917, p. 128. A very brief Heidelberg monograph, H. A. Snyder, *Thoreau's Philosophy of Life with Special Consideration of the Influence of Hindoo Philosophy*, n.d., will be found suggestive but not conclusive by the student of Thoreau.

2. Thoreau, *Journal*, I, 55.

3. A possible exception to this statement must be mentioned. Among Thoreau's college essays which Sanborn published in the volume cited in note 1, appeared "Books and their Titles." The following paragraph is taken from that essay (p. 127): "No people have been more prone to these extravagances than the Persians. Mohammed Ebn Emir Chowand Shah, who flourished in 1741, was the author of a voluminous historical work entitled 'Hortus Puritatis in Historia Prophetarum, Regum et Chalifarum.' A Persian-Turkish dictionary bears the title of 'Naamet Allah' or 'Delight of Gods.' 'The Gulistan,' or 'Flower-Garden,' a collection of moral fables and apophthegms, by Sheikh Sadi of Shiraz, being written in an excessively florid style, may aptly enough be compared to a garden of flowers, or a parcel of nosegays. We next come upon the ground of the 'Lebtarik or Marrow of History,' by the immortal (so far as his name is concerned) Abdolatif al Kaswini. Abu Said wrote a universal history from Adam to his own time, under the title of *?*. 'Historical Pearl Necklace.'" There was, of course, a great difference between this Persian literature and the Hindu, which later enamored Thoreau.

4. Thoreau, *Journal*, I, 261. See also I, 264, for comment on Manu. A week later the spell of Manu still remained. "I know of no book which comes to us with grander pretensions. . . ."

5. *Ibid.*, I, 266.

6. *Ibid.*, I, 267.

7. *Ibid.*, I, 268.

8. *Ibid.*, I, 277.

9. *Ibid.*, II, 4.

10. *Loc. cit.*

11. *Loc. cit.*

12. *Loc. cit.*

13. Thoreau, *Writings*, I, 44.

14. Thoreau, *Journal*, V, 271.

15. Thoreau, *Writings*, II, 351.

16. *Ibid.*, V, 331.

17. Thoreau, *Journal*, III, 266.

18. *Ibid.*, I, 224.

19. Thoreau, *Writings*, V. 240-41.

20. *Ibid.*, IV, 470-71.

21. *Ibid.*, II, 359-60. For other passages see *Writings*, I, 10; II, 134, 189, 190; IV, 303, 394, 395; V, 174, 412. Also see *Journal*, I, 170, 176, 246, 343, 370; II, 35, 298; IV, 15, 205; IX, 251; X, 54; XI, 65, 81.

22. *Ibid.*, IV, 387.

23. *Ibid.*, II, 105-06. The source is *Analects*, XIV. 26.1-2.

24. Ibid., II, 242; *Mencius*, IV.2.19.1; Legge, *op. cit.*, II, 201; Collie, "Hea Mung," p. 112: "Mencius says, the difference between men and brutes is but small. The common herd lose this difference, but superior men preserve it." Thoreau probably paraphrased this passage.

25. *Ibid.*, I, 23.

26. *Ibid.*, II, 98. *The Great Learning*, II.1. Legge, *op. cit.*, I, 225. Collie, "Ta Hea," p. 3.

27. Some of these papers are to be found in the Harvard College Library. They consist of an heterogeneous sheaf of notes, with an occasional page from some early draft of *Walden* or the *Week*. The source of this Confucian anecdote is *Analects*, XI.25.

28. For further use of Confucian material, see the marginalia in the Appendix.

29. The reproduction of this title-page will be found in the Bibliophile Edition.

30. Thoreau, *Writings*, VI, 175.

31. Thoreau, *Journal*, I, 279.

32. Alcott, *Concord Days*, p. 263.

33. Conway, *Emerson at Home and Abroad*, p. 280.

34. Thoreau, *Writings*, II, 18. Van Doren suggests (*op. cit.*, p. 17) that this passage had a Confucian model previously printed in the *Dial* (IV, 206); "Benevolence is man's heart, and justice is man's path. If a man loses his fowls or his dogs, he knows how to seek them. There are those who lose their hearts and know not how to seek them. The duty of the student is no other than to seek his lost heart."

35. Thoreau, *Writings*, II, 21. The italics are added.

36. *Ibid.*, II, 123-24.

37. *Ibid.*, II, 240. Note the following additional passage. *Writings*, II, 236: "I have found repeatedly, of late years, that I cannot fish without falling a little in self-respect. . . . Beside, there is something essentially unclean about this diet and all flesh."

38. *Ibid.*, VI, 395-96. See also William Ellery Channing, *Thoreau the Poet-Naturalist*, Boston, Goodspeed, 1902, p. 17.

39. Thoreau, *Writings*, V, 409.

40. *Ibid.*, VI, 42.

41. Radhakrishan, *The Vedanta*, p. 207.

42. Thoreau, *Writings*, II, 356.

43. See page 202.

44. A complete discussion will be found in J. F. C. Fuller, *Yoga*, London, Rider, 1925, pp. 38-45. For general purposes, these disciplines may be understood by the corresponding English phrases Fuller assigns to them: (1) Jnana Yoga—"union by knowledge"; (2) Raja Yoga—"union by will"; (3) Bhakta Yoga—"union by love"; (4) Hatha Yoga—"union by courage"; (5) Mantra Yoga—"union through speech"; (6) Karma Yoga—"union through work."

45. Cornelia Sarabji, *Woman's Outlook in India*, II, 669. Quoted in McKenzie, *Hindu Ethics*, pp. 207-8.

46. Mark Van Doren, *op. cit.*, pp. 96-97.

47. Thoreau, *Journal*, III, 400.

48. *Ibid.*, III, 147.

49. Thoreau, *Writings*, II, 84.

50. *Brihadaranyaka Upanishad*, III.5.1. Quoted in McKenzie, *Hindu Ethics*, pp. 88 and 213.

51. I may qualify this statement by reminding the reader that both Thoreau and Alcott at one time refused to pay taxes.

52. Emerson, *Journals*, VI, 82.

53. Henry Seidel Canby, *Classic Americans*, New York, Harcourt, Brace, 1931, pp. 208-9.

54. See pages 265-66.

55. *Chandogya Upanishad*, IV. 14.3; Cave, *Living Religions*, p. 37. The reference will also be found in Hume, *Thirteen Principal Upanishads*, p. 223.

56. *Kaushitaki Upanishad*, III. 1; Cave, *Redemption Hindu and Christian*, p. 74. See also Hume, *Thirteen Principal Upanishads*, p. 321.

57. Thoreau, *Writings*, VI, 93.

58. Thoreau, *Journal*, III, 108.

59. Channing, *Thoreau the Poet-Naturalist*, p. 271.

60. Thoreau, *Journal*, I, 176.

61. *Ibid.*, I, 280. The italics are added.

62. Note the other entries in his *Journal*, I, 263, 264, 266, 267, 268.

63. *Ibid.*, I, 279. The italics are added.

64. Jones, *Institutes of Hindu Law*, 1794, pp. 119-20.

65. *Ibid.*, p. 346.

66. Thoreau, *The Transmigration of the Seven Brahmans*, ed. Arthur Christy, New York. W. E. Rudge, 1931. A complete facsimile of the manuscript, together with the complete French source, will be found in this volume. The original manuscript is in the Thoreau collection of the Harvard College Library.

67. Thoreau, ed., "The Preaching of Buddha," *Dial*, IV (Jan., 1844), 395-96.

68. Thoreau, *Journal*, IX, 200.

69. Thoreau, *Writings*, I, 418-19.

70. Charles Wilkins, *The Bhagvat-Geeta*, 1785, p. 63. The general *Gita* reference is VI.11-12.

71. Henry Seidel Canby, "Thoreau, The Great Eccentric," *Saturday Review of Literature*, IV (Nov. 26, 1927), 338.

72. Thoreau, *Writings*, II, 29.

73. *Ibid.*, II, 7.

74. *Ibid.*, II, 4-5.

75. Sanborn was of the opinion that Thoreau went to Walden to prepare the *Week* for his publisher. In the light of Thoreau's confessions as to the manner in which he spent his time, this is not the only explanation.

76. Thoreau, *Writings*, II, 77.

77. *Ibid.*, II, 59.

78. *Ibid.*, II, 44.

79. *Ibid.*, II, 9.

80. *Ibid.*, II, 364.

81. *Ibid.*, IV, 348.

82. Emerson, *Works*, X, 485.

83. Sanborn, *Thoreau*, 1917, pp. 336-37.

84. *Pertaining to Thoreau*, Detroit, Edwin B. Hill, 1901.

85. *Ibid.*, p. 37.

86. *Ibid.*, p. 46.

87. *Ibid.*, pp. 24-25.

88. *Ibid.*, p. 26.

89. Van Doren, *op. cit.*, pp. 49-50.

90. Paul Elmer More, "Thoreau's Journal," *Shelburne Essays,* Fifth Series, New York, Putnam, 1908, p. 121.

91. Thoreau, *Journal,* I, 54. See also Kuno Francke, "Emerson and German Personality," *The International Quarterly,* VIII (Sept. 1903), 93-107; and Louise Pound, "Emerson as a Romanticist," *The Mid-West Quarterly,* II (Jan., 1915), 184-95. These articles are valuable discussion of the New England background against which Thoreau must ever be studied.

92. Van Doren, *op. cit.*, p. 114.

93. *Ibid.*, p. 115.

94. *Ibid.*, p. 116.

95. *Ibid.*, p. 117.

96. *Ibid.*, p. 122.

97. *Ibid.*, p. 123.

98. Thoreau, *Writings,* II, 356.

99. John Weiss, "Thoreau," *Pertaining to Thoreau,* pp. 133-34.

PART FOUR: ALCOTT

1. A textual examination of Alcott's published works reveals that quotations from the *Bhagavadgita* which deal with the subject of food predominate. An example is the following from *Tablets,* (p. 16): " 'All living things,' said the Bhagavad Gita, 'are generated from the bread they eat; bread is generated from rain, rain from divine worship, and divine worship from good works.'" The following is Alcott's commentary in the same context: "A creed dealing thus super-sensibly with the elements must have fertilizing properties, and bring the gardener to his task little tinctured by noxious notions of any kind. If he fall short of being the reverent naturalist, the devout divine, surrounded thus by shapes of skill, types of beauty, tokens of design, every hue in the chromatic, every device in the symbolic gamut, I see not what shall make him these. . . ." Another similar passage, with quotation from the *Bhagavadgita,* will be found in *Table-Talk* (p. 72). The most readable use of Oriental material in Alcott's books, in this connection probably taken from a Sufi poet, is to be found in *Sonnets and Canzonets* (p. 114): "One knocked at the Beloved's door, and a Voice asked from within, Who is there? And he answered, It is I. Then the Voice said, This house will not hold me and

thee, and the door was not opened. Then went the lover into the desert, and fasted and prayed in solitude. And after a year he returned, and knocked again at the door. And again the Voice asked, Who is there? and he said, It is Thyself. And the door was opened to him." The closest resemblance to a Confucian influence to be found in Alcott's work is the following from *Table-Talk*, (p. 60): "Reverence for superiors is the source of filial piety and obedience. We are told that the times of remote antiquity bore so great a reverence for parents as to venture to call them gods." Such a passage may equally be ascribed to Greek influence, however. In *Concord Days*, p. 117, Alcott wrote: " 'He that in the morning hath heard the voice of virtue,' says Confucius, 'may die at night.' And it were virtuous to rise early during our June mornings to breakfast on strawberries with the robins. . . ." The original Confucian passage source read: "If in the morning I hear of the right way, and in the evening die, I can be happy." (*Analects*, IV. 8.) Emerson had used the quotation in his *Works*, X, 117. The passage also appeared in the *Dial*, III, 493. Alcott, in what is probably his characteristic manner in quoting, garbled it.

2. Honoré Willsie Morrow in *The Father of Little Women*, Boston, Little Brown, 1927, has dealt mostly with Alcott's educational theories and their exemplification in the Philadelphia and Boston experiments.

3. I am indebted to Mrs. F. Alcott Pratt of Concord for the information presented here. The Alcott *Journals* are being held for publication in entirety at some future time. They are therefore not available for reference. Mrs. Pratt, however, graciously consented to my using a limited number of excerpts dealing with Alcott's Oriental interests, and to include the following unpublished paragraph, dated July 3, 1859: "Thoreau comes and stays an hour or two. Students of nature alike: our methods differ. He is an observer of Nature pure, and I discern her as exalted and mingled in Man. Her brute aspects and qualities interest him, and these he discriminates with a sagacity unsurpassed. He is less thinker than observer: a naturalist in tendency but of a mystic habit, and a genius for detecting the essence in the form, and giving forth the soul of things seen. He knows more of Nature's secrets than any man I have known, and of Man as related to Nature. He thinks and sees for himself in ways eminently original and is formidably individual and persistent."

4. See page 10.

5. *Tablets* appeared in Boston, 1868.

6. See Sanborn and Harris, *op. cit.*, I, 332.

7. Max Müller edited *The Sacred Books of the East*, which appeared 1879-1910. For statistics see Mudge, *Guide to Reference Books*, fifth edition, 1929, p. 87.

8. Abby and Louisa were Alcott's daughters. Mrs. Alcott's maiden name was May.

9. I am informed by Mrs. F. Alcott Pratt of Concord that the reference was to Alvin Adams, the founder of the Adams Express Company.

10. With Charles Lane for the Fruitlands Library.

11. Cory's translation will be found in *The Phenix*. See Appendix for the others.

12. These quotations were taken from *The Phenix*, New York, Gowan, 1835. The following completes the list which Alcott copied into his diary as texts for conversational meetings:

Ether "in which the things without figure are figured."

"Defile not the Spirit nor deepen a superficies."

"Enlarge not thy destiny."

"Oh how the world has inflexible intellectual rulers."

"All fountains and principles whirl round,
And always remain in ceaseless revolution."

"Never change barbarous names,
For there are names in every nation given by God,
Having unspeakable efficacy in the mysteries."

"Nature persuades us that there are pure demons,
Even the blossoms of evil matter are useful and good."

"From the cavities
Of the earth leap forth terrestrial dogs,
Showing no true sign to mortal men."

"Let the immortal depth of your soul lead you,
But earnestly extend your eyes upward."

"It is not proper to understand that Intelligible with vehemence,
But with the extended flame of an extended mind measuring all things
Except the Intelligible. But it is ignoble to understand this;
For if you incline your mind you will understand it
Not correctly, but it becomes you to bring with you a pure and inquiring eye,
To extend the void mind of your Soul to the Intelligible,
That you may learn the Intelligible
Because it subsists beyond mind."

"You will not understand it, as when understanding some particular thing."

"Things divine are not attainable by mortals who understand body,
But only as many as are lightly armed arrive at the Summit."

"Rhea, the fountain and river of the blessed Intellectuals,
Having first received the power of all things in her ineffable bosom,

Pours forth perpetual generation upon every thing."
"But the paternal mind receives not her will
Until she has gone out of oblivion and pronounces the word
Assuming the memory of the pure fraternal Symbol."
"The Soul of man will in a manner clasp God to herself,
Having nothing mortal she is wholly
For the glories in the harmony under which the mortal body exists."
"For thy vessel the beasts of the earth shall inherit."
"The Paternal Mind has sowed Symbols in souls."

13. In the appendix of this book will be found a list of the Oriental volumes in Henry Wadsworth Longfellow's library which Alcott might have used. It is not impossible that Emerson also drew from this source.

14. A note in Alcott's diary adds the information that William Goodwin was a Greek scholar of note and the husband of Ellen Channing. He was probably William Watson Goodwin, listed in *Appleton's Cyclopedia of American Biography* as born in Concord, Massachusetts, May 9, 1831. He graduated from Harvard in 1851, studied at Bonn, Berlin and Göttingen, and became Eliot Professor of Greek literature at Harvard in 1856. He was the first director of the American school of classical studies at Athens.

15. The identity of the persons mentioned by Alcott is probably as follows: Mrs. C. H. Dall, a later Transcendentalist and a blue-stocking. She is most interesting because of her marriage to William Healey Dall, the first foreign missionary of the Unitarian Church to India. Mr. Dall established himself in Calcutta in 1855, returning to visit his family once every five years. Emerson wrote in his *Journals*, X, 163: "In India, a Brahmin may be very poor, and perform daily menial tasks for the English, as porters or servants, but the natives still kneel to him, and show him the highest respect.—Mr. Dall testified this fact to me on his return from India." For the identity of Miss Parsons, see the preface, *Letters from Brook Farm* 1844-47, edited by Amy L. Reed, Vassar College, 1928. In this book appears a brief sketch of Anna Q. T. Parsons, who was a frequent visitor to Brook Farm, but never a member. Charles Eliot Norton needs no identification.

16. The date of the marriage is not in the account of Arnold's life given in the *Dictionary of National Biography,* Second Supplement. The death of Arnold's first wife occurred in the year 1864 and that of Mrs. Fannie Channing Arnold in 1889. Arnold's third wife was a Japanese, Tama Kuro Kawa, of Sendai.

17. Edwin Arnold (1832-1904) was the second son of Robert Coles

Arnold of Whartons, Framfield, England. He graduated B.A. from University College, Oxford, in 1854, and M.A. in 1856. For a detailed account of his life see *Dictionary of National Biography*, Second Supplement.

18. I found no review of the book in *The Journal of Speculative Philosophy*. It is singular that the book was not even listed under the head of "books received."

19. Sanborn's notice of the book, which appeared in the *Springfield Republican* of August 24, 1879, consisted principally of excerpts from the introduction and Channing's letter, the latter being biographical. Only in the last paragraph did Sanborn write anything of a contribution: "Unable to be present with his friends at the Orchard House, Mr. Channing sent Mr. Arnold's book to Mr. Alcott, Prof. Harris and Mr. Sanborn: but it arrived too late to be even a text for one of the conversations. It will, perhaps, be reprinted in Boston and thus become better known to the American public than it well could be in the London edition. Its poetic merits are considerable, but it has a higher value as an exposition in a sympathetic spirit of the true ideal that inspires the great philanthropic religion of Asia,—the harbinger, and, for half-civilized men the complement, of Christianity."

20. Little, Brown and Company, the successors to Roberts Brothers, have written me that they are unable to supply data regarding Alcott's dealings with the publishers. They stated that Mr. Niles was the publishing manager for Roberts Brothers and came in direct contact with the authors and editors.

21. I quote from a letter by a member of the Mills family, graciously written in response to my request for information of Charles Mills's friendship with Alcott: "Charles de Berard Mills was a student of Oriental literatures and philosophies. He was also a friend both to Emerson and to Thoreau. He exchanged visits and letters with them and the bond of mutual interests and sympathies was strong. . . . As a boy he knew when Alcott was expected for a visit as his father laid in a barrel of special apples and cheese for the vegetarian philosopher. . . . Mr. Mills secured a lecture for Emerson in Syracuse. . . . Of Mr. Mills's books I can give the title of three, *The Indian Saint or Buddha and Buddhism; Pebbles, Pearls and Gems of the Orient*, and *The Tree of Mythology*."

22. Channing gave four lectures in Concord in 1880. They were listed under the head of "Oriental and Mystical Philosophy." Specific titles were 1. "Historical Mysticism." 2. "Man's Fourfold Being." 3. "True Buddhism." 4. "Modern Pessimism." *The Journal of Speculative Philosophy*, XIV, 252-53, presents a prospectus of the lectures.

23. *Dictionary of National Biography*, Second Supplement. The italics are added.

24. See page 251.

25. O. W. Holmes, "The Light of Asia," *International Review*, VII (Oct., 1879), 345-71.

26. W. C. Brownell, "Recent Poetry," *Nation*, DCCXLIX (Nov. 6, 1879), 314.

PART FIVE: CONCLUSION

1. The Brahmo Somaj, literally "the congregation of God," was a movement of native Hindu origin, founded in Calcutta in 1828 as a theistic church. The body began to advocate far-reaching reforms, such as the abolition of caste, child-marriage and polygamy. In 1830 its leaders proclaimed Christianity to be a true religion, but the Christ it presented was hardly that of the Christian churches. It was rather an amalgamation of Hinduism, Mohammedanism and Christianity. For a fuller discussion see Maurice A. Canney, *An Encyclopedia of Religions*, p. 75. See also J. N. Farquhar, *Modern Religious Movements in India*, p. 29: "Of all the religious movements of the nineteenth century the Brahmo Samaj has, without doubt, proved the most influential. . . . Looked at from one side, it is one of a long series of attempts to found a spiritual religion on a genuine Hindu foundation, which have marked the religion of India from a very early date; while, from the other side, it is a new creation, finding the sources of its vitality in Christian faith and practice." Farquhar's extensive study of this movement is probably the best that is available for the student who would investigate the subject further.

2. *The Genius and Character of Emerson*, p. 371.

3. *Ibid.*, p. 367.

4. Herambachandra Maitra, "Emerson from an Indian Point of View," *Harvard Theological Review*, IV, 403 (October, 1911).

5. Mahatma Gandhi, *Young India 1919-1922*, New York, Huebsch, 1923, p. 931. See also Romain Rolland, *Mahatma Gandhi*, New York. Century, 1924, p. 91: "Gandhi is not planning civil disobedience for the present. He knows civil disobedience. He has studied it in Thoreau, whom he quotes in his articles, and he takes pains to explain the difference between it and non-coöperation." See pages 211 and 264-66 for fuller discussion of Gandhi and Thoreau.

6. Henry S. Salt, *Company I Have Kept*, London, Allen & Unwin, 1930, pp. 100-01.

7. Conway, *op. cit.*, p. 356.

8. Emerson, *Works*, IV, 51.

9. Wendel Thomas, *Hinduism Invades America*, New York, Beacon Press, 1930. A Columbia University doctoral dissertation.

10. John McKenzie, *Hindu Ethics*, p. 199.

11. Max Müller, *Ramarkrishna, His Life and Sayings*, New York, Scribner, 1899, p. 148.

INDEX

INDEX

DATE DUE

JUL 5 1967	DEC 1 '74	
AUG 1 1 1967	DEC 15 '72	
AUG 3 1967	FEB 12 '73	
OCT 8 1967		
NOV 1 2 1967	DEC 8 '75	
MAY 1 0 '68	DEC 2 6 1983	
NOV 1 2 '68	MAY 1 2 1986	
JAN 2 4 '69	OCT 1 3 1986	
	APR 0 3 1989	
NOV 1 7 1969	MAY 2 8 1990	
JAN 2 '70		
NOV 1 0 '70	DEC 0 3 1990	
DEC 2 2 '70	NOV 06 2002	
APR 2 '71		
NOV 2 1 '72		
GAYLORD		PRINTED IN U.S.A.